About Island Press

Since 1984, the nonprofit organization Island Press has been stimulating, shaping, and communicating ideas that are essential for solving environmental problems worldwide. With more than 1,000 titles in print and some 30 new releases each year, we are the nation's leading publisher on environmental issues. We identify innovative thinkers and emerging trends in the environmental field. We work with world-renowned experts and authors to develop cross-disciplinary solutions to environmental challenges.

Island Press designs and executes educational campaigns, in conjunction with our authors, to communicate their critical messages in print, in person, and online using the latest technologies, innovative programs, and the media. Our goal is to reach targeted audiences—scientists, policy makers, environmental advocates, urban planners, the media, and concerned citizens—with information that can be used to create the framework for long-term ecological health and human well-being.

Island Press gratefully acknowledges major support from The Bobolink Foundation, Caldera Foundation, The Curtis and Edith Munson Foundation, The Forrest C. and Frances H. Lattner Foundation, The JPB Foundation, The Kresge Foundation, The Summit Charitable Foundation, Inc., and many other generous organizations and individuals.

The opinions expressed in this book are those of the author(s) and do not necessarily reflect the views of our supporters.

COPENHAGENIZE

COPENHAGENIZE

THE DEFINITIVE GUIDE TO GLOBAL BICYCLE URBANISM

Mikael Colville-Andersen

ISLANDPRESS

Washington | Covelo | London

Island Press is a trademark of The Center for Resource Economics.

Library of Congress Control Number: 2018931245

All Island Press books are printed on environmentally responsible materials.

Manufactured in Canada

10 9 8 7 6 5 4 3 2 1

Keywords: A2Bism, arrogance of space, bidirectional bike lane, bicycle urbanism,
bike lane, bike superhighway, bus stop, climaphobia, contra-flow bike lane, desire lines,
infrastructure design, intermodal, life-sized city, protected bike lane, sharrow,
urban design

I wish to thank the many members of my team at Copenhagenize Design Company for their support and help in writing this book. In particular, Michael Wexler, James Thoem, Stephanie Patto, and Darcy Miller. Thanks to Lorenz Siegel and Christina Steinmayr for their amazing design and layout. In addition, a warm thank-you to so many people in my network around the world for their support and encouragement.

FOR MY CHILDREN, FELIX AND LULU-SOPHIA.
AND FOR RILEY, MY INSPIRATION.

Contents

Introduction

I have spent the past decade staring intently at urban cyclists in cities around the world and closely examining the role of the humble bicycle on the urban landscape and in the finely woven social fabric. All of the thoughts and observations that have welled up through that time have reached a critical mass, and this book, I suppose, is the vessel into which they flow.

In picking up this book, you may have a hunch that I'll be discussing bicycles and bicycle urbanism, and rightly so. Nevertheless, I want to make sure that we're on the same page before we begin.

Let's be clear from the get-go. This is a book about bikes, but it's also about urbanization. It's about how we possess the ability to move a lot of people through cities and to effectively reestablish the bicycle as a respected, accepted, and feasible transport form—all while making money off of the investment.

In many cultures—not least in North America—the bicycle is still sadly misunderstood. It remains a tolerated tag-along in the resplendent urbanism parade. Instead, I will build a pedestal for the bicycle as transport to stand upon, in order to accelerate the understanding of its role in the life-sized city and the transport equation, as well as to drive home once and for all the importance of best-practice infrastructure.

The global bicycle boom has been underway since 2007 and shows no sign of waning. The bicycle is returning as transport in our cities after an absence, in many places, of decades. We have entered into an exciting urban age of rediscovery, but there remains a lack of understanding, be it macro or micro, about the role of bicycle urbanism in our cities as both transport and as a social cohesive. It is high time we fixed that by presenting a clear and definitive guide to the hows and whys of embracing an urban future that includes the bicycle as the key tool for transport, design, planning, and social development. I firmly believe that the bicycle is the single most important tool in our urban toolbox for improving our cities. We need to ensure that as many people as possible are in the loop about how to use it efficiently.

Living in Copenhagen—the City of Cyclists—has offered me a solid pedestal from which I have been able to regard other cities. Through my work I have cycled in over 65 cities around the world, rolling effortlessly along gold-standard infrastructure but also navigating bizarre bike lanes and the worst asphalt imaginable. Studying and analyzing the designs and how they work or don't work. Observing the people cycling in a city and how they interact with the infrastructure or lack thereof, as well as all the amazing anthropological details and transport psychology relating to urban cycling.

Since I am the author of a book about urban cycling and bicycle urbanism, it may come as a surprise that I am not a cyclist. Perhaps quotation marks are in order: "cyclist." I don't identify in any way, shape, or form as one. I am just a modern city dweller who just happens to use a bicycle to get around because it is safe and efficient. I'll explore further along why citizens of Copenhagen—including myself—overwhelmingly choose the bicycle as transport, but for now it is important to establish that baseline.

When I leave my apartment to go to the bakery, I suppose I become a pedestrian if I walk, a motorist if I take a car, or a passenger if I take public transport. Likewise, I transform from being an apartment dweller to being a cyclist if I hop on my bike. For purposes of gathering data, we get sorted into these categories. Fair enough. The very word *cyclist*, however, has strong connotations in many parts of the world. If I am talking to someone in a bar in America and I say I am a cyclist, images will invariably appear in their head of me decked out in spandex, helmet, and clicky shoes, out for a long ride somewhere or trying to beat my record for speed or distance. In Denmark, we use the word *cyclist* to differentiate among traffic users, but very few people will identify as one.

This book isn't about bicycle culture any more than it's about vacuum-cleaner culture, which is how I describe bicycle-friendly cities like Copenhagen, Amsterdam, or Tokyo. We all have a vacuum and have learned how to use it. We don't have a stable of vacuums that we keep polished and oiled. We don't dress up in vacuuming clothes or wave at other avid "vacuumists" on the street. The vacuum cleaner is just an effective tool that makes our daily lives easier. Just like the bicycle.

I came to cycling late. Like any kid, I had a burning desire to learn how to ride, but my dad worked ungodly hours, and while my mum was a model matriarch, her skill set didn't include teaching a kid to ride. I think I was seven when my big brother Steven visited and took me out onto Fairview Crescent and worked with me until I nailed it. I'll never forget that moment. He had been jogging behind me, holding onto the high backrest bar on my banana seat—it was the 1970s, man—to help me keep my balance. Then, on one run up the street, I realized I couldn't hear his footsteps. I turned my head as best I could and saw him far behind me, standing in the middle of the street with a big smile on his face. I was cycling. Isn't it beautiful how most people remember that moment when they cycle for the first time? Despite decades of car-centric development, children still learn to ride a bike, even if they don't have anywhere safe to ride it afterwards. This remains the first powerful moment of true independence in our lives that we can remember. We're too young to recall sitting, crawling, or walking for the first time, but mastering the bicycle stays with us forever. The fact that learning to ride a bicycle is still a thing is, for me, one of the great poetic aspects of cycling.

I can't be bothered to repair bikes beyond the most basic fixes. Hey, I live in a city with 600 bike shops, so, like most of my fellow Copenhageners, I chuck a bike into a shop for my repairs. But I believe in the bicycle, not only as a brilliant symbol for this emerging urban age but also as the tool for reversing the damage done to our cities over the past century. The bicycle boom that started in early 2007 with *Cycle Chic* could have been a brief, viral window. A trend like acid-washed jeans in the 1980s (guilty as charged). But the bike stuck. It's as though, without knowing it, we were waiting for its return to fulfill its timeless role as a symbol of modernity.

In 2006, very few cities were considering the bicycle as transport. Ten years on, very few cities haven't at least had the conversation, and, more encouragingly, many are making serious efforts to capitalize on bikes.

I grew up in Calgary, Canada, the son of immigrants who had arrived from Denmark in 1953. While much of my childhood and youth was spent on bikes—cycling to sports, friends' houses, and the local shops, and generally disappearing on my bike until I got hungry and came home—I also lived in North America, where getting a car at sixteen was the default. A 15-minute walk to high school became a five-minute drive. No more bus rides to get to the mall. Nevertheless, I still rode my bike, enjoying the pathway around Glenmore Dam and trying to beat the personal best that I had timed.

At eighteen, I moved from Calgary to Vancouver and, for reasons I no longer recall, I would ride my bike from various apartments in North Vancouver to downtown over the Lion's Gate Bridge. I just liked it. This was 1986, and I don't remember seeing very many other cyclists on my daily routes. I also recall that I never experienced any animosity from motorists. (Things have changed.)

When, at 22, I ventured farther afield—leaving Canada, never to return—I often found a bike to ride for transport in the cities where I was living. Melbourne, Moscow, London, Paris. Even Suva City and Hong Kong. I was often regarded with curiosity and a bemused smile, but never ridicule. I never wore the spandex uniform of cyclists or had any gear on my trusty 10-speeds. I never intended to be demonstrative about my transport form. I was just a dude on a bike who liked moving around like that.

In retrospect, one pivotal event left its mark on me and continues to feed my inner aquifer with inspiration. In 1988, I was studying in Pasadena, California, and, while crossing the street at the corner with a friend, I was struck by a car traveling at about 60 km/h (about 40 mph), according to police estimates. I flew through the air like a football and landed 30 meters (98 feet) farther along. By all accounts, everyone who witnessed the accident was convinced that I was dead—no one could have survived such an impact. But I was a lucky man. My leg was broken in two places and my collarbone snapped close to my sternum from landing on my shoulder, but apart from that and some road rash, I was fine. Based on what I know now about death and injury rates from automobile impacts, I had only a 5 percent chance of surviving being run down at that speed.

The event dipped under the surface of my consciousness but never disappeared completely. It was only later in life that it manifested itself as a primary factor in my work and personal philosophy about urban development. I was handed a slim chance of survival and I was allowed to take it. Since that day in November 1988, I have tried to live life to the fullest and, through my work, design conditions in cities that will allow other people to live without the risk of the same situation or worse.

I moved to Copenhagen in 1994. I had intended to visit friends for a week before continuing my restless wandering from city to city around the world. Because of my family's heritage, I could work, so I decided to stick around for a bit. That was 24 years ago. I found the roots I didn't know I had been searching for.

I had hardly been in country more than a week before my friends made two things perfectly clear. One: if I was going to stay, FC Copenhagen would now be my Danish football team of choice. That was not up for discussion. Two: I needed a bike to get around. I was tossed a bike key and informed that the bike was somewhere in the backyard and was probably green. I found it and immediately hit the cycle tracks. No fireworks or rousing orchestral music. Just two wheels and a rusty chain. That bike key doubled as the key to the city. The absolute normalcy of using a bicycle in Copenhagen is something I can recognize now, but at the time I just slid right into it without much conscious thought. Isn't that the way it should be?

I continued my life in Copenhagen. Like most of my fellow citizens I was happily ignorant of the inherent beauty of being a part of the organic transport ballet of the Danish capital. Until the morning of November 14, 2006. I have shot street photography for many years, and that morning was no exception. I had a trusty camera in my pocket as I headed to work at Danish Broadcasting. According to the Exif info on the photo, it was at 08:46 that I took a photo in the morning traffic. The light ahead had just turned to green. A cyclist on the right was pushing off. A couple of cyclists were swooping in from a side street on the left. In front of me was a Copenhagener who hadn't yet moved. She was standing astride her bicycle. A pillar of calm in a world of chaos, lost in her thoughts. I snapped the shot and rode past her to work.

Later that day I put the photo on Flickr, where I had a bit of a following. I started receiving comments, mostly from the States, like "How does she ride a bike in that skirt and those boots?!" As though it was some bizarre thing to do on a bike. I didn't get it. These were odd questions for me, a Copenhagener. I had no idea what they were talking about.

When someone reacts positively to your work, be it photography or writing or whatever, the simple reaction is to continue in the same vein. I started taking more photos of elegantly dressed Copenhageners doing absolutely nothing special on their bikes, and viewers continued to express their amazement.

In early 2007, a series of these photos were published in *Magasinet KBH*, a local publication about life in Copenhagen, and I coined the phrase *cycle chic* as a title (*cykel chic* was how it was rendered in Danish). People kept reacting and I kept shooting. In mid-2007, I decided to start a blog. Hey, everyone and their dog was starting one at that point. I figured I could use the blog as a repository or gallery in case I took more shots of Copenhagen's bicycle life. What happened surprised me. Within a week, there were a few hundred visitors a day, and that continued to grow exponentially.

In mid-2007, streetstyle blogs were booming, and *Copenhagen Cycle Chic* walked right into this trend. In addition, I discovered that there were no blogs anywhere dedicated to urban cycling. I googled and googled and could only find blogs about sport and recreational cycling. *Streetsblog* had a few articles about urban cycling, but there wasn't much else out there.

My blog continued to explode and I upped the content contribution. The majority of the readers were—and still are—women. Even though the blog featured street photography, the streetstyle feel was the main draw, and the fact that we focus on bicycles made it unique.

Cycle Chic continued to snowball and, at its peak, there were over 200 copycat blogs all over the world. It was in the spring of 2007 that I started to ponder in detail why these photos were capturing so many imaginations. Something that was so completely normal to me and my fellow Copenhageners was getting people around the world excited. The simple act of riding a bike through a city.

I started researching how Copenhagen had ended up like this. My curiosity as a journalist led me down the path to start Copenhagenize.com, designed as a companion blog to *Cycle Chic*.

I had read an article about the "copenhagenization" of some city, used in a slightly negative way by a journalist. I let *copenhagenize* roll off my tongue a few times and liked it. The next, natural step was to google both *copenhagenise* and *copenhagenize* to see what was out there. There was nothing apart from a naval term dating from the early 1800s, used to describe the British strategy of bombing an enemy into submission from the sea and then sailing their entire navy away. The Brits did this to Copenhagen in 1807 and the term *Copenhagenize* originated there. Until 2007, of course, when I gave it a new meaning.

Others in my industry have hijacked the term and use it to describe all manner of urbanist influences coming from Copenhagen, but that was never my intention. I stick to my original meaning, which is the specific focus on the bicycle as transport.

The *Copenhagenize* blog, like *Cycle Chic*, exploded early on. This little blog seemed to fill a gap about the bicycle's role in cities as transport. Indeed, I have pondered the whole return of the bicycle. It is as though we were all waiting for something, anything, to act as a symbol of where we all should be heading with urban development and environmental concerns. The bicycle came back and slid effortlessly into the same role it had played after its invention in the late 1800s. Pragmatic, sensible, modern, societal change.

It is safe to say that very few cities were discussing the bicycle as transport in 2006. Now, there are very few cities where the bicycle has not been, at the very least, discussed. A strong *esprit de corps* has developed. A lone voice in the wilderness has morphed into a choir.

The role of these two blogs in reestablishing the bicycle in the public consciousness, however inadvertently, was not restricted to the rest of the world. The bicycle was an integral part of the image of Amsterdam, but in Copenhagen, despite having the same cycling levels, the bicycle was not a visible part of the city's branding or image. There were very few hotels that rented bikes to tourists in 2006; instead they sent visitors to a handful of rental locations. Now, a hotel without bike rental is a rarity and bikes appear regularly in the city's tourism material. Copenhagen's cycling life is a role model for other cities everywhere.

The bicycle could have enjoyed a starring role in just that one brief chapter of urban history over a century ago, but now it is back. Bigger and stronger than ever. It's time to cement it firmly in the urban narrative.

I approach the subject matter with fresh eyes, unencumbered by academic indoctrination. I draw upon my own thoughts and ideas, but also the experience I've gained while working for dozens of cities around the world on bicycle planning, strategy, infrastructure design, and communication.

After a century of urban confusion, of wrongly placed energy, of seduction by overcomplicated technology, it's time to clean up. To return to a spirit of *mater artium necesssitas*—necessity is the mother of invention. We need to act in order to save our cities—and us—from ourselves. To fix a century of broken with a tool that fixes.

Let's go.

CHAPTER 1

THE LIFE-SIZED CITY

Daddy, when is my city going to fit me?

Lulu-Sophia Modler-Andersen

I have a strange suspicion that we've been hacked. As people. As societies. We have been led to believe that big is best. That growth is good. For so many years that you can easily call it a century of living with the Cult of Big. Certainly regarding the economy. You can't mention the economy without mentioning growth. But I'm not an economist. I work in urbanism. In cities. And the same thing applies. Cities have to be bigger. Broader. They have to sprawl into the distance as far as the eye can see. That is what makes a city great and good. Or so we've been told for many, many years. Buildings have to be taller, shinier. Reaching for the sky. Breaking world records. Monuments to engineering and, quite possibly, phallic symbols for the male-dominated industries that design and build them. Roads and motorways have to be longer, wider, go farther. More capacity, improved flow, reduced congestion. It's one of the saddest ironies of urban planning that the only thing we have learned from a hundred years of traffic engineering is

Cyclists on best-practice infrastructure in Copenhagen.

Lulu-Sophia in Copenhagen in 2011.

this: if you make more space for cars, more cars come. It's sad if you think about all the kabillions of dollars we've thrown at this for the past century.

Megaprojects are all the rage. Never finished on time, always obscenely over budget, and yet they make up 8 percent of the global GDP. We're fascinated, obsessed by megaprojects. We, the people, the consumers, are told to spend more. Buy more stuff. The more we buy, the better it will be for the economy. For growth. Or so we have been told for a very long time.

Perhaps we've been hacked, but I believe that we still have the original code inside us. When you have been around for 300,000 years as homo sapiens, you possess that original code. The pure programming. We can be rational when we want to be. Everyone knows, deep inside, which ice cream will be more enjoyable to eat when choosing between a single, delicious scoop or a monster pile of ice cream. Once in a while we can go crazy,

but the single scoop will usually be the best experience. The same applies to food portions. We're hard-wired to understand the basics of urban life. Every one of us who lives in a city knows what a good street should look like. It's in our urban DNA to know that a human street that is friendly to pedestrians and cyclists and that has lots of green space is the best solution. We know intuitively and instinctively as a species that size doesn't matter. Luckily, somewhere in there, in the dark shadow of the Cult of Big, behind the mountain of obsessive growth, there is a lovely little place I call the Life-Sized City, where things are different.

The idea of the *life-sized city* has become a cornerstone in my working philosophy. The concept was handed to me by one of my life's greatest urbanist inspirations: my daughter Lulu-Sophia. We were walking around our neighborhood and waiting to cross a street, holding hands. She was quiet, looking around at the cityscape around her. Suddenly, she turned and looked up at me and said, "Daddy, when is my city going to fit me?" She was five at the time. I looked down at her quizzical face and assured her she would grow to fit her city better. She just shrugged and nodded. She knew the answer but in that moment she felt too small for her city, as so many kids must. But her innocent concept lodged itself in my head. I couldn't think of anything else and wondered about whether my city fits *me*.

There are many stretches in Copenhagen where it feels as though the place were designed for me and me alone. Riding over Queen Louise's Bridge on one-way cycle tracks over four meters wide, the city fits me like a finely crafted glove. Elsewhere, even though I have gold-standard infrastructure to cycle on, the buildings are out of scale, the roadway parallel to the cycle track is congested with noisy, polluting automobiles, and in place like these, I fail to achieve a sense of life-sized. Indeed, there are few places in the world where I, let alone Lulu, feel like the city fits me.

From that revelation coming from the mind of a child, the phrase *life-sized city* came to me—both as a way of describing cities at the moment and as a goal for how cities should be once again.

The idea of the life-sized city is complemented by the concept of *genius loci*—the spirit of place. Applying both of these notions to city planning will bring the scale back to normal. We all possess a universal, individual desire to feel like we belong in our surroundings.

Think about your home. Think about the effort you put into designing, crafting, and creating a space in which you have a constant, unwavering sense of belonging and well-being. Think also about where you work, where people (hopefully) have put a similar effort into making a space that inspires you to be a productive member of the workforce.

After decades of car-centric planning, the same can't be said for most of the cityscapes we move through on a daily basis around the world.

What is a city? When I travel, I often hear things like, "Oh, but that's Copenhagen . . . It's different there . . . " Civic pride is important. Absolutely. I wouldn't want to live in a city that did not give me a sense of ownership every single day, even with a tectonic political landscape that often fails to match my own desires. We have, however, allowed our cities to be engineered since we invented the automobile, even though cities are organic creatures, morphing themselves over time and space to accommodate shifting generational needs and demographic trends. They are defined by the citizens who live in cities here and now and who hopefully have an eye on the future of the place. You simply cannot engineer organic places populated by a wide and varied selection of humans. Nor do you need to.

Think about your home. Think about the effort you put into designing, crafting, and creating a space in which you have a constant, unwavering sense of belonging and well-being.

A city is a language. Each one has an ever-changing dialect and a unique tonal fingerprint that differentiates it even from the suburbs that surround it. These urban dialects contribute to the urban, global language spoken by those of us who see what improvements need to be made in order to make our cities better. And if a city is a language, the bicycle is the compound modifier.

_85 percent of kids in Denmark can
ride a bike by the age of five._

CHAPTER 2

BICYCLE URBANISM BY DESIGN

 Everyone wants progress, no one wants change.

Søren Kierkegaard

Here's the baseline. We have been living together in cities for more than 7,000 years. By and large, we used those seven millennia to hammer out some serious best-practices about cohabitation and transport in the urban theater and the importance of social fabric. We threw most of that knowledge under the wheels of the automobile shortly after we invented it and have subsequently suffered through a *saeculum horribilis* in the urban context. Our overenthusiasm for technology and our human tendency to suffer from short-term urban memory loss have further contributed to our zealous disregard for past experience.

Cities thrill me, but it has always been the streets that fascinate me to no end. Streets are the skeletal structure of the city organism. The veins pumping the lifeblood of a city from one end of the urban landscape to the other. For 7,000 years, the streets of a city were the most democratic spaces in the history of homo sapiens. We did everything in the streets. We transported ourselves, sure, but we also bought and sold our goods, flirted, gossiped, discussed politics. Our children played in the streets. They were an extension of our homes, of our living rooms. Urban development was natural and organic and was based on the immediate needs of the people living in the streets in particular and the city in general. Both logistical needs and societal.

Years ago, after I finished film school, I taught storytelling and screenwriting. After we, as homo sapiens, have secured our three basic needs—water, food, and shelter—our fourth need emerges: storytelling. For the better part of human history, we gathered around a firepit after the day was done—telling stories, forming bonds, and further building belief systems and cultural mythologies. Some might argue that sex is our fourth basic need, but telling or listening to stories is an important step toward having sex with someone.

When the automobile appeared in our cities, it was an invasive species and detested by citizens.

The firepit was our meeting place. Our anchor. As cities emerged and an indoor life became a part of our norm, the streets still remained as our urban firepit in which we told our stories and formed our bonds.

The automobile and the infrastructure required to move it through our cities sounded a death knell for the streets and for our urban firepit. After 300,000 years of homo sapiens and 7,000 years of democratic space, our perception of the streets changed drastically. The automobile industry

made quick work of it, too. Two things happened to change the perception. When the automobile appeared in our cities, it was an invasive species detested by citizens. Motorists were despised, and makeshift monuments were erected in many American cities to the alarming number of victims of car crashes—in particular, children.

There was an almost instant traffic-safety problem, and everyone was at a loss as to how to solve it. Engineers were the urban heroes of the day in our rapidly expanding cities. Figuring out solutions for how to get electricity and water to our homes and sewage away from them. That couple of generations of engineers were brilliant. Engineers were handed the task of solving the traffic-safety carnage. The best problem-solvers of the day were an obvious choice for tackling such a serious problem. What happened, however, was that streets went from being regarded as a subconscious democratic firepit to becoming treated as public utilities. Not human spaces but puzzles to be solved with mathematical equations.

The automobile industry also had a problem. It had shiny new products to sell, and yet everyone hated them. They knew they needed to change the public perception of streets, and so they employed marketing, spin, and good old-fashioned ridicule to start the ball rolling. This is where they cut their teeth on marketing their vehicles and carved out techniques still in use today.

It was one thing that engineers were tweaking the way traffic lights functioned in order to accommodate the rising number of cars, but the automobile industry saw an opportunity to start selling the idea that streetspace should be allocated exclusively to those cars.

The idea was simple: Everyone else get out of the way. It started with op-eds and ads in newspapers about pedestrians staying out of the streets and instead using the growing number of crosswalks. Boy Scouts were enlisted to hand out flyers, chastising pedestrians for their behavior. The timeless act of crossing the street in the middle of the block was gradually becoming socially unacceptable. Anyone who resisted this new school of thought was labeled as old-fashioned. Standing in the way of progress.

That very American word, *jaywalking,* was intended simply to ridicule pedestrians who were slow to adapt to the desires of the automobile industry. *Jay* was a derogatory word for a country bumpkin—someone who didn't know the ways of the big, cool city. If we live in cities, the last thing we want is to be considered outsiders. We want to feel a sense of collective belonging. One simple word, repeated *ad nauseam* was all that was needed.

The last great obstacle faced by those wanting to secure streetspace for cars was the angry mothers of America who kept seeing their children killed or maimed by cars in the streets. Enter: the playground. That little zoological garden into which we continue to put our kids was an invention of the automobile industry as a way to get the little rascals out of the way and to appease their mothers. Finally, the stage was set. The coast was clear of irritating, squishy obstacles, and the greatest paradigm shift in the history of our cities was complete. It took under two decades to reverse 7,000 years of perceiving streets as democratic spaces. We are still suffering from it. (Peter Norton's book *Fighting Traffic* is your go-to tome about this fascinating and depressing period in transportation history.)

What also happened was that our societal firepit was effectively removed. Doused in water, buried out of sight, and paved over with asphalt.

Firepits have reemerged in some cities. Pedestrian-friendly streets, public transport, and the bicycle have brought back the opportunity to gather with our urban flock. Whether we speak to each other or not, we are elbow to elbow with our fellow citizens, sharing a subconscious urban experience. In the Copenhagen rush hour, on every street small firepits are formed at intersections, allowing citizens to gather in clusters while transporting themselves through the city.

Our societal firepit was effectively removed. Doused in water, buried out of sight, and paved over with asphalt.

The urban anthropological advantages of having impromptu cycling firepits should not be underestimated. Motorists walk out of a house and into a garage to get into a car for a drive to work. They park and enter an office. There is little interaction with other citizens in such a vacuum-packed life. Cycling through a city, however, you are closely connected with the urban landscape, using all of your senses. Every morning, as I pass City Hall Square cyclists check the clock tower. They either slow down or speed up, depending on their schedule. I don't communicate directly with other people at red lights, but we are connected. I see human forms, I hear coughs or telephone conversations. I smell shampoo and perfume around me. I get ideas for shopping when I see clothes or shoes worn by someone else. I exchange flirtatious glances or smiles.

I will do the same as a pedestrian or aboard public transport, but there is an amazing dynamic on the cycle tracks and at red lights. Jostling for space, keeping our balance, soaking up sensory impressions before moving on to the next firepit.

The Danish novelist Johannes V. Jensen, who won the Nobel Prize for Literature in 1944, has many references to urban cycling in his body of work. In the 1936 novel *Gudrun*, he writes:

"And, like a large home, Copenhagen begins the day's work. Already down on the streets, one is at home, with loose hair, in long sitting rooms through which one travels sociably on a bicycle. In offices, workshops, and boutiques you are at home, in your own home. Part of one large family that has divided the city among itself and that runs it in an orderly fashion, like a large house. So that everyone has a role and everyone gets what they need. Copenhagen is like a large, simple house."

A Copenhagener checks the time on Copenhagen City Hall's clocktower. © Lorenz Siegel

Indeed. A home. With a much-needed hearth. And lest we forget, this was the norm in most cities on the planet for decades—from the bicycle boom in the late nineteenth century to at least the 1940s and 1950s. The bicycle was a normal form of transport from Manchester to Singapore, from Sydney to Seville. The modal share for bicycles in Los Angeles a century ago was 20 percent. Small, transportational firepits around which cyclists gathered were warming our cities.

The fledgling vocation of traffic engineering, granted carte blanche by the new paradigm, continued the radical engineering of our streets. Standards were developed in America through the 1930s and 1940s, in tandem with the rising belief that cars were the vehicle of a glorious future. The standards started to travel and were readily adopted by countries around the world. This development accelerated through the 1950s and 1960s. Cycling traffic in most cities of the world peaked in the late 1940s and then began a sharp decline. Even in Copenhagen and Amsterdam; 55 percent of Copenhageners rode a bike in 1949. By 1969, that number had fallen to around 20 percent as roads were widened to accommodate cars. The most surprising thing about traffic engineering is that it is largely unchanged in the decades since the 1950s. In our modern society we would be absolutely outraged if one vital profession lagged behind. Imagine if medical care were still using the same techniques and science as it did in the 1950s. Or education, or parenting. That would be bizarre and unacceptable. And yet we accept that traffic engineering has failed to modernize. Or perhaps just failed.

When you start to scratch just a little below the surface, you discover that we live in cities that are controlled by strange and often outdated mathematical theories, models, and engineering "solutions" that continue to be used despite the fact that they are of little use to modern cities.

One of them is called "the 85th percentile." It's a method that cities all over the planet use to determine speed limits. It's the standard. Nobody questions it. Certainly not the engineers and planners who, for decades, have swallowed it whole during their studies. Which reminds me of the old traffic engineer joke: Why did the engineer cross the road? Because that's what they did last year.

The concept is rather simple: the speed limit of a road is set by determining the speed of 85 percent of cars that go down it. In other words, the speed limit is solely set by the speed of drivers, and this is the basic rule that determines traffic speeds worldwide. Including the street outside your home.

The bicycle was a normal transport form from Manchester to Singapore, from Sydney to Seville.

It can, of course, be revised—but that rarely happens. The engineers will just shrug and say that the 85th percentile method is the only method and it can't be changed. The numbers don't lie. The problem is that human beings are not numbers. Here's the tricky part of the 85th-percentile method. It assumes the following:

The large majority of drivers are reasonable and prudent, do not want to have a crash, and desire to reach their destination in the shortest possible time; a speed at or below which 85 percent of people drive at any given location under good weather and visibility conditions may be considered as the maximum safe speed for that location.

"I'm a traffic engineer, but I'm a problem solver. Nobody has ever told me that there was a different problem to solve."

If they're assuming that the large majority of drivers are reasonable and prudent, then what about the rest of the drivers? Do we just assume that everything is going to be fine by handing over complete power of our streets to motorists? Not to mention mixing anthropological assumptions with pseudoscience?

This, on the other hand, is the traffic engineer's perception of "safety" and speed. Looking at the graph, their perception is rather different and rather out of date:

Imagine a street where the average speed is 50 kilometers per hour (30 miles per hour). If the speed is reduced by 5 kilometers per hour (3 miles per hour), then, according to this archaic model, the drivers are allegedly exposed to a higher risk. What is most shocking is that this entire concept completely ignores pedestrians and cyclists. Another horrific conclusion from this graph is that when you increase the speed, the crash risk is alleged to be less than for slow speeds.

All of this seems suspiciously like an argument to build more highways and freeways—because "with more speed comes more security,"

as they (once) said. The graph, still touted as the "latest research," is called the Solomon Curve. At the Copenhagenize Design Company office we all guessed how old it was, and our guesses ranged between 15 and 30 years old. But none of us were close. In reality, it is based on a 1964 study by David Solomon entitled "Accidents on Main Rural Highways Related to Speed, Driver, and Vehicle."

You read that right. "Main Rural Highways"— not city streets. It is still wholly endorsed by the US Department of Commerce and the Bureau of Public Roads, which was administered at the time of the study by Rex Whitton. He was also—surprise, surprise—a federal highway administrator. Okay, don't be surprised.

In essence, a study from 1964 remains the main argument to build more highways and freeways with faster speeds where the ends justify the means, even if the means ignore vulnerable groups such as pedestrians and cyclists and assume that public transport doesn't even exist. Even if the study is also now used to serve the automobile in densely populated urban areas, far from any freeways.

The Institute of Traffic Engineers once wrote that "the 85th Percentile is how drivers vote with their feet." The ITE failed to mention that, when it comes to establishing speed limits in cities, pedestrians and cyclists are excluded from their election. They don't even get the chance to go to the polls. All this is still happening right now as you read this. In your street. With your tax money.

Adam Millard-Ball is an assistant professor at the University of Santa Cruz. He has studied peak traffic and the future of traffic demand. He is highly critical of another key aspect of traffic engineering, namely traffic modeling, which attempts to map out future patterns of travel demand, patterns that, he says, have enormous implications for energy supply and the environment. In order to sell the need for more motorways and street expansions to politicians and engineers, they try to determine how far people will travel in the future and by what forms of transport. They employ techniques and mathematical equations that are guesses decked out in sheep's clothing. They are wrong almost every time.

Millard-Ball uses two examples. One is projections from the Department for Transport in the United Kingdom and from Washington State. The actual traffic growth is marked in black. Wild colored lines shooting for the stars show the projections. Millard-Ball says that it is a tendency all around the world to wildly exaggerate the increase in volume of traffic. Reality is quite different from the computer models, still employed by transport departments, that pro-

duce projections that influence politicians and affect the lives of millions. Such graphs are what politicians see and believe to be true. But the models are wrong and hopelessly out of date.

I could go on. It's no secret that I am critical of traffic engineering and the pedestal on which we place it as the sole solution for planning traffic in cities. I speak to this in the keynotes I give around the world. I am often approached by audience members who want to discuss it further after I come offstage. In six different countries, I have met six traffic engineers who came up to me after a keynote and said exactly the same thing, which I find fascinating: "I'm a traffic engineer, but I'm a problem solver. Nobody has ever told me that there was a different problem to solve…"

The same line, almost verbatim, spoken in English in six different accents by traffic engineers frustrated by the fact that other solvable

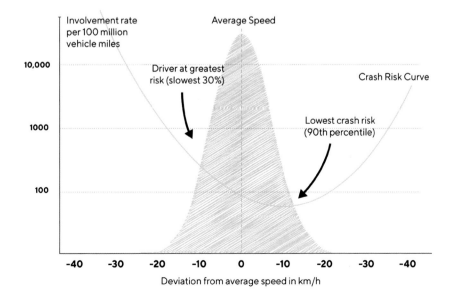

The Solomon Curve.

problems exist and they were kept in the dark. Like discovering there was ice cream in the freezer for ages but you were told there wasn't. Later in this book I will cover how we desperately need to change the questions we have been asking in cities for close to a century.

First, though, I want to offer up some alternative philosophies. We can rightly assume that there was "engineering" in play over the past 7,000 years that preceded the automobile. Roads and squares were built and buildings to go alongside them. The Romans, among others, excelled at construction and developing techniques. By and large, it was a much more organic process. Engineering responded to the immediate needs of the people who were living there and worked in tandem with them. Necessity was the mother of invention, as it should be. Although no longer, it would seem. We live in an overly tech-horny world where

we invent things because we can, not because we actually need them. No one has been able to explain to me what the phrase "smart cities" is supposed to mean. Believe me, I have asked. It's a fancy, seductive catchphrase but one without any specific definition.

In order to plan for our urban future, we need to look closely at our urban past. A few years ago I was watching *Back to the Future* with my son, who was nine at the time. The film ended and he asked me what year it was made in. I told him it was 1985. He laughed. "So Doc went 30 years into the future . . . that's like . . . NOW! But there are no flying cars and goofy clothes . . ."

Nope. He nailed it. A century of technological—and fashion—promises that failed to deliver. A *saeculum horribilis* from which we need to recover. Feel free to lump autonomous cars and the hype surrounding them into the same category. When

Left: Graph by Professor Phil Goodwin showing traffic projections by Britain's Department for Transport (in color) and the actual car traffic growth (black).
Right: Graph by Sightline Institute showing similar traffic projections by Washington State's DoT and the actual car traffic growth.

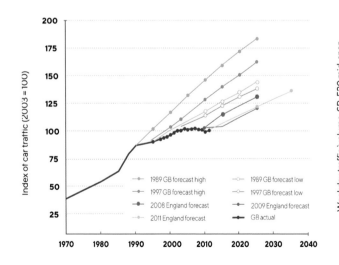

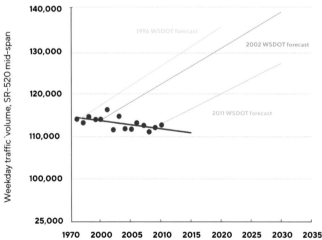

I speak of the importance of going to back to the future, I mean to a place where we were rational and realistic. Back to a time—or times—where we did things that made sense.

Bicycle urbanism by design is the way forward. We are surrounded—if not bombarded—by products to buy in our daily lives. Take a look around you at the many products you have acquired. Your smartphone, toothbrush, remote control, mouse, chair. They all have one thing in common. There was a designer or a design team dedicated to ensuring that you would have a positive design experience when using it. The team that produced my smartphone was employed by a multinational corporation that is intent on increasing profit margins, sure, but the designers bent over backwards to make sure that the phone was easy, intuitive, and enjoyable to use by me, my ten-year-old daughter, and my 88-year-old father. And everyone in between. It was a human-to-human process from idea to purchase. Their sole task was thinking about the human on the other end of that process. That can't be said of traffic engineering and even traffic planning in most parts of the world, where mathematical models focused on moving cars around is the primary focus.

It's a simple question: What if we designed our streets like we design everything else in our lives? Like we expect everything we use to be designed? It's no secret that Denmark is a design culture. The phrase "Danish Design" is swathed loftily in quotation marks, and my kids have design classes in the third and fourth grades here in Copenhagen. The three principles of Danish Design are carved in stone: Practical, Functional, Elegant. Humans love chairs and have been constantly designing them for several millennia. As well as interpreting them. Designers and architects have been trying to funk up the chair since forever. All manner of interpretations have seen the light of day, from the interesting to the wacky. We can regard chairs at exhibitions that have been dressed up like an octopus or a shopping cart and either love them or hate them. The point is that none of us have four crazy interpretations of the chair in our living room for guests to sit on.

It's a simple question. What if we designed our streets like we design everything else in our lives? Like we expect everything we use to be designed?

Chair design can be relevant as a metaphor for bicycle infrastructure, however. A chair like the design by Peter Bristol might just be a fair representation of a cycling map for most cities in the world. There are bits and pieces of it, it doesn't really connect up in any coherent network, and there are many sharp edges—but the man is showing us that it "works." Funny. Interesting. At the end of the day, however, we still don't have six of these around our dining table. *All people want is a chair.* You're probably sitting down as you read this. Think about the chair or sofa you're on. You walked over to it, turned, and sat down. You didn't have to circle the chair, pensively scratching your chin, wondering what the designer's intentions were. It wasn't necessary to search for an on/off button. You were not concerned at any point about

The cycling map of your city? Bits and pieces of infrastructure. Doesn't really connect up in a coherent network. Lots of sharp edges.
Photo: "Cut Chair" by Peter Bristol

whether or not the chair would disappear from under you while reading these words. You sat down. It was easy and intuitive.

Imagine if cycling or walking in a city were as easy and intuitive as that. Well, a well-designed bicycle infrastructure network is like a well-designed chair. It is practical and functional and requires little interpretation to use it. If it is also elegant, then so much the better. Mark my words, it's not a pipe dream. It's a reality and it's attain-able. In the study "Understanding the Seduc-tive Experience," designers Julie Khaslavsky and Nathan Shedroff explore the seductive nature of design. To paraphrase: *The seductive power of design can transcend issues of price and performance. They have the ability to create an emotional bond with their audiences, almost a need for them.*

Do I swoon every time I cycle around Copen-hagen on best-practice infrastructure that is kept swept and smooth? No. Nor do I fall to my knees in awe of the beauty of the "7" chair by Danish architect Arne Jacobsen in my living room or sigh wistfully every time I pull out my Samsung Galaxy S8 smartphone. All have seduced me, however. The thrill of the seduction bubbled to the surface in the early stages of my emotional relationship with such objects, but now it has been absorbed into my subconscious. I do not doubt that I experience pleasure when using such objects, but damn, I need them. I need that constant sense of well-being I experience when using them. I don't need to think about them, they just need to work and to look spectacular. In the case of bicycle infrastructure, I need to be safe and feel safe and get to where I'm going without having to put much thought into it.

The seduction of design became apparent to me while playing a car-racing game on our Xbox with my son, Felix, when he was ten years old. It's a game where you get to select which car you want to race with, and you can choose cars from all the major brands and throughout the history of the automobile. As Felix was scrolling through the selection, I noticed how every now and then he would say, "Daddy . . . cool car."

My kids, I've calculated, spend no more than five hours a year in a car in our daily lives in Copenhagen. We may rent a car in the summer holidays, but the rest of the year, cars simply don't register on their radar. Ours is not an anti-car home, as such; we just have no cause to talk about cars, since we never use them. So it was all the more interesting to see Felix look at vintage cars and react to them positively. As he scrolled, I started to keep track of which cars he was reacting to. I wrote them down and looked them up. Every single car was pre-1972, whether it was a Volvo, BMW, Ford, you name it.

Back when car design was cool and not the generic blur of anonymous, colorless vehicles we see today. The kid saw cool design and knew it was cool without having any investment in the subject. Don't worry, I also have a bike-related anecdote about young Felix, although it is reversed. Where cars don't figure into our conversation, bikes most certainly do, simply because they are our primary transport form. In a city where 62 percent of the population ride a bike to work or school, bikes are a key element in our transport habits, but they are also incredibly anonymous. I noticed that Felix, as he graduated from bike to bike since learning to cycle at four years old, would invariably choose bikes that looked liked everyone else's—particularly his schoolmates' bikes. Among children, the desire to conform is strong.

You sat down. It was easy and intuitive. Imagine if cycling or walking in a city were as easy and intuitive as that.

Until one day when he sent me a photo taken at one of the bike racks outside his school, accompanied by the text, "Daddy! Must have!" It was a photo of a vintage Schwinn chopper, complete with banana seat and backrest. This learned-to-cycle in the 1970s Dad was thrilled, but it was odd that he was reacting to a bike design so far outside the typological norms of his contemporaries. "It's just really cool," was Felix's response when I asked. So I embarked on a mission to accommodate his request, ending up finding him a Raleigh chopper to ride. Apart from enjoying his new ride, he started to experience something unusual in the Copenhagen context: people noticed his bike. In a forest, it's hard to appreciate one particular tree, which is the case with bikes in Copenhagen. But Felix would roll up to a red light and men would look down at the bike, nod approvingly, and say, "Cool bike, kid." Small kids would point at him cycling past and exclaim, *"Wow! Cool bike!"*

After cycling anonymously for years, Felix was discovering how his personal design choice was received positively among strangers. He was seduced by design rather than performance, because—let's face it—choppers are uncomfortable to ride.

The citizens of Copenhagen have been seduced by the bicycle infrastructure network. It is practical and functional, getting them where they want to go quickly and conveniently. There is elegance in the smooth, structured uniformity and high level of maintenance. The smoothest asphalt in Denmark is always found on the cycle tracks. Even when the weather is miserable, which is more often than not in Copenhagen,

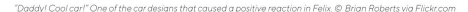

Take care of it. Keep it clean, polished, beautiful. Cherish it.

"Daddy! Cool car!" One of the car designs that caused a positive reaction in Felix. © Brian Roberts via Flickr.com

the seduction continues. Seventy-five percent of Copenhageners cycle all winter. There are better days for cycling in the city, but despite the challenges, it's still the quickest way to get around. The City knows how to make cycling a feasible option throughout the year. In the winter, the official policy is that all the cycle tracks are cleared of snow by 8:00 a.m. The goal is "black asphalt" by the time the citizens head out to go to work or school. As in many cities, the streets are divided up into categories for snow clearance; it's just that the bike infrastructure sits at the top of the list. If a snowstorm is more intense, it may prove difficult to keep the infrastructure clear of snow. The citizens know that it's temporary and

that the City is on the way and doing their best. The journey home will be much more pleasant, despite the subzero temperatures.

When you invest in a designer chair, table, or lamp, you take care of it. Why should it be any different with a comprehensive network of bicycle infrastructure? Keep it clean, polished, beautiful. Cherish it. Design is seductive, and design also possesses great power—the power to change human behavior, no less. Wherever you are as you read this, you have probably heard the same kind of comments about cyclists. You might even have uttered them yourself. "Those damn cyclists . . . breaking the law . . . " Insert whatever local expletives might be relevant. The first thing

Felix on his chopper in 2012.

Top: *Map of the on-street bicycle infrastructure network in Copenhagen.*
Bottom: *Map showing the infrastructure prioritized for winter maintenance.*
Data: City of Copenhagen

I say when I hear this—and I hear it all over the planet—is that it is completely unacceptable to scold cyclists when the city hasn't given them best-practice infrastructure or, even worse, none at all. I can't scold my children for stealing cookies if we don't even have a cookie jar.

Through design we have positively influenced human behavior.

Homo sapiens react to design, either positively or negatively, with their behavior. If you don't like their behavior, it's important to take a long hard look at the cause before going ballistic. Homo sapiens, by nature, do not like to break laws or partake of socially unacceptable behavior. We are a largely conservative species of herd animals. I don't look around for rocks to throw every time I pass a window. Nor do you. I just want to go about my daily life enjoyably and efficiently without spending much time contemplating the hows and whys. I cycle on a network designed for me and others like me, one that limits my need to deviate from the legal norms.

Indeed, Copenhageners are the world's best-behaved cyclists, due to the uniformity and intuitive design of our bicycle infrastructure. I'll get into the methodology later in this book, but after studying over 80,000 cyclists in Copenhagen intersections with Copenhagenize Design Company's Desire Line Analysis Studies, we can conclude that only 5 percent of cyclists smash through the Danish traffic laws.

Through design we have positively influenced human behavior. A cluster of cyclists at a red light in Copenhagen is a study in fidgeting, phone checking, city glancing, or straightforward staring. Not much else. Beautifully dull.

Afternoon traffic in the snow on a February day on Søtorvet in Copenhagen.

Even when stopped by a red light, we know that we'll still get to where we're going on time and more quickly than we would when using other transport forms. If you want to tackle the issue of cyclist behavior, first build a network that keeps them safe and separated from the other traffic users. Create a unique space for cycling—a luxury that has long been afforded to motorists and pedestrians—and prioritize cyclists at intersections, and then . . . and only then . . . do you have the right to criticize them.

Although, by that point, you'll only be criticizing a small group of bad apples and will prefer to enjoy the view of the ripe orchard. Well-designed infrastructure levels the playing field. Those who use it take care of it and defend it. It's asphalt democracy. By using basic design principles for the human users of the bicycle and the urban space, instead of flawed mathematical models employed by traffic engineering, we will accelerate the journey towards a bicycle-friendly urban future.

CHAPTER 3

THE BICYCLE'S ROLE IN URBAN LIFE

One sits on it either straight-backed, as though at a festive dinner party, or hunched painfully forward, as though one just failed an exam. All according to the situation, your inclination, or your inborn characteristics.

Johannes Wulff

The bicycle, since its invention, has had an amazing transformational effect on city life. The rising number of cyclists in our cities may seem new to many, but the parallels to the first rise of the bicycle in the late 1800s and early 1900s are important to highlight. To be honest, reading a book like *Bike Boom: The Unexpected Resurgence of Cycling,* by Carlton Reid, is absolutely the best way to get into the subject of the rise of the bicycle in history. I want to cover the role of the bicycle in our cities and our societies. While it may seem glaringly obvious to some, there is still a great deal of misunderstanding, which is regrettable now that we're trying to figure out how to weave the bikes back into the spectacular urban fabric.

We suffer collectively from short-term urban memory loss, and that is the first challenge to deal with. The entire NIMBY (Not In My Backyard) approach is firmly rooted in the conception that "This is new. This has never happened before. I don't want it." I hear the same thing all

Afternoon traffic on the world's busiest
bicycle street, Nørrebrogade in Copenhagen.

over the world. That cycling won't take off since "we never cycled here." (Look forward to the Mythbusting chapter later in the book, where I tackle comments like that.)

It is no secret that bicycles were shoved out of the way by the bullying influence of American traffic engineering standards that were exported from the 1940s through the 1960s. Not to mention pedestrians and public-transport users. We tend to see what is right in front of us, or in the recent past, or near future. Not much else.

The story of the bicycle is being retold. How it transformed human society and transport more quickly and more efficiently than any other invention in human history. From being a fun and expensive toy for rich boys, the bicycle morphed into something quite remarkable after the diamond frame was invented. Mass production began and the price plummeted. I doubt that anyone at the time could have guessed what

lay ahead in the last couple of decades of the nineteenth century. The bicycle liberated women and the working class, providing them with an affordable form of independent transport that radically increased their mobility radius. Women no longer needed to be reliant on their husbands to get around. Workers could travel farther to get to work or to look for it. As well as being able to ride farther in search of a mate. There is strong evidence that the bicycle improved the human gene pool. In birth and death records in the United Kingdom, surnames that had been locked to one small town or county for centuries started appearing farther away, thanks to the bicycle.

Where horses were a luxury transport acquisition, bicycles were accessible to The 99%. It's interesting to ponder just how society regarded the bicycle back then. It was a freedom machine as well as the ultimate symbol of modernity. The future was glorious and the bicycle proved it to

Left: Two friends having a conversation as they ride through the city. Photo: Zane Kraujina
Center: A musical ride.
Right: Heading home with the family tree on a cargo bike.

be so. You can imagine my surprise, then, when I first visited the photo archives of the Copenhagen Museum several years ago. I had put it off for a while but finally found the time to be there during their brief opening times. Damn, I was looking forward to it. I donned the requisite white gloves and ceremoniously requested "The Bicycle Material." The employee shrugged and wandered off, returning with just three archive boxes.

"That's it?! Three boxes for over a century in one of the world's great bicycle cities?!" She explained that the archive was categorized according to streets or squares. I could get the material for certain places and there would probably be bikes in them. Talk about anticlimactic. Sure, I found some amazing photos and documents in those three boxes, but I was still surprised that the massive influence of the bicycle on the city's history was not somehow better recorded. It was like discovering a lack of material about ships while researching the history of ports. I have heard the same from friends and colleagues elsewhere in the world who go exploring bicycle history in their local archives. When you dig deeper, you find a lot of material, but photos of bikes were never archived in any great detail. As archives and museums digitize, the search is getting easier, but for more than a century, photos of bicycles in cities lay largely undiscovered. The answer as to why is simple. The bicycle was so completely ordinary and unremarkable in cities that we never thought to record or preserve its history.

Through my network, photos have emerged from a number of cities around the world. Perfect ammunition for the increasingly tiresome "we never cycled here" discussions. Armadas of bicycles outside a cinema in Cairns, Australia, in the 1940s. Office workers cycling to work in Singapore in the 1950s. Bicycle cops keeping the peace in 1920s Los Angeles. Quotes emerge that reveal how normal it all was, like this one from John Woodeforde's book, *The Story of the Bicycle* (1970): "In the late nineteenth century, large numbers of women were already using bicycles to get to work, women office workers and shop assistants wending their way each weekday morning from the suburbs to the town. They found the bicycle a convenient form of transport for distances up to, say, ten miles." Meh. Easy peasy. The bicycle was just there. Doing its thing. Serving its purpose in making our daily lives easier and more convenient. A humble and yet integral part of our urban narrative. It just was.

Understanding the role of the bicycle in cities is merely an extension of understanding the role of pedestrians. The gap in time since the

bicycle was a normal sight on city streets has caused us to forget this simple fact. Bicycles operate at street level and at speeds that are conducive to both urban life and the human ability to gauge speed. Homo sapiens lose the ability to visually register things they are passing when they move faster than 30 kilometers per hour (about 20 miles per hour).

For those living in Copenhagen, it's easy to see how it works. How the bicycle contributes to daily life. Some days, I ride along in my own thoughts. Going quicker if I am late for a meeting. Most of the time, I am experiencing my city without being conscious of it and I see hundreds of examples of my fellow citizens doing the

Left: Bicycles parked outside a cinema in Cairns, Australia in 1937. Photographer unknown. Courtesy State Library of Queensland

Right: Homo sapiens lose the ability to register visually things they are passing when their speed increases.

same. Checking the time on clock towers, window shopping as they pass storefronts, waving at friends and stopping to chat with them. Doing everything pedestrians have done for millennia, just at a quicker pace. The average speed that 400,000 daily cyclists in Copenhagen settle upon in their collective subconscious is 16 kilometers per hour (a little less than 10 miles per hour). In Amsterdam, it has been measured at about 15 km/h (a little more than 9 mph).

The bicycle was just there. Serving its purpose in making our daily lives easier and more convenient. A humble and yet integral part of our urban narrative.

It all seems so simple. All that potential and opportunity. And yet therein is a fundamental flaw in the perception of urban cycling that is rife in many parts of the world. In Danish and Dutch planning, cyclists are regarded as a species of the same genus as pedestrians in the unwritten taxonomic hierarchy of urban dwellers transporting themselves. In other parts of the world, where traffic engineering dominates, cyclists are wrongly lumped together with cars and trucks and are separated from pedestrians. It's as though someone thought, "Hmm. Wheels. Everything with wheels should go together." It was a mechanical decision-making process that excluded any human considerations. And once this flawed categorization was established, what followed was subjecting cyclists to all manner of car-centric traffic laws. Traffic laws are necessary, of course, but many of the laws that were spawned to serve the automobile back in the day fail to consider the transport psychology of the

urban cyclist. It's like forcing badminton players to use the rules of rugby in their tournaments—which is quirky, but it doesn't make much sense.

The flawed categorization goes hand in hand with the perception, largely in regions like North America and Australasia, that if the bicycle isn't used for sport or recreation, then the only possible use for it is commuting. It's all a macroscale perception based on longer distances and an extended product of a bicycle industry that only produces bicycles for a demographic that only uses them for speed, without many of the accessories of daily urban cycling. For example, when it rains in Copenhagen, the most socially unacceptable behavior in traffic is not having a fender on, at least, the rear wheel. You want to roll up to the person at the light and give them money to buy one. But I digress.

The bicycle belongs in cities. It's transport, it's a shopping cart, it's a family adhesive, it's an analog dating app.

The bicycle can get you to work, absolutely. What needs to be part of the discussion is how the bicycle can do everything else as well.

We can look to traffic engineering—as ever—in order to identify our primary antagonist, but challenges also appear where you don't expect them. It is apparently the nature of our modern culture to invent a whole bunch of phrases to explain stuff that was the norm in cities for seven millennia, and one of them is the American concept of placemaking. According to Wikipedia: "Placemaking is a multi-faceted approach to the planning, design, and management of public spaces. Placemaking capitalizes on a local community's assets, inspiration, and potential, with

the intention of creating public spaces that promote people's health, happiness, and well-being. It is political due to the nature of place identity. Placemaking is both a process and a philosophy."

Man, that sounds cool, doesn't it? A bit over-the-top academic-y. But it is cool. What I have noticed, however, is that modern placemaking, especially in the United States, has failed miserably in recognizing the role of the bicycle in cities. It is rarely mentioned. Every time I see a presentation about the subject at conferences, I count the bikes in the images. Actually, to be fair, there are often bikes featured—bikes always look great in dreamy city shots—but that is where it ends. The placemakers don't know how to proceed from there. Or perhaps they don't want to, having grown up in a society that has misunderstood the bicycle's full potential for a couple of generations.

I'll get into the nature of subcultures later in the book, but it's interesting to consider how the placemaking community is built around and focused on their gurus: namely, Jane Jacobs and William H. Whyte. Apparently Jacobs rode a bike around, which is awesome. But back when they penned their holy scriptures, bicycle planning just didn't feature at all, so maybe that's why it gets the short end of the stick. Placemaking has an enormous focus on pedestrianism, which is important and fantastic, but I sometimes feel that the bicycle is seen as competition to this specific focus on walking. But hey. Placemaking is a self-described movement that claims its goal is to change the world. What could possibly have more impact across all aspects of urbanism than the bicycle?

One thing is moody academics pondering paving tile designs and bench aesthetics in creatively cluttered NoHo offices, another is "starchitects" who suddenly stick their noses into urban planning. Yes, you, Norman Foster. A couple of years ago, a fanciful idea came out of the British architect's office. It was originally a student's idea, and Norman dusted it off and thrust it rudely onto the Internet. He suggested that London build cycle tracks atop the city's many elevated railways—he called it SkyCycle.

Now of course this isn't a good idea. It's classic "magpie architecture." Attempting to attract people to big, shiny things that dazzle but that have little functional value in the development of a city. Then again, Foster is a master of building big, shiny things.

Ideas like his are city killers. Removing great numbers of citizens who could be cycling down city streets, past shops and cafés on their way to work or school, and instead placing them on a shelf, far away from everything else. All this in a city that is so far behind in reestablishing cycling as transport that it's embarrassing. With most of the population already whining about bicycles on streets, sticking them up in the air, out of the way, is hardly going to help us to return bicycles to the urban fabric of the city.

Now more than ever before, when urban planning is heading back to the future—back to when cities were life-sized places with rational and practical solutions for moving people around—ideas like SkyCycle stand out like a sore thumb.

As Canadian author Chris Turner, whose book *The Geography of Hope* is a must-read, responded on Twitter when I criticized the idea: "You say that as if Foster and the starchitect league have ever attempted to understand how streets work in general." Indeed. We'll get into that later.

Foster grew up in Manchester, back in an age when that city had around 30 percent modal share for bicycles. Instead of realizing that modern urban planning is seeking to return our cities to their pre-car state, he insists on dishing up city-killing Blade Runner fantasies. You would hope that Foster would harken back to his roots and embrace the kind of city he grew up in. His bizarre idea has spawned a flurry of others. A floating cycle track on the Thames. Bikeways in disused subway tunnels. All ideas that fail to address the basics of a bicycle-friendly city and that continue to cement the car-centric status quo that has failed our cities—and us—so miserably.

My colleague Marie Kåstrup, head of the City of Copenhagen's bicycle office, says that even if Copenhagen had the money to build the Skycycle solution above our railways, it wouldn't. Taking bikes away from street level is not a goal for the Danish capital.

The bicycle can get you to work, absolutely. What needs to be part of the discussion is how the bicycle can do everything else as well.

The bicycle belongs in cities. It's transport, it's a shopping cart, it's a family adhesive, it's an analog dating app. With the rise of the cargo bike, it's an SUV. It's everything you can imagine, anything you wish, and whatever you want it to be—and it's been all that for 130 years. This most human form of transport represents the perfect synergy between technology and the human desire to move. It is the most perfect vehicle for urban living ever invented.

One of many demonstrations for safer cycling
conditions and infrastructure in Copenhagen.
The sign reads: "City traffic is bicycle traffic."
1980. Photo: Søren Svendsen

CHAPTER 4

THE RE-DEMOCRATIZATION OF CYCLING

The great city is that which has the greatest man or woman: if it be a few ragged huts, it is still the greatest city in the whole world.

Walt Whitman

After those 7,000 years of urban democracy, we have suffered 70-odd years of transport dictatorship in every corner of the globe. Our streets were expropriated in favor of what we now know to be a flawed transport form in our cities. The bicycle, that most democratic of inventions that had transformed human society in such spectacular fashion, was declared persona non grata and exiled to suburban driveways, parks, fragmented stretches of infrastructure, and remote country roads. It was oppressed, humiliated, and ridiculed, but despite best efforts it could not be eradicated. Bicycles remained hidden in garages, in summer houses, and in cellars, like dusty but sturdy musical instruments awaiting a new orchestra, without ever knowing when it would arrive. Cycling is like music—you will never be able to rid the world of it.

The bicycle is a darling of both sides of the political spectrum. For the left, it is a dreamy vehicle that embodies all the potential for social equality and cohesion and achieving environmental goals. For the right, it is the ultimate freedom machine, providing unrivaled independent mobility with a watertight return on investment. Ride a bike for society. Ride it for yourself and no one else. The bicycle doesn't care. It serves as it always has. It always will.

I actually don't know much about bikes, but I know a great deal about people riding bikes. No matter how much I try to maintain a cool, Nordic pragmatism about the role of bicycles in cities, I feel emotion well up inside when I think about what the bicycle has done for us and what it continues to do.

The moment I learned to ride a bike is so completely and deeply embedded in my memory as a defining moment in my life that just sitting here and writing this brings tears to my eyes. I piggyback shamelessly on the memories of my children, remembering in brilliant detail the moment their brains mastered the physics and coordination and achieved the momentum required to ride. Remembering all the hard work leading up to that moment, practicing with them, sharing their trials but focused on that singular goal. My parental pride at teaching them to ride a bike was happily relegated to second place in order to allow their glorious moment of true independence to take the pedestal. This non-cyclist cyclist could have left it at that, but now I have wedded my life not to teaching people to ride but to teaching cities how to embrace the bicycle as transport in order to afford their citizens a second wave of freedom and independence.

I think I have lost track of how many cities I have visited through my work. Combine the client cities I have worked in with Copenhagenize Design Company and the ones where I have given a keynote, and we're well over a hundred. The common denominator is the people in all those places who share the vision of using bicycle to make cities better.

After delivering a keynote in São Paolo, Brazil—my first in that country—I was standing with a group of audience members who were asking me questions. A young woman stood off to the side, waiting patiently for her turn. Finally, she interrupted the flow, saying she only had a quick comment. "I just want to say that I have been reading your blogs for years, and you are the reason I now ride a bike in São Paulo. Thank you." She shook my hand and left. Just like that.

Without bicycles Denmark would grind to a halt, which would negatively impact the production of food and risk riling up the population.

I have the privilege of meeting people all over the world who share my passion and inspiration, but for me, that one woman sums it all up. Sao Paulo is not a city I would want to ride in every day—or any day, really. It's so far behind the curve. And yet the bicycle persists. A musician has picked it up and played it. The orchestra is forming once again. For decades, nobody needed to ask who "owned" cycling simply because everyone did. The bicycle was a humble tool, anonymous in nature, that just helped us get things done. On occasion, the power of the bicycle was regarded as a threat.

Hitler, despite having been an army bike messenger during the Great War, did what he could to pass anti-cycling laws in favor of cars, and he banned cycling clubs if they had socialist leanings. During World War II, the German occupation force in the Netherlands first prohibited Jews from riding bikes in July 1942, but a week later this prohibition was extended to everyone. The Germans would confiscate all bikes during raids, even children's bikes. For many years,

*Massive demonstration on City Hall Square in Copenhagen where
citizens demanded safer cycling conditions in 1979. © Søren Svendsen*

when the Netherlands played Germany in football, the Dutch fans had a tradition of taunting
their opponents with this chant: *Ik wil mijn fiets
terug*—"I want my bike back." The bicycle simply provided a dangerous level of mobility for
citizens and the resistance. Farther north, the
German occupiers in Denmark were faced with
a similar problem. Cyclists were hard to control
and catch, and the resistance always had a head
start on their bikes. The Germans at the highest
level discussed whether or not bicycles should
be banned altogether, as in the Netherlands.
After much discussion, though, it was decided
not to ban them. The Germans exploited Denmark as a breadbasket to feed their armies, and
without bicycles Denmark would grind to a halt,
which would negatively impact the production
of food and risk riling up the population. The
bicycle was considered dangerous . . . but kind of

like Mahatma Gandhi was considered dangerous.

We all owned cycling. It was universally anonymous. This continues today in countries like the
Netherlands, Denmark, and Japan. Bicycles are
tools. You invest in them, sure, with the purpose
of using them, and of course it is frustrating if
they get stolen—although it is often the sudden
reduced mobility that is frustrating, rather than
the loss of the object.

I once made a mistake in Copenhagen when
I left my Bullitt cargo bike parked in front of my
apartment instead of in my back courtyard—and
I only locked it with a wheel lock and not with
a chain around a fixed object. Cargo bikes are
expensive and the quality Danish brands maintain a high resale value, so I was asking for it.
I schlepped down the stairs with my kids the
next morning. It was Saturday. Felix had to go
to football practice and Lulu-Sophia was off to a

That magical moment when the author's daughter, Lulu-Sophia, learned to cycle was a joy for the whole family. Learning to ride a bike is the first act of independence in our childhood that we remember.

birthday party. Afterwards, I had errands to run. When I realized that my bike had been stolen, my first thought was My entire day is screwed . . . In my mind's eye I only saw logistics—all the places I needed to go and things I needed to do. I got on the phone to borrow another bike from a friend. When I was close to figuring out the logistics, Lulu-Sophia, who was four years old at the time, said, "I liked that bike." Which then made me think, So did I. It was an afterthought. I needed that tool and it was gone. But it was a nice tool. The story ended well. Through my social media network, the bike was found and I took it back.

Around 18,000 bikes are stolen each year in Copenhagen. For a couple of decades, the standard myth has been that Eastern European gangs round up random bikes into trucks and ship them home. It's a flawed myth in that run-of-the-mill upright bikes are all but worthless

on the Eastern European market, since very few people ride them, until recently at least. Sporty racing bikes? Sure. They are pretty universal and have a resale value all over the continent.

The fact is that most bike theft in Copenhagen is done by Copenhageners who don't have a bike at that moment but need one. Through the years, I have seen many a survey where Danes were asked if they have stolen a bike. Such a question, of course, yields only declared-preference answers, which is tricky. One of the more recent surveys tells us that 20 percent of Danes between the ages of 18 and 29 have stolen a bike. Just over 8 percent of citizens between 30 and 39 have done it, and for Danes between 60 and 74 years in age, the number is 2.4 percent.

I asked my teenage son if his friends have stolen bikes, and he shrugged and said yes. He doesn't need to because I can always get ahold

The bicycle as a tool and symbol for demonstrations.

of a bike for him, but bike theft isn't regarded as odd behavior among his 15-year-old friends. He added that, as a rule, it is unlocked bikes that are nicked. I asked if they stole other people's smartphones or stuff like that, and his face changed. No way! Not stuff like that! He was indignant on behalf of his friends.

In a way, it's built into the system. I have a friend who has a drinking bike that he uses on weekends when painting the town red until the wee hours. I adopted the idea, and when heading out on the town I would take an old black upright bike with a step-through frame, rusty chain, and stickers all over it. Sturdy, reliable, but completely anonymous. I never locked it. After two years of nocturnal excursions, I walked out of a bar at four in the morning and discovered that it was gone. Somebody needed a bike to get home and found one. My 10-minute bike ride turned into a

30-minute walk, but I had been waiting for the day—or night—so I shrugged and got on with it. Many people I know will slap stickers on a new bike or add an ugly basket in order to make it less attractive. Still, they accept the odds that it might be expropriated to serve the transport needs of a stranger at an inconvenient moment.

Yes! It's wrong! We can all agree on that. Bike theft is also a huge problem in emerging bicycle cities. Bikes are a shiny new commodity with the potential for a quick resale. But this is Denmark. This is not the Wild West. This is the world's happiest nation. The world's least-corrupt nation. A pillar of prosperity and social welfare. My son's friends live in an affluent neighborhood and want for nothing. And yet there is a sense under the surface that bicycles belong to all of us.

Another contributing factor is that there are so many bikes. There are 5.6 million people in

Photo shoot for Madmoiselle magazine during an actual cycling demonstration in San Francisco in 1972. Photo: Jean-Pierre Zachariasen/Mademoiselle © Condé Nast

Denmark and they buy 500,000 new bikes each year, but 400,000 bikes are scrapped. That is one million extra bikes in the country every decade. Cities are in a constant circle of clearing *herreløse*—ownerless—bikes from bike racks. I live next to a bar popular with young students. At least twice a day, I walk past the small square where they all park and make a mental note of the bikes. Many of them are parked permanently. Three months. Six months. Until the City, together with the police, comes and removes them.

Even in my back courtyard, shared by around 80 apartments, we clean up unused bikes twice a year and there are 15–20 bikes every time, some completely trashed but many perfectly fine save a flat tire or rusty brake cables. Interestingly, if the cluster of unused bikes are not shipped away and are allowed to remain leaning up against the wall, they slowly either disappear or start losing seats, wheels, or baskets. They are put back into circulation either whole or in part. Even this is illegal, of course. A bike is always someone's property in Denmark. Either the owner or the insurance company. And yet my own neighbors will see these bikes, wait for a while, and then start recycling the parts for personal use.

You and I can share our anger and frustration about bike theft, but I remain fascinated about how, on some deep, social level, bicycles are perceived as things that belong to all of us. How they became some binding element and a democratic tool for sharing—long before the sharing economy was a thing. Maybe it's just the world's largest bike-share system. *I have a little pocket full of poetic to pepper up my indignation.* It's all very confusing. I have also confused others by saying that you can measure the success of reestablishing the bicycle as a mainstream transport form by counting how many bikes end in the harbors, lakes, and rivers of a city. The more there are, the better. The bicycle is a vital tool, but also one that is completely ordinary and not fetishized.

The global bicycle boom in the 1970s, during the oil crises, brought the bike back. In Denmark, this was the catalyst to rebooting our infrastructure. In many parts of the world, the bicycle was virtually forgotten as transport, and the boom had a narrower focus on sport and recreation. The result is that cycling has an elitist feel to it. The enormous focus on having the right gear, the right bike, the bragging rights for the latest, coolest stuff. All this objectification doesn't serve making the bicycle an accessible object.

I clearly remember speaking to two New Yorkers, both Caucasian males in their late twenties or early thirties, after a keynote in the city. I commented on how amazing it is that there are so many deliveries made by bike and added that I regarded these people as amazing working-class heroes. They should be regarded as an important piece of the puzzle in making New York more bicycle-friendly. The two dudes with whom I was speaking were taken aback. One said, "But they're not like us. They have to ride, because they're immigrants and have little money. We *choose* to ride . . . " Cue my realization that urban cycling has an extra layer that only impedes our goal of not only bringing the bikes back but also regarding it as a democratic tool.

The same perception can be seen in cities in Central and Latin America where, bizarrely and fantastically, bikes and cargo bikes are still used for deliveries in great numbers. The Brazilian cycling NGO Transporte Ativo calculated that there are over 11,000 deliveries a day by bike or cargo bike in the Copacabana neighborhood of Rio de Janeiro. Everything is moved by bike there. Dry-cleaning, mattresses, pet food, groceries. The hip young cultural elite I have spoken to in the city are just as surprised as the guys in New York when I put all these delivery bikes in both cities into the same democratic box.

The response I received regarding the *Copenhagen Cycle Chic* blog that I started in 2007, on the other hand, showed me the power of the bicycle.

Most of the readership are women from around the world, and I have received scores of inspirational comments and emails over the years. The bicycle was instrumental in the emancipation of women when it first appeared in our societies in the late 1800s.

I can understand why many people feel that the subcultural fraternity of avid cyclists is an entry barrier, but I have learned firsthand that many women feel particularly alienated. Here are four examples:

On some deep, social level, bicycles are perceived as things that belong to all of us.

"Thanks to your wonderful blog, I've finally started wearing proper work clothes while riding my bike. I started bike commuting by necessity in May, and now I love it. All of your photos convinced me to try wearing a dress, which I did last week. Today, I wore a dress and heels. It's much easier than I expected, and I'm thoroughly enjoying it. People are shocked when they see me, but I tell them it's easy and fun. Style Over Speed is my new mantra."

"You're converting people, one photo at a time. Your comments and photos offer a glimpse into something so beautiful, and I am very jealous. I love this website, I really do. *Cycle Chic* influenced my decision to ride in the winter, to ride in a dress, to ride in heels and not care what anyone else said about it."

"In my small city, I ride my bicycle(s) almost exclusively for transportation. Your Cycle Chic movement has inspired me to celebrate being a woman and celebrate bicycling by wearing skirts and dresses on my bike."

Let's be clear. It is the women and men of Copenhagen who are the source of inspiration.

I was just the messenger bringing photos to the Internet. But if the blog helped in some way to broaden the democratic and demographic appeal of urban cycling, then it achieved a great purpose.

It's great that people regard cycling as a hobby, sport, recreational activity, passion, or lifestyle. But it shouldn't stop there. It never used to. For decades, citizens around the world never gave their bikes names or fetishized them. Personally, I find it bizarre, this anthropomorphism. Attributing human traits and emotions to inanimate objects. And, man, don't even get me started on object-oriented ontology. I don't pull out my friend Archie, plug him in, and vacuum the floors, lamenting to friends on Facebook how he just doesn't seem to like having to go under the sofa and how I'll need to have a talk with him about it. I don't employ the services of Princess the power drill—I hope she's not moody today—when building a new table (I think I'll call her Brigit). No. Wait. Brigitte—because she just feels French, you know? I suppose I reserve a place wherein I understand how a fantastic invention like the bicycle inspires some people to give them names and talk about them as though they were alive. Sure, people do the same thing with cars and trucks. I just think the goal should be a return to a place where the bicycle is considered a powerful, useful tool that we can't live without but that garners little attention. In Danish, we still use generic and affectionate nicknames for bikes like *jernhest* or *havelåge*—"iron horse" or "garden gate"—which sums up the bicycle nicely for us, without the need for anthropomorphic naming.

Do you want to know what the most popular bike on the planet is? Any old bike. The massive rise of the vintage bicycle market is a testament to both the quality design and construction in the past as well as the desire of regular citizens to get into the game. The corporate bicycle industry has been late to the party. Countless small bike brands have emerged around the world in the past decade, and they largely draw upon clas-

sic designs akin to most vintage, upright bikes. Fair enough, the big bike brands are huge. They need more time to launch new products, adapt production schedules, and whatnot. It was comical, though, to see new corporate fixies appear at bike fairs two years after the cool kids stopped riding them. Despite a century of readily available blueprints for the design of upright bikes, Big Bike has struggled to reinvent itself and respond to the amazing emerging market.

Do we not have the inherent right to move about the urban landscape as we see fit? It has been so for most of human history.

Bikes are being produced called hybrids, which I think tries to marry the desire for speed and performance with utility. Apparently, 40 years of making bikes solely for sport and recreation is a big monkey to get off your business back. This is why vintage bikes are rocking it. They are filling a void with their solid, no-nonsense build and sensible functionality. The price is attractive as well, especially in a market with a focus on performance, weight, and tech bling. I read articles now and then about how, in order to get Americans to ride bikes, speed is a major factor. No, it's not. Comfort, safety, and functionality are. Homo sapiens are the same everywhere.

I have been hired by a number of bike companies, including Batavus and Biomega, to produce trend analyses of the growing market in order to help them target their products better. As an extension of that, I have done a market survey that ended up with a few thousand responses from around the world and which included questions about what type of bike the person would buy, what color it should be, and what accessories they would choose. Most of the respondents were not sporty cyclists, just regular citizens. The results were clear-cut. Even though the list of colors was long, black overwhelmingly won the day. A black upright bicycle with either a basket or pannier bags. The most utilitarian choice in history is a desired object. In many regions, such a normal bicycle is still difficult to get ahold of. It is clear that the market for bicycles is populated by people who are ready and willing but who don't have the option of buying such a bike.

Look at the ease with which bike-share in over 1,000 cities has rooted itself in our transport habits. To regular citizens, these are practical and efficient bicycles. To the avid cyclists, they're heavy and cumbersome tanks. Anyone who actually knows how much their bicycle weighs is probably not someone you want advocating cycling for The 99%. The day that one of the huge American bike brands like Trek puts in an order in Taiwan for 50,000 basic, black upright bikes, you'll know that change is right around the corner.

It's all about the redemocratization and reallocation of our urban space—and it's about the bikes themselves. It is also about something as grand as basic human rights. Do we not have the inherent right to move about the urban landscape as we see fit? It has been so for most of human history, after all.

If the answer to that question is yes, then surely this means that we need to bend over backwards to make our streets safe for all users, including those who wish to cycle. Reluctantly squeezing the bicycle into a car-centric Matrix serves very few. A massive effort to redemocratize our streets and our cities is the greatest urban challenge we face.

Top: The bicycle. Freedom machine since the 1880s.
Bottom: The author and his son, Felix, on holiday on the Danish island of Bornholm.

CHAPTER 5

TAMING THE BULL IN SOCIETY'S CHINA SHOP

>> **There comes a time in the affairs of man when he must take the bull by the tail and face the situation.**

W. C. Fields

It's a fine metaphor: society as a china shop. A stylish, brightly lit room with a diverse selection of lovingly crafted and valuable porcelain. It's been in business for 7,000 years, but a century or so ago someone let a bull loose inside. If you actually owned a china shop and someone actually let a bull inside, you would be rather dismayed. Don't you think you would drop everything and channel all your energies into getting the bull out?

When you call for help, however, you're told that there is nothing you can do. You're directed to websites that advise you to don safety equipment and issue the same to any customers who venture inside. Your porcelain? Time to start buying kilometers of bubble wrap and packing it all in. Meanwhile, the bull just crapped on the floor in aisle 9 and knocked over another shelf.

Welcome to a century of cars in our cities. Everyone can agree that we have, indeed, let a bull loose inside our cities, but there is little desire to do anything about it on a global level. The best option would be to eliminate the danger.

Cyclists shouldn't have to run with the bulls. Photo: Zane Kraujina

Either lead the bull out of the shop or kill it and have a celebratory barbecue. Until that happens, shouldn't we at least minimize the danger? Lasso the beast, tether it in a corral in the corner in order to restrict its movements. What about castration or medication? There are numerous options, and yet, on a societal level, we choose to completely ignore the bull. We stand with our back to it and hand out safety wear to anyone who comes in. If they refuse to put it all on, accusing fingers are pointed in their direction, accompanied by tiresome, victim-blaming monologues about "safety" and how ridiculous it is that you choose to enter the china shop without assuming "your share of the responsibility."

In the time it took you to read that previous paragraph, one human somewhere in the world was killed and around 50 people were injured by the rampaging bulls. In both Europe and America, there is a car-crash 9/11 every single month—and every single month for the past 60 years—and yet there is no war on this particular terror.

What is interesting is that for the first time in decades, Big Auto is a bit worried.

More than anyone else, the automobile industry is really quite keen on our ignoring the bull. It's all well and good believing in the bicycle's role in our societies, but we are faced with a daunting antagonist: a century of car culture and car-centric planning. How do we begin to take the battle to Big Auto? You would think that the companies that produce such dangerous vehicles would be held accountable or would at least make serious efforts to stop people from dying. For all the air bags and ABS brakes and seatbelts, though, the killed and seriously injured (KSI) numbers remain stable. Nothing is happening.

What is interesting is that for the first time in decades, Big Auto is a bit worried. I first noticed a shift in focus in car commercials back in 2009, and it started with Audi. You know how car commercials usually work. They have honed their marketing skills for generations in a market where they've had little competition. Cars roaring across breathtaking landscapes or down unrealistically empty city streets. Freedom, sex, adventure, and coolness with insane production value and astronomical budgets. But the Audi ad for their A3 model employed new tactics. The bike boom was well underway and talk of improved public transport was rising. The ad just showed the other options. A wobbly cyclist in pouring rain, a bus passenger getting jostled around by fellow passengers, and a dorky dude on a Segway. All looking stupid and pathetic. Then, the money shot. A beat-up station wagon with a "Powered by Vegetable Oil" bumper sticker is crawling up a hill, and the A3 blows past it—overtaking on a curve, which is not at all safe.

The bemused male voice-over: "Many people are trying to do their part. Some just have more fun doing it. The new Audi A3 TDI Clean Diesel."

This is just one of many commercials in the same vein that I've identified over the past eight years, from a wide variety of carmakers. The tactics invented and employed by the fledgling automobile industry back in the Anti-Automobile Age lay dormant for decades until now. Ridicule, arrogance, and spin. Ready to pull out of the drawer and slapped into an expensive commercial. The reason for the return to these tactics is, if you think about it, positive. The bicycle reappeared on the urban scene in about 2006 or 2007, and the car industry identified it as a competitor and went after it, tossing public transport into the mix.

It's not just the automobile industry. Companies from industries like insurance and car-share are in on the act. There are, it must be said, examples of car companies greenwashing with bikes in the commercial, filming the car in the city from bikes, and even producing bikes that fit in the trunks of their cars.

They're worried and they don't know exactly what to do. Two of the main Big Auto players, BMW and Ford, are trying to reinvent themselves as "mobility companies," but largely the industry is still stuck in its ways. Add to this the concerted effort being made to hype electric vehicles and autonomous vehicles as the next big thing that will change the world. The former only eliminates one aspect of the problem—emissions. The latter brings new problems with it. I recall reading a quote on Twitter that "In Amsterdam, a Google self-driving car would park itself after a few minutes and start crying." Both of them still occupy an arrogant amount of urban space.

I spoke at the State of Design Festival in Melbourne a few years back. The event was book-ended by two keynote speakers. The American, Chris Bangle, who is the former head of design at BMW, would kick it off, and I would wrap it up a few days later. Bangle is a charming and personable guy and entertaining as a speaker. I was looking forward to a Big Auto representative speak at a design and sustainability festival.

The program featured this blurb about his talk: "We are becoming more aware of 'personal mobility,' the choice we make for moving around. However, Bangle perceives the need to consider 'personal emotional mobility' if we are to seriously tackle behavior change and develop more sustainable mobility products. People have developed 'emotional' attachments to their modes of transport, so if we want change we need to provide new experiences that act equally as a catalyst for emotional connection and sustainable outcomes."

No Henry Ford without Albert Augustus Pope. No selling their products gorgeously without the massive success of early bicycle marketing.

Okay, no mention of the environment or sustainability, but there was a fancy new catchphrase: *Personal Emotional Mobility*. How hip and cool does that sound? It was the pivotal point of Bangle's talk. The car industry needs to rethink their design so that people can experience a heightened emotional attachment to their cars. He highlighted how the number of 16- to 18-year-olds in the United States who aren't bothering to get a driver's license is rising. The same thing is happening all over the world. But then Bangle said it: "We have to hook them back to the car." Yep. That's what he said. To those sitting in the audience, it was remarkable to see how many people turned their heads to the person next to them with quizzical looks on their faces, silently asking each other, "Did he just say that? Really?"

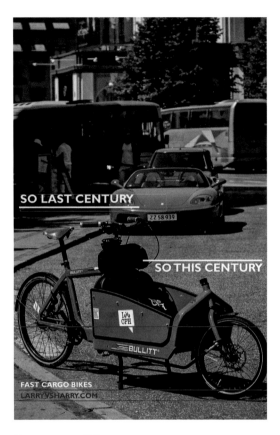

SO LAST CENTURY

SO THIS CENTURY

FAST CARGO BIKES
LARRYVSHARRY.COM

It's a new century, kids.

I had my son, Felix, with me on the trip, and he was busy with his Nintendo during the talk—fair enough when you're eight—but he did look up at one point and whisper to me, "Daddy . . . isn't it funny that he's talking about cars and you're here to talk about bicycles?" Well spotted, my boy.

We shared a car with Bangle from the airport when we arrived, and we discussed various aspects of our respective fields. Bangle asked me two questions in the course of the conversation. Did I think that bikes should be registered like cars? I said no, of course. It's a ridiculous idea. He then asked an interesting question about whether bikes are the top end of pedestrian traffic or the bottom end of car traffic. I replied that bikes were the former. Cyclists move faster than pedestrians but are capable of pedestrian-like movement and spontaneity.

During his talk he referred to our conversation and added a bit of bike-bashing for good measure. He mentioned the top-end/bottom-end question and suggested that cyclists want to be both. Delivered with a crooked smile and a roll-of-the-eyes expression on his face. He also chucked out the line that "somebody has to pay for the roads." Something that the good people at the I Pay Road Tax website would have a field day with.

I approached him at the restaurant we all went to that evening and mentioned this myth about "paying for roads." "Oh, I know . . . ," he replied with a smile. So he knew . . . but still chucked out the line to the audience. Felix made himself famous in Melbourne that evening. He was drawing at the table, on yellow post-it notes. He asked me how to spell *bicycle* and I helped him, not knowing what he had planned. He tiptoed over to Bangle and put a post-it note on his back. He had simply written: "I ❤ Bicycles."

Big Auto Dude took it with a laugh, but a whole bunch of the people at the table fired off text messages about this innocent but effective eight-year-old's bicycle-advocacy activism.

So. What is Personal Emotional Mobility? The car industry would love you to mutter *"Oooh, baby"* as your hands caress the carefully chosen material on your steering wheel and *"Oh yeah . . ."* as you look down the elegant slope of your hood. They want to trigger emotional reactions in people. All while those people are incarcerated inside their vehicles—completely and utterly cut off from the society in which they live. Isolated and alienated. It's no secret that the car industry has borrowed freely from the bicycle industry throughout the past century. No Henry Ford without Albert Augustus Pope. No gorgeously selling their products without the massive success of early bicycle marketing.

So here's what we should do. Pluck this catchphrase of Personal Emotional Mobility from the clutches of the car industry and plant it firmly in the blossoming garden of urban cycling. Because you know what the great thing about Personal Emotional Mobility is? It describes perfectly what the bicycle can offer the person who rides it. It is a brilliant description of what I, personally, get out of riding a bicycle in cities. My personal and emotional attachment with the cityscape, as well as with my fellow citizens, whether on bicycles or on foot, is intensified, heightened.

I interact with my urban landscape as I roll down the cycle tracks or streets of my own or any other city. The bicycle is independent mobility and on it I am an integral, active, and visible element in the city. Offering yet another human thread that strengthens the social fabric. Thank you, Bangle. Thank you BMW. Your desperate attempt to sell

cars has given us the perfect phrase with which to describe the beauty of the bicycle in cities.

It is a bit of a departure, though. Think about all the car commercials you've ever seen. Think about the logos of carmakers. Proud stallions, imposing rams, fearsome birds of prey, big cats, mythical dragons. Virile symbols of power. Now we see Big Auto either ridiculing the competition or trying to get all warm and fuzzy. But it's like that aunt or uncle at the family gathering who has had too much to drink and wants to hug everyone. Awkward and comical.

So perhaps Big Auto is struggling to rediscover its role in a society that is rapidly changing, what with all this talk of bikes, public transport, liveable and life-sized cities, but their legacy remains unchanged until further notice. Ever since they orchestrated the paradigm shift in our perception of streets, generations of citizens have just accepted it without any critical thought.

Traces of car-centric planning are everywhere, like scars on our cities' skin.

Traces of car-centric thinking are everywhere. Study every nook and cranny of your neighborhood. Every crack in the sidewalks. Every centimeter of bike infrastructure. Each and every crosswalk and intersection. Traces of car-centric planning are everywhere, like scars on our cities' skin. Individuals, organizations, and policymakers in every country subconsciously do the bidding of Big Auto, even though they may feel their intentions are good.

Traffic safety organizations abound. Local, national, international. My company did a meta-analysis of the communication techniques used by a selection of them. From the Danish Road Safety Council to FIA—the international automobile association. It was easy to find their common denominators. Their techniques are firmly rooted in the Culture of Fear, so aptly described in the book of the same name by British sociologist Frank Furedi. They're all about scaremongering, but none of it is rational or helpful to encouraging cycling or pedestrianism. In fact, most of it attempts to brand cycling and walking as dangerous. If they do focus on car safety, the general theme

is your safety inside the car and that of your passengers. Very few campaigns focus on your high odds of killing someone outside your car. Science doesn't feature high on the list of their communication strategies. The Danish Road Safety Council is notorious for handpicking one or two studies that support their ideology about bike helmets, for example. They place them on a pedestal and haughtily declare, "See? Proof!" Then they cross their arms and refuse to discuss further. All the campaigns and rhetoric from these organizations are vague and based on the failed notion that putting up cute signs suggesting people slow down will change behavior. There is little evidence that such campaigns

Below: Campaign by RACC, the Catalan Automobile Association. "In Barcelona, 1 out of 3 traffic accident deaths are pedestrians. Attention, we are all pedestrians!"

Opposite: Funky victim-blaming campaign from New York's Department of Transportation.

Credits: New York City Department of Transportation Art Program and John Morse Curbside Haiku © 2011, www.StarDogStudio.com. Image used with permission of the artist.

have any measurable effect. Global organizations use the same vague tactics and no real-world solutions apart from financing helmets and reflective clothing. Firmly slapping the responsibility on the vulnerable roadway users with emotional propaganda and car-centric arrogance.

Desperately trying to cement, in the public consciousness of its citizens, the rather outdated philosophy that cars rule supreme and everyone else is a mere pawn to be swept aside without regret.

When look at similarities between all these organizations, one thing is shockingly clear. None of them will ever say that a drastic reduction of cars would save lives. It's all talk and no serious action. They also have a tendency to support electric vehicles and autonomous vehicles, not at all aware of the irony that such vehicles still take up public space and will still contribute to death and injury.

None of them have urban-planning experience, or if they do touch upon it, they never mention it. They spend most of their time vehemently protecting their status as "traffic safety authorities." I know this from personal experience. I have been interviewed in various Nordic newspapers about the science of bicycle helmets and the negative effect that promotion and legislation have on cycling levels. I learned from some journalists that the Danish Road Safety Council had contacted them with the intent of discrediting me as a source. I have the emails. It's amusing. Colleagues in other countries experience similar situations with their local or national versions.

The point is that such organizations love their status, and if you question it—which we obviously should—they come out like a raccoon backed into a corner. A pattern you often see when ideology is elevated over science.

Cities employ various methods in order to draw attention to themselves. Tourism campaigns, posters on bus stops for events or municipal services, and the like. City Branding is also a thing. Countries and organizations do the same. Usually the money is spent on highlighting positive angles. It's a basic marketing concept to be positive. What often goes unnoticed is that cities have a tendency to broadcast the sad and undeniable fact that they are often completely inept at keeping the streets safe. They try, unsuccessfully, to disguise their incompetence as "safety" campaigns. It's not exactly billboards declaring "*We Suck!*"—but it's close. These campaigns are often funded by taxpayers, so you would think there were some sort of moral check-and-balance to the process.

Examples from around the world could fill an entire book. There are American cities that buy flags and put them in buckets at crosswalks, telling pedestrians to grab a flag and wave it vigorously above their head while walking across a crosswalk where they already have the right of way. Seriously. You can't make stuff like that up.

Even here where I live, in Frederiksberg in the heart of Copenhagen, we cannot escape the city advertising its incompetence. It rhymes in Danish, but reads: "He listened to music but died in traffic." What a stupid pedestrian. Cars are everywhere and they're not going away anytime soon. It's his own damn fault for impeding their route. Think of the poor motorist who had no choice but to run him down as music blasted from his earbuds. The driver was just a regular citizen on their way to or from work. Not only were they forced to suffer the mental anguish of killing a text-messaging pedestrian (shockingly sans walking helmet), but they were made to wait around at the scene of the accident to be interviewed by the police, and they were probably late for dinner or work.

The Danish Road Safety Council was granted permission from the City to paint bright yellow graphics pictograms on the cycle tracks. They read, "Keep an eye on the side roads." I checked to see if there were corresponding signs for motorists on the side roads reading, "Keep an eye out for cyclists and pedestrians who have the right of way," but in vain. It was a campaign placing responsibility on the cyclists, even though they are protected by laws that dictate that cars must stop.

Some stickers appeared on sidewalks around my neighborhood a few years back. "Cross at the intersection." With arrows pointing in either direction. I saw one on a long stretch of street, and the intersection to the left was 250 meters (273 yards) away. To the right, it was 350 meters (383 yards). So much for prioritizing pedestrians in Denmark's most densely populated city. Send them on epic detours instead.

Consider the simple idea of school crossing guards. It's a concept well known around the world. Hey, I used to be one back in the day (and I remember hating having to do it). This concept is merely an advertisement for municipalities that have failed to make their streets safe, despite the existence of solutions that would actually do so. So just slap children onto the front lines and dress them up as clowns.

Let's face it—if a city had safe, human streets, then they wouldn't need school crossing guards.

Let's face it—if a city had safe, human streets with intelligently low speed limits, modern street design, and a sincere will to prioritize pedestrians and cyclists, then they wouldn't need school crossing guards. In New York City, the Department of Transportation consistently produces fancy ad campaigns seemingly aimed at maintaining the status quo of the automobile's role in society.

Seriously . . . I can't think of any other city on the planet in recent times that has spent so

Car-centric campaign on a cycle track from the Danish Road Safety Council. "Keep an eye on the side roads." Motorists were not bothered with corresponding signs.

Victim-blaming in my neighbourhood. "He listened to music and died in traffic." Because the city couldn't keep him safe.

much advertising money on finger-pointing and "behavioral" campaigns aimed at the vulnerable traffic users of their city. Desperately trying to cement, in the public consciousness of its citizens, the rather outdated philosophy that cars rule supreme and everyone else is a mere pawn to be swept aside without regret. Stand in the way of a queen, you're stupid. You'll get taken. And you know what? We can afford to lose you.

This *New York Postian* attitude from New York's DoT towards a city that otherwise has great potential for being much more pedestrian-, public-transport-, and cyclist-friendly is the primary reason why New York is so far away from reaching any sensible level of life-sized. Paris makes New York look like the illegitimate love child of Robert Moses and Le Corbusier. This approach is right out of *Mad Men*. "Cars! They're toasted!" If I were a walking/cycling New York taxpayer, I'd be rather irritated that the city was chucking money into campaigns like these. A single #fail campaign is one thing, but this is just a continuation of a theme. A few years back, they had a series of funky haiku posters going after pedestrians. "She walks in beauty / Like the night. Maybe that's why / Drivers can't see her." "Oncoming cars rush. / Each one, a three-ton bullet. / And you, flesh and bone."

I would rather see a campaign that announces a citywide plan to redesign all the streets to slow down cars, prioritize pedestrians and cyclists, and improve safety. New York City has a budget for campaigns with a high creative bar and amazing design. But they throw it all away.

I've spent years seeking examples of campaigns that are focused on the actual problem, campaigns that place responsibility on the heavy hitters in the traffic equation, rather than on the vulnerable traffic users (or the "soft traffic," as it is in Danish). One example, or rather exception, is the annual campaign described above. It is a staple around Denmark when the kids start school. "Watch out for Laura, she is new in traffic." Simple and effective communication, yes,

but then again, quite useless without modern road design to slow down cars. Such positive campaigns are rare. Easily 90–95 percent of the campaigns I've seen from all over the world are car-centric and use victim-blaming communication. I could go on. And on. Instead, how about a quick and dirty list of ideas and campaigns that turn the tables? If we were to apply rationality and a focus on the rampaging bull, we could consider these:

HEALTH WARNINGS ON MOTOR VEHICLES
What started out as a fun thought experiment back in 2008 turned into something surprisingly realistic. Cigarette packaging now has to include health warnings to make people aware of the

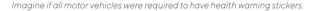

Imagine if all motor vehicles were required to have health warning stickers.

dangers of cigarette smoking. A common-sense idea and something most of us can get behind. Back in 2008, the European Union had standards in place that required 30–50 percent of the cigarette packaging to be covered by these warnings.

Instead of campaigns that scare people away from a life-extending, healthy, and sustainable transport form, wouldn't it be more appropriate to campaign about the real and present dangers of automobiles? Many people in car-centric countries no longer regard cars as dangerous. Or maybe that knowledge is there, under the surface, but the car is such an ingrained part of the culture that the perception of danger rarely rises to the surface of people's consciousness. What if we just cut to the chase? Only a couple of decades ago, cigarettes were an integral part of life, whether you smoked or not. That has changed radically. I gathered all the approved health warnings for cigarettes and asked a doctor friend if they would also be appropriate for use in car-related health warnings. The answer was a resounding *"Yes."* Every single one.

Car emissions cause emphysema. / Driving causes cancer. / Driving clogs your arteries. / Don't transport your children by car. / Driving—A leading cause of death. / Quitting driving will improve your health. / Driving harms unborn babies. / Driving is addictive. / Car emissions are toxic.

Removing the status associated with driving is something that is slowly evolving in this, the Age of Demotorization. Speeding that process might be a good idea. We don't even have to mention bicycles, because it's not all about that. It's about reducing societal harm caused by car crashes, harmful emissions, and noise pollution. In Denmark, an estimated 4,000 people die every year because of the health hazards related to cars—and that's twenty times greater than the number of people actually killed in car crashes. Respiratory illnesses, heart disease, stress-related illnesses caused by noise pollution, etc. The numbers are just as nasty everywhere. Very few people are aware that the levels of dangerous microparticles from exhaust are actually higher inside the car than if you're cycling next to it. So let's focus on this fact and, hopefully, encourage motorists to think twice about their last-century transport form.

Where is the legislation dictating that 30 percent of the surface area of cars must feature health warnings? Seriously. Imagine carmakers having to plaster 30 percent of the surface of each side of the car with health warnings. On the sides of trucks, the message would be massive. Imagine the impact it would make on the public psyche from one day to the next. If we think practically about implementing this idea, certain clauses would be necessary. Electric cars might be exempt from displaying the dangerous emissions warnings, though not the ones about how driving kills, etc.

Removing the status associated with driving is something that is slowly evolving in this, the Age of Demotorization.

In the first phase, car owners would be required to purchase large stickers with heavy-duty adhesive and in various sizes, depending on their vehicle. Using reflective material so the warnings are visible at night would be a good idea. A little cottage industry would pop up, with companies offering to stick the warnings on, while you wait. Consumers could choose from a list of approved warnings instead of just being stuck with whatever they're given.

In time, carmakers could implement the warning labels directly into the design and paint job of the car, as long as they adhere to the directive's requirements for size and font. Public transport companies would benefit, and they could propose targeted warnings that would benefit trains, buses, and even bicycles. If there is a fee involved with purchasing the stickers for your car—which there should be—the proceeds could go to planting trees in cities, or to charities dealing with obese children or illnesses caused by car pollution. A good idea whose time has come—and one that is backed by science.

EXTERNAL AIRBAGS ON CARS

This idea started as a crazy "what if" article in the magazine of the Dutch Cyclists Federation (Fietsersbond) back in 2008 but quickly morphed into something very real. Current airbags protect the car occupants to some extent but do little for cyclists or pedestrians. If we are serious about placing the responsibility where it belongs—on the most dangerous animal in traffic—placing airbags that deploy externally is a simple and intelligent idea.

The idea captured the imagination of Dutch authorities and they first financed a feasibility study and then moved into actual prototyping and crash tests. The airbags would add a couple of hundred euros to the price tag of a car but would ultimately save lives. Volvo's V40 now has pedestrian airbags, although TNO, the company tasked with developing bags that would also benefit cyclists, found that the placement of them varies for pedestrians and cyclists. The technology is there, ready to use. This should be standard on every new motor vehicle.

STRICT LIABILITY

One would hope that laws are balanced, rational, and fair to all, but that isn't always the case—certainly not with the dominating force of car-centric thinking. The easiest way to kill someone in America is to hit them with a car. The repercussions are minor. Many countries in Europe have strict liability. Indeed, only five countries don't, including the United Kingdom. Strict liability—rendered also as presumed liability—simply

means that a person is automatically legally responsible for any damage to persons or property caused by their actions, regardless of fault. From the moment you get into your car, you are presumed liable simply because you are driving a dangerous vehicle. France introduced such a law in 1984 after a dark period of many cyclist fatalities. Making the motorists liable reduced the number of fatalities by 60 percent over the next twenty years. If I get hit by a car, the motorist is responsible for paying full damages as long as the collision was unintentional—meaning neither of us tried to hit the other.

> One would hope that laws are balanced, rational, and fair to all, but that isn't always the case—certainly not with the dominating force of car-centric thinking.

If I ride through a red light in the middle of the night without any lights on my bike and get hit, the motorist is still responsible for paying 50 percent of the damages. In the Netherlands, if the cyclist is under 14 years old, it is always 100 percent regardless of fault. As the vulnerable traffic user, I am not obliged to prove the motorist's negligence or intention. Talk about leveling the playing field. We've not seen a lot of action on this front but in 2017, the province of Onatrio, Canada, proposed a law that would raise the fine for careless driving to CA$50,000. A bold and rational move.

ESTABLISHING 30 KM/H (19 MPH) ZONES

Back in 1983, a pilot project was started in the small German town of Buxtehude. The speed limit was lowered to 30 kilometers per hour (19 miles per hour) in order to see what effect it

The risk of injury or death increases drastically with higher speeds.

would have on traffic safety. It was a success and the "30kmh" movement was born. Well over 100 European Union towns and cities have 30 km/h as their baseline speed. In the United Kingdom, the "20's Plenty" movement (20 miles per hour being approximately 30 kilometers per hour) is encouraging more British cities to adopt this as a norm.

While I was writing this chapter, Paris announced that 85 percent of the city with the Peripherique motorway will be a 30 km/h zone by 2020. That is nothing short of amazing. Barcelona is pursuing a similar goal. The 30 km/h movement has truly arrived. Lowering the speed limits to 30 km/h has multiple effects, and all of them are positive. The body of science that supports the idea grows yearly. First, it drastically reduces death and injury levels. If you get hit by a car doing 30 km/h while cycling or walking, you only have a 5 percent chance of dying and a 15 percent chance of walking away unharmed. At 40 km/h (25 mph), you have a 50 percent of dying, and at 60 km/h (37 mph) it's 95 percent. Right there, we can see that the reduction of societal harm is massive at lower speeds.

The flow of motorized traffic is unaffected by the speed; in fact, it is often improved. Vehicles traveling through a city at this speed do so quietly. Noise pollution decreases by up to 40 percent. In my city, millions of Danish kroner are spent on fancy noise-reducing asphalt, which is only really effective for a few years. Lowering the speed limit is much cheaper, and the noise-reduction levels are the same.

Then there is the all-important sense of safety and comfort. Riding a bike or walking next to cars driving at 30 km/h is an amazing game-changer. The city just feels slower and more civilized. I often spend summer holidays in Barcelona with my kids, and they both noticed the slow speeds of cars in the densely populated neighborhoods. It was obvious to them. Especially coming from our neighborhood, where cars still zoom past our apartment at 50 km/h (31 mph).

Lowering the speed limits to 30 km/h has multiple effects, and all of them are positive.

Changing the speed-limit signs and enforcing the law are important. Road design, however, is also a factor. I did an experiment a few years ago here in Copenhagen. I drive in my own city only every couple of years. I was in a car-share car and it was Sunday, so the roads were empty. I decided to drive through a residential neighborhood at 30 km/h. The streets were wide and, damn, it felt slow. So we absolutely need to alter the road design and, in the process, win back space for pedestrians and cyclists.

48% CARS

26% LEISURE

13% MOTORBIKE

9% WORK

2% CRIME

1% CYCLING

1% WALKING

WHAT'S LIKELY TO GIVE YOU A HEAD INJURY?

LET'S GET SERIOUS ABOUT SAVING LIVES

MOTORISTS DISMOUNT TO CROSS ROADWAY

Top: What's likely to give you a head injury?
Data: German organization ZNS
Hannelore Kohl Foundation
Center: *Commercial motoring helmet*
from Davies, Craig. ©Carlton Reid
Bottom: *Copenhagenize graphics*
applying a rational approach.
Opposite: *The Hierarchy of Hazard*
Control applied to urban cycling.

MOTORING HELMETS

Helmets for car occupants emerged as an idea in Sweden in the 1960s. The first commercial model appeared in Australia in the 1980s, produced by a company called Davies, Craig, which produces cooling systems for car engines. The box reads: "You have made a sound decision to purchase your Davies, Craig Motoring Helmet. Wear it and don't feel self-conscious. Driving even for the most proficient is dangerous. Ultimately, motoring helmets will be commonplace, but in the meantime, you will be a leader whilst those who may consider your good sense misplaced will follow." In the instruction manual, more advice is offered:

"Davies, Craig recommends you wear your Motoring Helmet at all times when motoring but particularly at the following, documented high-risk times:

» After consuming any alcohol.
» When other drivers are likely to have consumed alcohol, especially 4:00 p.m. to 2:00 a.m. Fridays and Saturdays.
» After dark and during twilight.
» In rain or when the roads are wet.
» During long trips when you may become tired.
» Within five kilometres of your home or destination
» Christmas, Easter, and long weekends.
» If you are aged under 25 or over 60."

Basically, don't wear it if you're 30, driving on a short trip in the sunshine eight kilometers from home on a Tuesday. Otherwise, strap

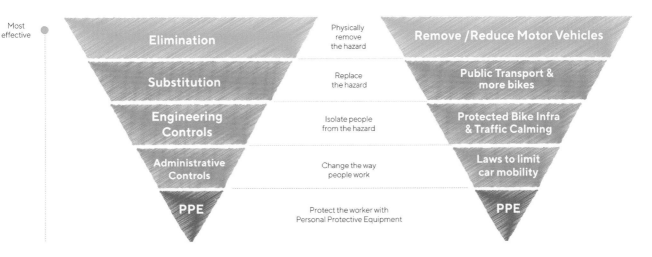

it on your head. Fun, right? Quirky. Goofy. Well, listen to this. In 2000, a report came out of the Road Accident Research Unit at the University of Adelaide entitled *CR 193: The Development of a Protective Headband for Car Occupants* (Andersen, White, McLean 2000). It was commissioned by the national government's Australian Transport Safety Bureau, which was trying to find solutions to the massive number of head injuries in car crashes. The prototype that was developed ended up being more of a headband, since that zone is where most head injuries occur in car crashes. It's rare that a head strikes the ceiling of the car, which is padded anyway.

The report estimates that the potential benefit of the headband would be as high as AU$380 million in reduced societal harm, even with seatbelts and airbags. Considering the fact that half of all serious head injuries happen inside cars, this product makes sense. The car industry, of course, won't touch this with a ten-foot pole. Imagine if the word got out that driving was dangerous? Not good for business. And business, for the car industry, is more important than safety. We cannot

credibly promote or legislate helmets for cyclists without extending that to pedestrians and motorists. If we really want to take safety for cycling seriously, we should be applying the Hierarchy of Hazard Control to the discussion. It's a system used in industry to work towards minimizing or eliminating workers' exposure to danger. It's standard practice. Here's what it looks like if we apply it to cycling and pedestrian danger in our cities.

What about these quick and easy ideas? If intersections are the most dangerous places for crashes, why don't motorists have to stop, push a button, and wait for permission to proceed? Or better yet, in a rational take on the Cyclist Dismount signage, let's force the motorists to do it. They'll get some exercise, too. All good.

The economist Gordon Tullock once joked that if the government wanted people to drive safely, they'd mandate a spike in the middle of each steering wheel. Traffic fatalities would plummet immediately.

Finally, simply make car horns just as loud inside cars as outside. Imagine the peace and quiet that would descend upon your city.

THE
LEAR
CURV

Here we all are. A decade or so into the triumphant return of the bicycle to our cities as transport. Cities around the world are wondering what to do and how to do it. In the global narrative, there are cities that inspire and cities that still fail to get it. What is the state of the urban bicycle nation? Where is the fence lowest, and where are there imposing walls? In order to understand where we are—and where we are headed—let's look at some of the primary challenges our cities face.

NING
E

CHAPTER 6

COPENHAGEN'S JOURNEY

This city is what it is because our citizens are what they are.

Plato

With good reason, hundreds of delegations come to cities like Copenhagen and Amsterdam every year to study and learn from the cities' consistent efforts to make the bicycle a respected and equal transport form and solve all manner of traffic and societal challenges. Copenhagen wasn't always Copenhagen—and that is so incredibly important to remember. Mistakes have been made, both large and small. This city was as car-clogged as anywhere else on the planet through the 1950s and 1960s. From a cycling peak in 1949, we took the on-ramp to the motorway of two decades of dismantling the city to make space for cars. A great deal of the bicycle infrastructure we had built was removed in the race for automobile space.

From a peak of amazing daily scenes like on Nørrebrogade during the 1940s, cycling started to decline. Following the American lead, plans were drawn up in many European cities for massive motorway systems that would carve their way through the urban landscape. Helsinki, Oslo,

Copenhagen's new bicycle and pedestrian bridge, Inderhavnsbroen.

Stockholm, Copenhagen, and Amsterdam were among the many cities that fostered such plans.

In Copenhagen in 1958, City Plan Vest (West) was hatched as a part of the plan for Søringen — the Lake Ring—and it was bombastic. A massive motorway would sweep down from the north and the ferry from Helsingborg, Sweden, and carve through neighborhoods, turning right and roaring along the iconic lakes to the north of the city center until it hit the Vesterbro neighborhood, where a huge spaghetti junction would be built on the bulldozed remains of a poor, densely populated area. It could not possibly have been more Robert Mosesesque.

From 1962 to 1976, Copenhagen had a lord mayor with one of most ironic names in political history: Urban Hansen. He had a big bucket o' car Kool-Aid and drank it. His vision for Copenhagen revolved entirely around the car. In 1972, he even removed the city's amazing tram network, which had been serving the citizens since 1863. The City Plan Vest and the Lake Ring advanced so far that

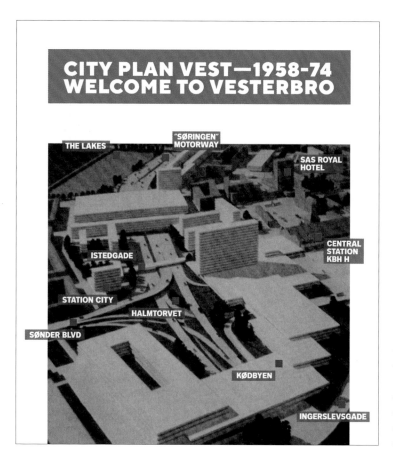

CITY PLAN VEST—1958-74
WELCOME TO VESTERBRO

THE LAKES

"SØRINGEN"
MOTORWAY

SAS ROYAL
HOTEL

CENTRAL
STATION
KBH H

ISTEDGADE

STATION CITY

HALMTORVET

SØNDER BLVD

KØDBYEN

INGERSLEVSGADE

Left: Rush hour traffic on Nørrebrogade in Copenhagen in the 1940s.
© The National Museum of Denmark
Right: *Model of the proposed Lake Ring motorway junction that would have destroyed part of the Vesterbro neighborhood. © City of Copenhagen*

apartment blocks were knocked down to make space, and large buildings were erected in anticipation of the coming motorway. The National Hospital and the Panum Institute are two of them. In Vesterbro, to the west of the Central Station, a strangely out-of-scale building stands on Halmtorvet Square and currently houses a police station. It's the tall building on the left of the model.

Amsterdam had their bulldozers in action as well, paving the way for a massive motorway development. Luckily, Copenhagen, Amsterdam, Oslo, and Helsinki, as well as other cities around the world like Vancouver, didn't complete the vision due to lack of funds. Sweden was neutral during the Second World War, and the ironic joke in Scandinavian urban planning is that they were never bombed so they bombed themselves after the war. Stockholm, like countless cities that embarked upon such car-centric plans in the 1950s and 1960s, is now struggling to figure out how to rid itself of wide motorways that restrict access to its harborfront. Some cities, like Paris, are ahead of the curve, reclaiming the space allocated to cars along the river—like the Georges Pompidou Expressway—and creating public space instead. They're giving the citizens their river back.

To say that the two oil crises in the 1970s hit Denmark hard is a massive understatement. Today it's almost impossible to imagine in a country with such a high standard of living, but families in apartments in the neighborhood where I live had to huddle around wood-burning stoves in one room during the winters.

Later today, after I write this paragraph, I will be heading out with my daughter, Lulu-Sophia, to enjoy Car-Free Sunday in Copenhagen. The first of its kind in Denmark was on November 25, 1973, and was an initiative by the government to save fuel. In many cities in Denmark, every second streetlight was turned off for the same reason.

There were public demonstrations on City Hall Square with tens of thousands of people with their bicycles, demanding safer conditions for cycling.

Sadly, the first oil crisis came only a year and a half after the last tram rolled through Copenhagen. Buses had replaced them, but gas prices went through the roof. At that point, the bicycle had almost completely disappeared in most cities in the world. In Copenhagen, the modal share

for bikes was still around 20 percent. The bicycle as a transport form had not been eradicated altogether, though, and people once again took to two wheels to get around. The problem was that cycling fatalities spiked to an all-time high in Denmark due to the lack of proper bicycle infrastructure. The people needed their bikes, but they weren't safe any longer. But hey, it was the seventies, man. An age of public engagement and of politicians who were willing to respond. At least in Denmark. There were public demonstrations on City Hall Square with tens of thousands of people with their bicycles, demanding safer conditions for cycling.

Efforts were made to improve both mobility and safety and to meet the demands of the people. It wasn't until the early 1980s, however, that there was the will and the budget to start rebuilding the protected network of bicycle infrastructure. It was a slow process at first, but it slowly accelerated through the 1980s and into the 1990s before really picking up the pace.

The first dedicated space for cycling was in Copenhagen, on Esplanaden, in 1892, when an equestrian path was reallocated for bicycles. The first protected, on-street cycle track in the world, however, saw the light of day in Copenhagen on Østerbrogade in 1915. Despite many decades of high cycling levels, the legacy of two car-centric decades proved challenging when city planners had to go back to the drawing board.

The biggest difference was that there was now a daunting armada of cars and trucks dominating the streetspace. Planners and engineers were initially loath to reclaim space from cars, just like most of them around the world still are today. Cyclists were returning to the streets, and while the safety-in-numbers concept was prov-

A CITY

**WHERE CARS &
PEDESTRIANS CAN GO**

**WHERE "THEY" THINK
CYCLISTS WANT TO GO**

**WHERE CYCLISTS
ACTUALLY WANT TO GO**

Cyclists don't want detours. They want full access to the city like everyone else.

ing to be true and the rates of cyclist fatalities and injuries started to fall, the space dilemma was at the forefront of planning.

In countries like the United States, we have recently seen the emergence of ideas like the Bicycle Boulevard. That has a nice ring to it, doesn't it? Some marketing thought was put into thinking that up. A boulevard—all wide and fancy-sounding—for bicycles. As though cycling is being prioritized and nurtured. The reality is quite different. A bicycle boulevard is, in fact, a detour that keeps cyclists away from the natural desire lines of a city—out of sight, out of mind—and does little to prioritize cycling as a transport form. Lazy bicycle planning. Band-aid solutions by politicians.

I hear the same thing in many countries. "But it's nicer to cycle away from traffic. That's what cyclists want . . . " Regardless of transport form, most people don't want to be forced to take detours. They want to go from A to B. I've seen many recreational paths for cyclists in the United States that have a wavy form with curves, even though there are no obstructions and a

straight line is totally doable. This is the result of non-bike-riding engineers designing bicycle infrastructure with preconceived ideas like "Must be boring to ride straight. Let's curve this puppy up a bit."

This bicycle boulevard lark was tried out in Copenhagen in the early 90s. Cycling levels along the main artery, Nørrebrogade, were increasing exponentially, but there was no infrastructure. Well-meaning city planners thought that cyclists would prefer a less congested and safer route, so a parallel street was blinged up with infrastructure. "There you go, cyclists! THAT'S where you'd rather ride, right?"

Nope. It was a flop. Nobody actually prefers detours. If you have ever visited an IKEA and only needed one specific item, you know how infuriating the labyrinthian route that IKEA has knowingly designed can be. Similarly, when you are heading for work in the morning, you don't want to be forcibly deflected from your route to roll down side streets. In most cities, the preferred routes have been laid out for a very long time—the natural desire lines to and from the city. Send-

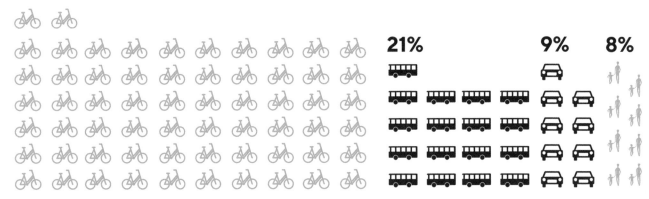

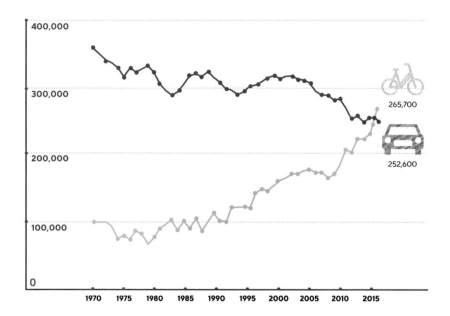

400,000

300,000

265,700

200,000

252,600

100,000

0

1970   1975   1980   1985   1990   1995   2000   2005   2010   2015

Graph left: In 2016, the number of bicycles entering Copenhagen's city center exceeded the number of cars for the first time since 1970. Data: City of Copenhagen

Opposite. *The statistics for how citizens of the City of Copenhagen arrived at work or education in the city in 2016. Data: City of Copenhagen*

ing cyclists onto a National Geographic expedition to foreign neighborhoods is not promoting or prioritizing cycling; it is reluctantly tolerating them. With a barely audible sigh and a furtive roll of the eyes. "Let's hope THAT shuts them up . . . "

To the City of Copenhagen's credit, they learned quickly from that crucial mistake, understanding that urban citizens on bikes should be afforded equal opportunity to get around. This was one of the catalysts that started the modern age of bicycle urbanism in Copenhagen. The focus switched to reallocating urban transport space on the main arteries leading to the city center. It was certainly tougher in the nineties than back in the twenties, what with the all the cars that now occupied urban space, but this was the way forward.

Slowly but surely, the network was expanded and cycling levels rose accordingly. The learning curve was steep but short due to the fact that there was still infrastructure in place outside of the city center, so there wasn't a need to start from scratch and rethink the designs.

For a couple of decades, a rigid transport engineering system had been implemented and adhered to. I liken it to the film *The Matrix*, and it feels like we, the citizens, just wander around in a fabricated reality, controlled unawares by complicated—and outdated—mathematical models. It was time to punch a hole through the code and start hacking the city back to a place that made sense.

The focus switched to reallocating urban transport space on the main arteries.

All around the world, the Matrix persists. Firewalls and security systems are in place in many countries, making the hacking more difficult, but progress is slowly being made.

The City of Copenhagen had a head start thanks to decades of planning and the establishment of best-practice standards back in the 1920s, but the game had changed. There were attempts to squeeze the bicycle into the Matrix, much like what we see in many parts of the world, but it was clear that if reestablishing the bicycle as transport were to succeed, it would require dedicated space.

Attempts were made to play around with bidirectional, on-street cycle tracks on one side of the street. It's classic lazy planning, and in Danish bicycle planning this design was thrown out twenty years ago because it wasn't safe enough and it proved difficult to connect bidirectional tracks up with unidirectional infrastructure. We'll get back to best-practice design later in the book, but the point is that mistakes were made and then they were fixed. From the oil crises to today, the Copenhagen journey is, in many ways, identical with the journey in Amsterdam and other Dutch cities. The worldwide oil embargo, the crushing blow dealt by OPEC, was handled with simple pragmatism—and the results are spectacular.

One of the trademarks of the cultures of the Nordic countries is a strong desire to seek compromise—to make sure everyone is appeased. On many levels, it is an admirable quality and avoids constant butting of heads in both political and social contexts. Years ago, the City of Copenhagen made a rough guideline for traffic planning, saying that the modal share for bicycles and public transport should never be allowed to fall below 30 percent, and that car traffic should never exceed 30 percent.

The primary data set that the City uses is how people arrive in the City of Copenhagen to go to work or to school. In 2016, the numbers indicate that the 30-30-30 goal is intact. In the current political climate in Copenhagen, it seems that this preestablished compromise is now a hurdle blocking efforts to move forward. The City now

has a declared political goal that 50 percent of trips to work and school arriving in the City will be by bike. The original goal was to achieve 50 percent by 2012. Then it was bumped to 2015 and now it is set for 2025. Cycling is increasing in Copenhagen. For the first time since 1970, the number of bikes entering the city center exceeded the number of cars, and the current modal share of 42 percent is impressively high. It is worth mentioning that among people who have an address in the city of Copenhagen, 62 percent will ride a bike to work or school. In order to move forward, however, more space is needed and the old compromise needs to be readjusted to reflect reality.

LEARNING FROM FAILING LIKE A CHAMP

For all the investment and drive in Copenhagen over the past 40 years in general and ten years in particular, you would think that expensive mistakes would be avoided. Unfortunately not.

One recent mistake occurred when the City decided to play around with the surfacing of cycle tracks. The default, quality asphalt, is always fine, but out in the new Ørestad development, paving stones were implemented. Experimenting is never a bad idea, but this one went south in a hurry. The quality of the stone was substandard and it cracked easily, especially in the winter. The paving stones were replaced with better-quality ones.

Then, in the city center, in conjunction with the street redesign of Vester Voldgade, it was decided to use the same paving-stone concept. There is a clear visual difference between Copenhagen's sidewalk design and the otherwise clear asphalt on the cycle tracks. On this street, the paving stones were used for both, without any physical demarcation. At first it seemed weird to most Copenhageners, but we had it figured out

The recently redesigned Vester Voldgade street with cycle track surfacing chosen for an aesthetic instead of logic. © Lorenz Siegel

in no time. The problem is the number of tourists in this area, most of whom aren't accustomed to looking for bikes, let alone recognizing a cycle track.

The City has now added some paint to illustrate the two different zones in an attempt to fix the problem, but at City Hall Square, in order to keep tourists off the cycle track they also added a pedestrian barrier, which is never a good idea. If you have to fix a design with extra infrastructure, it wasn't a good design to begin with.

One of the more recent additions to the bicycle-culture arsenal is the Inner Harbor Bridge—Inderhavnsbroen in Danish—that spans Copenhagen Harbor at a key strategic and iconic point. It links the city center at the end of the postcard-perfect Nyhavn with the Christianshavn neighborhood and the southern neighborhoods beyond. The bridge opened in July 2016 and is one of a series of 17 new bridges or underpasses for bicycle traffic that have been added to the City's transport network in the past few years. Let me be clear: I'm thrilled that we have a brand-new, modern link over the harbor to accommodate bicycle traffic and pedestrians. I am over the moon that the number of cyclists crossing daily exceeds all pro-

Fresh skid marks on the Inner Harbour Bridge leading towards the warning markings.
If you need to put warning signs on a design, it's not a good design.

jected numbers. The City estimated that between 3,000 and 7,000 cyclists would use the bridge, but the latest numbers as of mid-2017 are 16,000.

So it's a massive success. But sometimes you *can* see the forest for the trees. I'm sorry, but Inderhavnsbro is a stupid, stupid bridge. Yes, it fulfills its primary function of allowing people to cross a body of water. But it is a cumbersome, beastly thing that is completely and utterly out of place in the delicate urban, historical, and architectural context of its location. A fantastic overcomplication of the simple, timeless art of building bridges that open and close. Designed by an architect named Cezary Bednarski from an architecture bureau with roots in two countries where cycling is no longer mainstream transport, Poland and the United Kingdom, it has failed miserably in respecting the basic concepts of bicycle urbanism and the established standards for infrastructure and facilities.

Crossing the bridge by bicycle involves two sharp turns—two chicanes. Chicanes designed by someone who doesn't ride a bicycle. Cyclists are shunted sharply and rudely towards the middle of the bridge and then back out to the side again. Best-practice standards for details like chicanes have been in place for a century. We know what degree of curvature works best for comfort and for safety. These chicanes, however, pose serious problems that are clearly visible for anyone to see. You can see from the bicycle tracks on a rainy day that people just cut the corners.

A more serious concern is the many skid marks you see on the bridge as you head downwards in either direction. I stop and study them every time I cross. Have a look if you visit it. There are always fresh ones. People crown the bridge in the middle and then get their speed up, but many people fail to realize that the architect wasn't capable of a straight line and they have to slam on the brakes and sometimes actually hit the glass. I don't know if anyone has gone over the edge into the water, but the physics provide

a perfect storm of things that can go wrong. The City has realized there is an issue and they have slapped up a large red-and-white warning sign on the glass barriers to inform people that it's a dead end. Once again, let's face it. If you need to put warning signs on a design, it is basically a crappy design. Period.

The incline grade to climb the bridge also ignores best-practice standards for bicycle infrastructure, most of which were established in the 1920s and 1930s. The architect probably thought "bike," and a spandexy dude on a racing bike popped into his head. The bridge is too steep. It is not designed for a mainstream bicycle city, and the architect didn't bother researching the fact that in Copenhagen we have 40,000 cargo bikes filled with kids and goods.

The basic principles of Danish design—practical, functional, elegant—were sadly forgotten in the choice of this bridge.

On all the other bicycle bridges in Copenhagen, a simple boom will drop along with the sound of a pleasant but insistent ringing bell to stop cyclists and pedestrians when the bridge is opening. Compare that simple design to the huge, groaning barriers that rise like creatures from the black lagoon on the Inderhavnsbro.

Another detail is that there are no ramps on the stairs on the pedestrian side—unusual in Copenhagen, but necessary in this case. That is easily fixed, compared with the rest of the nightmare. The bridge was also funded by a philanthropic fund—but does this mean that we don't have to be rational when we get free stuff? I can easily and rightfully criticize the architect who failed miserably at his task, but, lest we forget, there was a jury of Copenhageners who actually looked at this and voted "YES!" So there are many fools at this party.

With so many moving parts, breakdowns become inevitable. It's already happened a number of times, with ships stuck on the wrong side because the bridge couldn't open. A fancy-schmancy bridge in Kiel, Germany, ended up having so many problems that another bridge was built next to it, to be used when the fancy bridge breaks down. Is that where we are heading in Copenhagen?

The bicycle is returning but unfortunately it is without any decent design consistency. I see weird stuff out there.

The bridge is nothing more than "magpie architecture"—a shiny object that attracted the favor of the people who selected it. Seduced by bling and fake innovation instead of being guided by timeless rationality and the basic principles of Danish design—practical, functional, and elegant. They were sadly forgotten in the choice of this bridge. The shine will wear off and, I fear, we'll be faced with more-expensive problems. It is important to make mistakes but it is paramount to learn from them.

INTERNATIONAL CHALLENGES

My work is a roller-coaster ride of emotions. I travel constantly to cities, whether to do a keynote or to work with a client city. I see what is happening all over the world, in the most unlikely places. I am, by nature, an optimistic idealist. I seek out the positive first and drink from glasses that are half full. I get excited to see progress being made in designing for bicycle traffic and reallocating urban space for intelligent transport forms. The bicycle is returning, but unfortunately it is without any decent design consistency. I see weird stuff out there.

And I see a pattern. A mayor sends a directive down the pipeline. "Let's build some infrastructure for bikes." You can almost hear the groans coming out of the engineering departments. Much like back in the day when engineers were handed the task of improving traffic safety without any experience or knowledge, engineers are now sent out to squeeze bikes into their Matrix.

Crappy examples of bicycle infrastructure could fill a book on their own, but there are some examples that stand out where the wrong people were sent out to design for bikes. You can see this in the photo from Ljubljana, Slovenia. A classic example of ignoring a great deal of available space off to the left and instead taking space away from pedestrians. Bizarre bollards are added to the mix. Whoever put this in expressed no regard for logic, safety, or the human experience, and was blatantly ignorant of it all. Luckily, the street has been since redesigned for the better.

In 2017, I saw a new design for bike lanes in Barcelona. I laughed out loud when I stood there looking at it. It simply doesn't make any sense. I showed my two kids this design. "What do you think of this?" Lulu-Sophia studied it for a moment and concluded that "it doesn't look very clever." Felix, in the midst of his moody teenager phase, just snorted and said, "That's so stupid," and went into his room. Both of them are absolutely right. Bizarrely, the next intersection further along had a completely different spaghetti-serving of painted lines. There is a sign up on a light post to educate people about how to use it. As ever, if you have to put up a sign to explain a design, it's a crappy design.

Barcelona is a city that is a bit ahead of the curve. They are looking seriously at the bicycle as transport once again and putting money where their mouth is. But they will not accelerate towards a bicycle-friendly future if they let people freestyle like this. They risk having the designs fail, which is ammo for the sceptics.

I don't know what individual was responsible for the first bike lane in the door zone. It's easier to make up a list of city planners and engineers in far too many cities in the world who have put them in since. This is not good infrastructure. In fact, it's not infrastructure at all. It's paint. Putting cyclists between the door zone in a single-occupant vehicle society and moving traffic is insanity. It makes me throw up a little bit in my mouth. It does nothing to protect cyclists or to encourage cycling. It does a lot to let politicians claim they are all bicycle-friendly without spending much money or making any serious effort.

Sharrows? OMG. Don't get me started on sharrows. The unwanted and unloved child of bicycle urbanism. I am so pleased that studies out there are now proving what we knew all along: that sharrows are completely useless. Cities shouldn't be allowed to count sharrows when they publish the total length of their bike lanes. Hastily painted pictograms in the middle of car lanes are not infrastructure. They are the awkward watermark of lazy politicians and lazier transport professionals.

Hastily painted pictograms in the middle of car lanes are not infrastructure.

Then there are center-running lanes. These are the Donald Trumps of bicycle engineering. (Appropriately, Washington, DC, has installed one.) Initially, my international team of planners and urban designers at the Copenhagen Design Company headquarters had a good laugh when we saw a photo of it, but then it sinks in: this is actually a thing. Someone was tasked with put-

Top: *Bizarre and failed attempt in Ljubljana to squeeze bicycles into the car-centric Matrix.*
Center: *One of the world's most confusing infrastructure designs for bikes in Barcelona.*
Bottom: *The stupidest place to put bicycles: in between the door zone and moving traffic.*

Right: *The dreaded sharrow in its natural environment*
Bottom: *Center-running bike lanes in Washington, DC ©Ole Kassow*

ting in bicycle infrastructure and this is what a city ended up with. Taxpayers' hard-earned money was used. I suggested on Twitter that the person responsible should be identified and promptly fired. A flippant remark—but still a serious one.

Why, then, do we see crap like this showing up on city streets? Who, in their right mind, would actually choose to put cycling citizens in the middle of a street with speeding cars on either side? Certainly not anyone with an understanding of the bicycle's role in urban life as transport, or with a sincere desire to encourage cycling and keep people safe. My first thought when seeing the photo was: *How am I supposed to get to a destination in mid-block?* Do I go up to the next intersection and walk my bike back? What if I'm cycling with my kids or older people? Would I really would I want to cycle with them on a barren wasteland as motorists fly past like it's 1962? No humans were considered in the development of this solution. There is no respect for access or safety, and no broader idea of an intelligent,

cohesive network. "Oh, but it works!" someone mutters from the shadowy wings of urbanism. What works, exactly? Cycling down this stretch is possible, yes. But it's not safe. The sense of safety is fake at best and probably nonexistent. We are planning our cities for the next century of transport. It is important to plan properly, drawing upon solutions that are tried and tested. Using cyclists as guinea pigs in solutions whipped together by lazy, car-centric engineers is ridiculous when we know the best way to approach it.

The proponents of this center-running lark call it "context-sensitive design." Just using the word *design* is an insult to generations of bicycle planners who worked so hard to establish best-practice. Perhaps the context of which they speak is idiocy. This DC solution is engineering in sheep's clothing. Built by people who don't understand human-centric design and who think that bikes are cars. But for those who insist on putting humans in the wasteland, what about just going all in? I tested the theory at my local wine bar the other evening. Didn't feel at all comfortable. "Oh, but they have them in Barcelona!" Yes they do. And in Nantes. And in Sao Paulo. You know where they *don't* have them? In countries that have been doing this for while.

Just because a couple of other cities have made the same mistake doesn't make it a good idea. Just because Ugg boots or Crocs cover your feet and keep them warm or dry doesn't mean they make sense as footwear. All that happened is that these cities allowed themselves to put their faith in engineers instead of designers or bicycle planners.

I have ridden on the center-running lanes in Barcelona several times, on holidays with my kids and while working in the city. There is no access to destinations or points of origin in mid-block. There are wide, arrogant intersections that force you to speed across them. The traffic lights are coordinated for car traffic, so you have to muscle it to catch the flow, which proved difficult with a nine-year-old kid. We spent days waiting at the lights at the end of every stretch of stupid. Luckily, the City has been made aware that such solutions are counterproductive to safety and growing cycling in the city, and local advocates have taken up the battle.

The center-running lane in the center of the French city of Nantes is also crappy design, but it is shouldered by low-speed car and tram lanes that allow easy access back and forth across the street. It fails, however, because it hardly provides any separation. It's a sieve through which anyone can meander. But, at the very least, it has a calm, low-speed feel to it. The one slicing down the middle of São Paulo's iconic boulevard Avenida de Paulista is an even bigger brain fart than the one in DC. A complete scandal.

One difference about Barcelona, like Nantes, is that much of the city is a 30 km/h (20 mph)

zone. The City is focused on slowing the whole place down in order to save lives, reduce injuries, and create a more life-sized city. The center-running lanes lead to large roundabouts, which make at least a bit more sense than throwing you headlong into a car-centric intersection. The infrastructure in DC is focused on the fit and the brave, not The 99%. Hardly an intelligent way to grow cycling as transport.

Bidirectional cycle tracks pose a much higher risk to the cyclists than two one-directional ones. The difference on crossings is by a factor 2.

One rule of thumb to consider is a simple one: If you don't see a particular infrastructure design in the Netherlands or in Denmark, it's probably a stupid infrastructure design. If you wouldn't put pedestrians in a center lane between moving traffic, why the hell would you put cyclists there? A rule of thumb for the ages. Don't worry. The engineers and planners we need to fire will probably get other jobs. There's other engineery stuff to do.

Bear with me on this rant. I get so incredibly frustrated thinking and writing about such designs. A major bone to pick is the on-street, bidirectional cycle track or bike lane. For clarity, when I say *on-street, bidirectional* I mean the creation of one lane for bicycles separated by a dotted line, allowing for two-way traffic—on city streets. I am not referring to a two-way path through a park or other areas free of motorized vehicles.

In Denmark, the on-street, bidirectional facility was effectively thrown out of the standards for bicycle infrastructure over two decades ago. That in itself should be an alarm bell to anyone paying attention. These two-way cycle tracks were found to be more dangerous than one-way cycle tracks on each side of the roadway. Having bicycles coming from two directions at once was an inferior design. It also proved difficult to connect them up with the unidirectional network. Two jigsaw puzzles that got mixed up.

We tried it out when we were getting the bike back into our cities, but this was also in an established bicycle culture where the cycling citizens and motorists are accustomed to one another. When I see this design being implemented in emerging bicycle cities where bikes are still being reintroduced, it makes my toes curl.

This isn't about building stuff out of asphalt. We are planting seeds in the hopes that lush gardens will grow.

There are bidirectional cycle tracks in Copenhagen, and I'll get into the best-practice standards in due time. They run through parks and down greenways, separated from motorized traffic, and on occasion they run on streets that have no cross streets. At all times they are placed where they actually make sense, to eliminate the risk of collision with cars and trucks. Cycle tracks are like sidewalks . . . you put them on either side of the street, except you keep them one-way.

I asked Theo Zeegers, a scientist who used to work at the Dutch national cycling organisation, Fietsersbond, about this issue. You see bidirec-

tional cycle tracks in Dutch cities. He told me that:

"Bidirectional cycle tracks pose a much higher risk to the cyclists than two one-directional ones. The difference on crossings is about a factor of 2. So, especially in areas with lots of crossings (i.e., built-up areas), one-directional lanes are preferred. Not all municipalities get this message, however."

Imagine removing a sidewalk on one side of the street and forcing pedestrians to share a narrow sidewalk on the other side of the street. You wouldn't do that if you wanted to prioritize walking. You shouldn't do it if you were serious about safety and prioritizing cycling.

The bidirectional cycle tracks we see in emerging bicycle cities can't possibly be put there by people who know what they're doing or who understand the needs of bicycle users or who really want cycling to boom. You can also see that in the width allocated to many of the tracks—incredibly narrow, making it a lip-biting experience just to pass oncoming cyclists and even making it a bit too hair-raising just to pass cyclists heading in the same direction.

Montreal has long been North America's premier bicycle city, having been ahead of the curve since back in the late 1980s, when they started putting in bike lanes, most of them bidirectional. In 2017, the City is finally planning on building unidirectional lanes along the sidewalk, but they are discovering the difficulty in connecting them up with the existing infrastructure. My team studied an intersection in Montreal with our Desire Line Analysis Tool, and the cyclists we observed highlighted the difficulty in making the design work.

Another oft-muttered excuse is, "Well . . . it's better than nothing"—usually spoken in a defensive tone. This is a flawed argument, lacking vision, commitment, and experience. A chair with two legs is better than nothing if you want to take a load off. But it's not a long-term design solution, especially when we're planning for the future.

This isn't about building stuff out of asphalt. We are planting seeds in the hopes that lush gardens will grow. We have the seeds we need. They are fertile, natural, and ready to grow with minimal maintenance. Instead, though, people are choosing bags of GMO seeds from traffic planning's Walmart. Limited fertility, modified for the simple needs of visionless gardeners. Potted plants instead of gardens. If someone advocates infrastructure like this and actually believes it is good, they probably shouldn't be advocating bicycle infrastructure. If I proposed any of the above in a Danish city I would be a laughingstock. Let's face it: the United States has given the world loads of brilliant, world-changing ideas

and technology since the Industrial Revolution, but bicycle infrastructure is not one of them.

After decades of pumping out the same hard-core, failed infrastructure, American traffic engineers finally pulled something new out of their bag. Behold the DDI: Double Diamond Interchange. It is hailed by their industry as revolutionary, but really it's nothing more than a tweak. In fact, it's the world's most expensive transport tweak, which will help them continue to get massive funding for their highways.

Copenhagenize Design Company's client city, Long Beach, California, has been told by the California Department of Transportation, CalTran, that they'll be getting two of them to lead the Los

Desire Line Analysis of an intersection in Montreal showing how bidirectional infrastructure has inherent flaws.

Conflict Zone 1 - mid-intersection

Angeles freeway system into their city. The city has always been fortunate in its location in Los Angeles. Freeways ended there but didn't carve up the cityscape. Long Beach has said they don't want the DDIs—but Uncle CalTrans gets to decide.

We were tasked with improving bicycle and pedestrian mobility through the new interchange. I put a whole bunch of brains on the project to try and figure it out. The engineers who spawned this monster certainly haven't helped. When you look at the designs, you notice areas marked "non-highway feature." That is traffic-engineering-speak for sidewalks, which are considered so irrelevant that they aren't even called *sidewalks*. Bicycle infrastructure? Completely nonexistent.

After a couple of weeks of brainstorming, we realized that there was no hope for redesigning the DDIs in any coherent way to improve bicycle and pedestrian mobility. Here is what we came up with instead. Sure. Ignoring the bull. But improving the transport network of Long Beach in doing so.

Along with these physical additions to the urban landscape, you can add various campaigns like Share the Road, Take the Lane, and moves to stipulate a minimum passing distance. Less demonstrative than paint, asphalt, and concrete and, no doubt, devised by people who mean well, they are still a declaration of transport bankruptcy. They are still awkward admissions that cars dominate and bikes are regarded as an invasive species.

Top: Highway in Montreal with what engineers refer to as a "non-highway feature." You know it as a sidewalk.
Bottom: *Copenhagenize Design Company's solution to make a Double Diamond Interchange in Long Beach, California, bicycle and pedestrian friendly? We simply ignored it. Architect: Kan Chen*

Copenhageners bound for
home on a winter's afternoon.

CHAPTER 7

CLIMAPHOBIA & VACUUM-PACKED CITIES

You can't create music in a vacuum.

Brian May

As I write this, I'm in a vacuum-packed tube hurtling through the air high above Europe. At this point I'm pleased to be vacuum-packed. I'm grateful that a few generations of designers and engineers have perfected the technology to allow me to avoid the −70°C (−94°F) temperature outside this aircraft and to sip a coffee while penning these words. I remain amazed that this is possible. Like the American comedian Louis C.K. would have it, "You're sitting in a chair in the sky! You're like a Greek myth right now!"

A few years ago in Edmonton, Alberta, I did a keynote at a conference with a unique angle. The Winter Cities Shakeup, held in February. It was all about design and urbanism, focused on life in winter cities. I have also spoken a couple of times at the niche Winter Cycling Conference that rotates between host cities with a wintry climate. While I like these two unique angles for conferences, I couldn't help wondering why they are even necessary. Where have we come to in the development of our cities and societies that we find it necessary to discuss life in cities with extreme(ish) weather conditions? Battling a recent—"recent" in the history of cities—development regarding people's perception of weather conditions.

The chain of thoughts about this started in Bangkok, where my team and I were working on a project for a client. The project required us to be driven all over the city, not only on work-related matters but also on sightseeing jaunts, thanks to the unstinting hospitality of our hosts. We also spent a great deal of time outside and on public transport. I soon noticed a pattern in our hosts' behavior.

We have morphed into climaphobes. We fear the weather as soon as it ventures out of our comfort zone at either end of the temperature scale.

The minivan was air-conditioned, as are the trains and every damn building we ventured into. Every time we entered an air-conditioned space, our hosts—fanning themselves and exhaling in relief through pursed lips—would comment on how great it was to be out of the heat. Even after a mere 20-meter (66-foot) dash from minivan to building entrance.

It was hot in Bangkok, sure—30–35°C (86–95°F) and muggy. This, however, is not unusual. It's basically been the same weather for the past few . . . millennia. At the very least. It is in these weather conditions that the ancestors of our hosts in this country were born and lived their lives. Working, raising families. In the course of a few decades, as air-conditioning units became widespread, the heat had become an unwitting

antagonist, simply because it was there. People have been conditioned to fear the heat.

An inverted meteorological condition affects northern cities like Edmonton and Calgary and many others. There, it is the cold—performing its standard seasonal routine—that has become the bogeyman. From growing up in Calgary, I know well the icy rage of a prairie winter. I remember how it was growing up in the seventies and eighties in those winters. Playing hockey on outdoor rinks at –25°C (–13°F). Simply because there was nothing else to do and I was an average young man with energy to burn. I walked to high school in highly unsuitable footwear—boat shoes were the thing at the time, and socks in boat shoes were a no-go. I hated hats, and on mornings when I washed my hair and didn't have time to dry it, my hair froze to ice on the 20-minute walk to school. Which I always thought was kind of cool.

Was I a hard young man? No. I was just an average dude in a winter city. I do remember discovering, at about the age of nine or so, that the thermostat in the house went up to 30°C (86°F). It baffled me that my dad had it set at 22°C (72°F). Why 22 when 30 was possible?! I kept turning it up to 30° until he approached me and gruffly explained the concept of heating bills. I was promptly sent back to the "put a sweater on" culture into which my mother had introduced all of us kids. Maybe my doppelganger in some Thai city at that time was being told "fan yourself if you're too hot." That "suck it up, buttercup" school of parenting is something I am pleased I experienced and something that my kids have certainly been introduced to.

Something has changed. In Bangkok. In Calgary. In Edmonton. I laugh when fellow Copenhageners feel they have to buy a fan during heatwaves in the summer where temperatures skyrocket to . . . oh, about 28°C (82°F). But something has changed in Copenhagen, too. And all over the world.

I decided to give it a name: *climaphobia*. Fear of the weather. Not extreme weather like destructive hurricanes, but just the normal weather.

We have morphed into climaphobes. We fear the weather as soon as it ventures out of our comfort zone at either end of the temperature scale. In Denmark, the comfort zone is narrow. After more than 20 years of living in Copenhagen, I have noticed that the perfect temperature for the Danes is 25°C (77°F). At 24°C (75°F) they bitch about the lousy summer. At 26°C (79°F) they gasp theatrically for breath. When the temperature stays above 20°C (68°F) at night, the Danish Meteorological Institute declares it a "Tropical Night." This is rarely a happy announcement, but more of a dire warning.

My dad grew up on a farm in Northern Jutland. He would tell stories about the legendary winters that were the norm back then. 1940/41? That was a winter. He lived in Calgary from 1953 to his death in 2015, so the winter temperatures were just a bit chillier than during his childhood. He would smile and almost chuckle when telling me of this or that cold snap in Calgary over the phone. He almost sounded disappointed when the temperature on winter days rose above zero (32°F).

The shrug his generation reserved for adverse weather rubbed off on my generation, too, but now climaphobia has struck. Coupled with our sensationalist media culture, a cold winter becomes a Polar Vortex. El Niño and his bride La Niña have produced a cull of unruly children named in order to imprint them on an entertainment-hungry society. Sure, nasty hurricanes deserve names, but weather has been celebritized much more generally than that. Previously undramatic weather conditions are elevated to the status of reality-show stars. These celebrities are always cast as the bad guys.

As a film, *Climaphobia* would be lame. If hackers found it on Sony's servers, they would have deleted it instead of distributing it as a torrent. The protagonist would be a regular person living a regular life, perhaps plagued by less-than-optimal blood circulation so their feet and fin-

gers were often too hot or too cold. The gallery of antagonists would be named to strike fear into our hearts—Henry Heatwave, Roger the Raindrop, Cold-Snap Charlie. The heroes would arm themselves with battery-operated fans, hair dryers, super-umbrellas—depending on which sequel we're watching.

Climaphobia is a thing because we have spent obscene amounts of energy and money desperately trying to engineer the weather out of our lives. Attempting to create a world like this tube I'm sitting in at 10,000 meters (33,000 feet) above Poland.

Climaphobia is a thing because we have spent obscene amounts of energy and money desperately trying to engineer the weather out of our lives.

Montreal has its underground (hence indoor) shopping center, but the city of Calgary is infamous for its Skywalk system—or the Plus 15, as it was called when I was young and they started developing it. The skyscrapers in the downtown core are connected by sealed-in walkways above the street that allow you to walk in shirtsleeves (even on frigid winter days) from A to B via a complicated and not-very-direct route. Below, cars roll along unencumbered by bothersome pedestrians. Edmonton and Minneapolis have similar networks.

Let's face it: the Skywalk concept is a direct product of a car-centric society. Keeping people out of the weather was an added bonus to keeping the streets clear for cars. It's a dystopian world. Sit in your warm house, with your car plugged in or parked in a heated garage. There are even remote-control devices that allow you to start your car from your dining table. My dad had one and loved it. This gadget would let him start his car and let it run and get warmed up before he made the five-meter dash to it. Then drive in a vacuum-packed bubble to the downtown core, enter a car park, dash five meters to the elevator and into the building to spend the rest of the day until it was time to retrace his (very few physical) steps. If Le Corbusier were alive, he wouldn't watch porn. He would google images of the Skywalk to get his kicks. To get your kicks, you have to see the satirical film about it, called *WayDownTown*. It's a great companion film to *Radiant City*—another must-see mockumentary about sprawl. Both films are by Gary Burns and both take place in Calgary.

> Let's agree from now on that anything with the word Sky in it is probably not conducive to city life.

The downtown cores in Edmonton and Calgary are, like so many other cities, doughnuts outside of working hours. Devoid of life after the workers head home. These cities effectively amputated their streetlife and replaced it with artificial limbs in the air. Back in 1970, Calgary tried to funk it up by making a stretch of 8th Avenue car-free and renaming it Stephen Avenue. The idea has never really worked, and parts of the street have since been handed back to cars, and it's a poor cousin to so many other pedestrianized streets around the world.

The Skywalk system and other concepts like it are simply attempts to put streetlife—and people—on a shelf, out of the way. Remember Norman Foster's SkyCycle? Let's agree from now on that anything with the word Sky in it is probably not conducive to city life.

A conference like Winter Cities Shake-up is the unwitting offspring of society's climaphobia. Its goal is to get people to enjoy outdoor life—even in the winter. Something homo sapiens have been doing since we wandered northward out of Africa. Don't get me wrong—the Shake-up was a great conference with brilliant speakers from 60 cities around the world. I'm just trying to wrap my brain around the societal developments leading up to it.

Is it enough to merely try and communicate the fact that "Hey! Winter's okay!" and work to inspire citizens to "rediscover outdoor winter pleasures"—especially when their perception has been warped by a generation of vacuum-packing?

No. It's not enough.

To battle the bad guys, we need urbanism and design. But lurking in the wings of our B-film is the kingpin—Eddie Engineering. As with most nemeses, it's not really his fault. He had a bad childhood, growing up in a neighborhood built on last-century engineering traditions. In an age where it was thought that engineering alone would save the world. In a region that bought into it.

We are left with one of the greatest challenges facing the modernization of our cities: how to change the perception of the citizens? Perception of life outside the bubble. Perception of how people can transport themselves around cities.

Telling is less effective than showing. In the information age where we are inundated with things to learn—more things than we can ever hope to understand—telling through communication is losing its effectiveness. Ten thousand hours of television is produced for every hour you're alive, and that doesn't even include the Web's content. We need to get our game face on. Engineering was allowed to build with few checks and balances. We need a carte blanche to start improving, fixing, and future-proofing our cities.

Okay. I've calmed down. For now. The challenges we face are many. Design, as well as tried-and-tested infrastructure, can solve them all. We're still faced with the challenge of society in general—and planners, engineers, and politicians, in particular—to understand urban cycling.

I had a conversation with a dear friend recently. Riley Westerfield is a teacher from Eugene, Oregon, who works with special-needs kids, specifically kids with autism. She was explaining the challenges she and other teachers in her field face, not only with the kids she cares for, but also with society's perception of autism, which we are only just beginning to understand. She speaks so passionately about her work. As she put it to me, kids with autism need a system designed for them. You have to learn how to communicate with them. It's all about trying to figure them out. Teaching them, however, involves giving them the tools and skills to navigate a world that isn't at all designed for them. Teachers have to learn how to pantomime a system that is alien to these kids but completely normal for those of us who are neurotypical. They will always be autistic and will forever be forced to try to act in ways that appease the neurotypical society around them.

At this point I said to her, "Just like cyclists in cities." She nodded. "Exactly. A city like Portland has been designed for years to be car-centric. A system was developed. People in the suburbs learned this system early and car dependency is the result, simply because there is really only one system. Cyclists are expected to adapt to that system. No real effort is made to understand them and their needs. Cyclists are the autists of the current transportation system."

She's right. Damn. She's right. In countries like Denmark and the Netherlands, efforts have been made to understand cyclists and their unique transport psychology and their needs. In most of the rest of the world, they're just expected to conform to an "auto-typical" society that wasn't designed for them.

What should we do in a perfect world? The learning curve is as steep and long or as short and gentle as you want it to be. In some cities, the politicians get it, but their ideas die on the doorstep of the engineering department. In others, the professionals get it, but they lack politicians with the chutzpah to make it happen. For every visionary, there is a whole pile of lazy.

CHAPTER 8

THE ARROGANCE OF SPACE

None are more hopelessly enslaved than those who falsely believe that they are free.

Johann Wolfgang von Goethe

Freedom is what you do with what's been done to you.

Jean-Paul Sartre

When we describe cities, we have a tendency to give them human character traits. It's a friendly city. A dynamic city. A boring city. Perhaps, then, a city can be arrogant. Arrogant, for example, with its distribution of space.

If you're afraid of heights, the rule of thumb is "don't look down." When you work with life-sized cities, transport, and bicycle urbanism, it would seem that this rule applies as well. Standing atop the Eiffel Tower with my kids a few years ago, I failed to heed that advice. I looked down at the Quai Branly intersection where it meets the Pont d'Iéna over the Seine. This is easily one of the busiest pedestrian intersections in the world, considering that 7 million people visit the Eiffel Tower each year.

I looked down and the Arrogance of Space leered back. Wide, sweeping corners engineered in the 1950s to afford cars a smooth turn without having to slow down too much. I decided to slap a filter on it, in order to map how much space was allocated to the different users of the inter-

Shibuya Crossing in Tokyo, Japan.
The world's busiest pedestrian crossing.

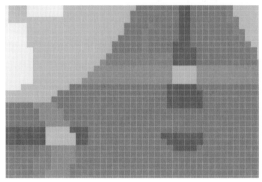
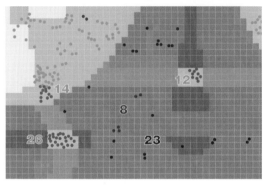
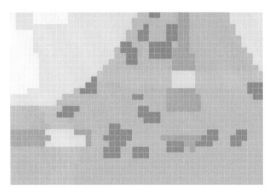

Top: *The Arrogance of Space in Paris. Mapping out how much space is allocated to each traffic user group. Such car-centric intersections can be modernized.*

Opposite: *Wide car lanes like these in Calgary can easily be narrowed to create space for bicycle infrastructure.*

section. I estimated a square meter (square yard) with each square. When color is added, that sea of red really stands out.

I decided to count the number of humans using the different space. At the time I took the photo, only 23 humans were passing through the space allocated for motor vehicles, whereas 38 pedestrians were clustered on traffic islands waiting for permission from the traffic-engineering models that dictate crossing times to be allowed to get to or from the damned tower. Some symbolic space had been reserved for cyclists and eight were visible, including those on sidewalks, although I also counted the passengers in the pedicabs. This is clearly a space dominated by last-century traffic engineering. It is museum for failed, car-centric solutions—sad and amusing all at once.

Luckily, best-practice is a thing. After fifteen minutes of sketching and a couple of hours in Photoshop, it's possible to show how to modernize this intersection and every one like it. Paris has a declared political goal that the city will the "World's Best City for Cycling" by 2020. Squeezing bikes into the city while ignoring the Arrogance of Space is not an effective way to reach such a lofty goal.

The Arrogance of Space is not unique to Paris. It is, regrettably, rather universal. Cape Town, São Paulo, Barcelona, Moscow.

I once stared down at a street in Calgary from a hotel balcony for a week, waiting for vehicles that actually filled out the whole lane. I never saw one. Car lanes, especially in North America, are wider than some European countries—an Arrogance of Space that also presents opportunities. Narrowing car lanes improves safety. Drivers have to concentrate—which is a rather good idea in cities. If the vehicles are not using the space, then let's reallocate. I took away the unused space from the car lanes and, presto! There is space for a 2.3-meter-wide cycle track off to the side

The Arrogance of Space exists even right here in Copenhagen. Our most infamous relic of last-century, car-centric planning roars canyon-

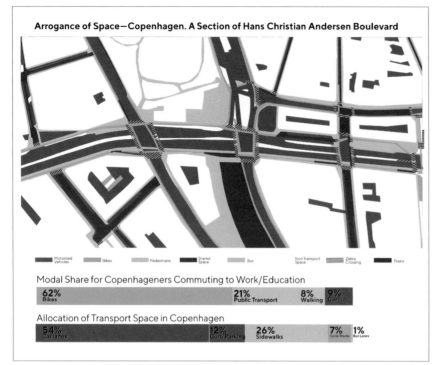

Arrogance of Space—Copenhagen. A Section of Hans Christian Andersen Boulevard

Motorised Vehicles · Bikes · Pedestrians · Shared Space · Bus · Non Transport Space · Zebra Crossing · Trains

Modal Share for Copenhageners Commuting to Work/Education

| 62% Bikes | 21% Public Transport | 8% Walking | 9% Car |

Allocation of Transport Space in Copenhagen

| 54% Car Lanes | 12% Curb Parking | 26% Sidewalks | 7% Cycle Tracks | 1% Bus Lanes |

Left: The Arrogance of Space is apparent even in Copenhagen, where 66 percent of the transport space is allocated to cars.

Bottom: The author's conceptualization of three buildings in the center of Hans Christian Andersens Boulevard in the center of Copenhagen.

Design: Mikael Colville Andersen / Kan Chen

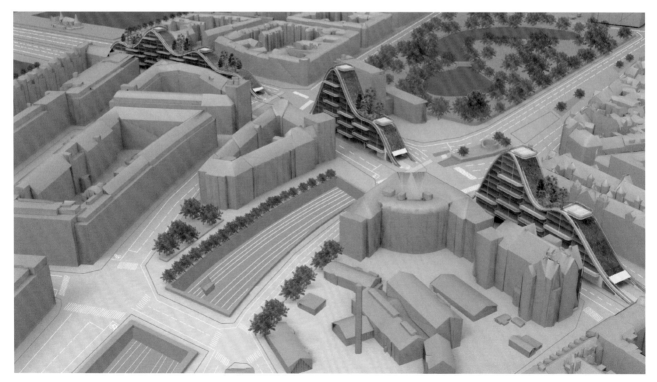

like through the heart of the city, creating a formidable divide that has been discussed for decades. Hans Christian Andersens Boulevard ain't no fairytale, sunshine. Denmark's busiest street carries 50–60,000 motor vehicles a day. Pollution levels continue to exceed the European Union's targets. For many years there has been talk of burying it, but politicians grumble about the high cost. A recent citizen movement has called for the long stretch leading to it—Åboulevarden—to be dug up and the original river that was buried years ago to be brought back to the surface, a project inspired by a number of other cities that have done it, like Aarhus and Seoul.

A whopping 64 percent of the transport space in Copenhagen is allocated to cars—both car lanes and curb parking. Even though, in 2016, 91 percent of Copenhageners didn't drive a car daily when heading to work or education in the city.

A whopping 64 percent of the transport space in Copenhagen is allocated to cars—both car lanes and curb parking. Even though, in 2016, 91 percent of Copenhageners didn't drive a car daily when heading to work or education in the city. So, if politicians can't figure out what to do with the street, allow me to offer a suggestion. We need affordable housing in the city, so I designed The Slopes: three iconic buildings providing 507 apartments of 50 square meters (538 square feet), three sections of green space below the structures, over 500 square meters (5,380 square feet) of public space on the green roofs, and some serious topography in the heart of the Danish capital. When your politicians fail to deliver, you have to do the work yourself.

Nature can play an important role in exposing the Arrogance of Space, as well. In the United States, it's called a "neckdown" when curbs are extended to provide pedestrians with a short, safer crossing distance. Clarence Eckerson Jr., from Streetfilms.org, thought up "snowy neckdown" and, in collaboration with Aaron Naparstek, Streetsblog founder and former editor-in-chief, the latter gave the world the word and hashtag "sneckdown." It describes how snowfall in a city reveals how much unused space there is on the streets. This is a fantastic whistleblower technique. The sneckdown is the Edward Snowden of urbanism. As ever, the hashtag is great to explore.

Dress for your destination, not your journey.

CHAPTER 9

MYTHBUSTING

The great enemy of the truth is very often not the lie, deliberate, contrived, and dishonest, but the myth, persistent, persuasive, and unrealistic.

John F. Kennedy

Anyone who knows me know that I am an idealist with a company and not a businessman with ideals. If I were the latter, I would have figured out how to monetize mythbusting. How to make €1 for every time I have to sigh, roll my eyes, and bust a tired, uninformed myth about urban cycling? While time-consuming and often frustrating, it still, however, appears to a necessary part of the narrative we're trying to cement in the public consciousness around the world. It's interesting how uniform the misconcep-

tions about cycling are, regardless of where in the world I hear them. It's equally interesting to sometimes hear them coming from people who cycle, not just people who don't.

People have short—or selective—memories, apparently. They look around their city and assume that it has always just been like that. Civic pride seems to play a role as well. People in winter cities are proud of their winters and look down their noses at cities that have a milder climate. The same applies to cities with hot weather. People in topographically challenged cities enjoy mocking cities with a flat landscape.

More often than not, the people uttering their misconceptions about cycling are merely projecting their own personal opinions onto the population at large—without any experience or data to back up their claims. It is invariably one of two angles: "I won't ride a bike here, so nobody will" or "I ride a bike here, I'm hard-core, and not everyone is as badass hard-core as I am."

We know that infrastructure is the key to increasing cycling levels. We know that, as individuals, we do not dictate what others will or won't do. If you make the bicycle the fastest way from A to B to C in a city, people will ride. San Francisco may never have 62 percent of the population on bikes—as in Copenhagen in 2016—but 20 percent is certainly a respectable and achievable target for any city. Here's a Top 11 list of myths that I can bust once and for all.

MYTH 1: PEOPLE WILL ONLY RIDE WHEN IT'S FLAT

Damn you, Netherlands. Your flat little postage-stamp-sized country is making mythbusting hard. "Oh, but the Netherlands is flat"—this has to be the excuse that I hear most often all around the world. (Sometimes it's accompanied by "and so is Denmark/Copenhagen.") Punctuated with dramatically crossed arms as though the discussion is sooo over.

But it's not. Sure, the Netherlands is a carpenter's dream. Do 26 percent of the population ride a bike each day because the terrain is flat? No. That helps, to be sure, but it's all about the infrastructure. Simply put: the bicycle is the fastest way from A to B. To work or school or that train station.

Copenhagen, too, is rather level. At least the Copenhagen that 95 percent of the tourists visit.

Cyclist in Tokyo

They don't cycle very far outside the city to the north, to the hills where the 2011 Cycling World Championships placed their finish line or the forests where mountain bikers do their thing.

Looking around the rest of the nation—which nobody we talk to ever does—you see topography that is considerably more Rubenesque. In fact, the hills and valleys are proudly lauded in the Danish national anthem. Some people google "highest point in Denmark" and use that to say, *"See?!"* As though a rolling landscape and steep streets are not possible if you don't have a Mont Blanc on your map. Indeed, if you ride around Denmark's second-largest city, Aarhus, you'll feel some thigh-burn as you head home

with groceries in your bike basket. And yet in 2015, 24 percent of all trips in the city were by bike—and that figure is expected to rise.

For decades, people rode bicycles in hilly cities. Back in an age when bicycles were machines that we would regard as incredibly heavy today. They rode in heavy dresses and thick fabrics, to boot. Modern bicycles have leveled the playing field, as well as the topography.

Looking at North America, two of the cities that are doing the most to reestablish the bicycle on the urban landscape are San Francisco and Vancouver. I rolled up and down the hills of San Francisco on a one-speed Biomega, together with friends on upright bikes. I was unimpressed. And

I'm just a normal schmuck in normal clothes, not some Captain Spandex dude. The citizens in San Francisco have done the wayfinding around the steep bits and called the route The Wiggle, now marked with official signage to guide bicycle users. Vancouver is also moving forward with infrastructure and urban planning for bikes, pedestrians, and public transport, and is ignoring their topography in doing so. Just getting on with it.

Another city doing the same is Oslo, Norway. Not only is the City planning on making the city center, within the Ring 1 road, free of private cars, they are also hell-bent on building bike lanes and removing car parking. I spent a great deal of time in the city in 2016, and while I never developed a fondness for their hills, I did learn to accept them. The wildly successful bike-share system in the city, Oslo Bysykkel, uses bikes with three gears. It's perfectly easy to get up the hills on those or even on my Bullitt cargo bike.

Let's cast a glance at Japan. The third-greatest cycling nation in the world with a 15 percent modal cycling share nationally. Tokyo, too, has 15 percent modal share, and I can tell you from experience that they have a rolling landscape. Like so many other cities where people used to cycle and are cycling again.

It's not about everyone cycling everywhere all the time. It's about going after the low-hanging fruit. When people say, "What about a city like Lisbon?,"

Opposite: Afternoon traffic in the snow on a February day on Søtorvet in Copenhagen.

Botttom: Cycling on a hot summer's day in Rio de Janeiro.

Top: Vintage photo from Rio de Janeiro's proud cycling past. Photographer: Unknown
Bottom: Cargo bike transport in Nanortalik, Greenland.
© Theis Mortensen

for example, you know that they aren't from there but visited on holiday. They remember the thigh-burn from walking up hills to Bairro Alto or Alfama to see the touristy stuff. The ripest fruit in the city is the 85 percent of the city that is under a 5-percent grade, much of it on commuter routes. That is where you start. The same applies to Bergen, Norway. Most of the city is in a valley. Just like you wouldn't leave your bike at home because it might rain three days from now, you shouldn't refrain from designing a city for bicycles just because parts of it have hills.

Hills are what gets talked about, but it's surprising how often the wind is left out of the equation. Not out of the equation in Denmark and the Netherlands, though, since we are constantly at the mercy of the blustery whims of the North Sea.

The Dutch pro cyclist Johnny Hoogerland has said what all the Danes and Dutch know to be true. He compared riding in the wind-swept Netherlands to riding in the Pyrenees. A stiff headwind can be the same as a mountain climb, basically.

Indeed, we did some calculations at Copenhagenize Design Company. The average wind speed in the winter is about 10 meters per second. That's 22 mph or 36 km/h. Cycling into that headwind corresponds to cycling up an

8-percent grade. Welcome to our life for several months a year here in Copenhagen. Furthermore, hills end, the wind doesn't. Believe me.

MYTH2: IT'S TOO HOT!

"Yes, Mikael, but people won't ride here, you see. It's too hot." Oh. Really? Get thee to a passport office. Travel to . . . oh, let's say . . . Seville. The city went from 0.2 percent of the population on bikes to 7 percent in just four years. Why? Did they pull a Truman Show and encapsulate the city in an air-conditioned dome? Nope. They built a network of infrastructure to enable people to cycle around. Go there in the summer and see citizens cycling around in 40-degree heat (104°F). City officials didn't mumble and groan about the heat or use it as an excuse not to invest in bicycle urbanism. They just did it. What about one of South America's best cycling cities, Rio de Janeiro? Or Barcelona? Or any number of hot, muggy places where the bicycle thrived before and is thriving once again.

An average windspeed in the winter is about 10 meters per second. That's 22 mph or 36 km/h. Cycling into that headwind corresponds to cycling up an 8 percent-grade.

Australia? "Too bloody hot, mate . . . " Not, apparently in Queensland, where archive photos reveal incredible scenes of bicycles parked outside a cinema in Cairns in the 1940s or bike parking at City Hall in Mackay. The proof is in the archives.

MYTH 3: BUT WE HAVE WINTER HERE!

Meteorological circumstances are very often married to civic pride. Back in 2008, when I posted some photos on Copenhagenize.com and CopenhagenCycleChic.com of Copenhageners cycling in the snow, men from primarily Montreal and Minneapolis were quick to comment on the fact that that wasn't winter. "We have winter." Adding links to Wikipedia about Denmark's mild climate. Mild compared to theirs, of course. Weather as a phallic symbol, apparently.

The winters of 2009/10 and 2010/11 in Denmark, however, were far more lively with regards to weather. Long, hard winters, the both of them. After I started posting photos of rush hours in snowstorms, it all went a bit quiet. The occasional peep about "real winter temperatures" was heard, but generally the photos hammered the point home. Check out the #VikingBiking hashtag. Winter cycling is a thing, and has been since the bicycle was invented.

The Winter Cycling Conference started in Oulu, Finland, a city of almost 200,000 people shiveringly close to the Arctic Circle, but where 14 percent of the population cycle all winter. Winnipeg, Minneapolis, Montreal, and Moscow have also been host cities. Montreal continues to debate whether they should leave their Bixi bike-share program on the streets year-round, but other cities like Chicago and New York just do it.

Yes, winter cycling is nothing new. It happened everywhere for decades. Nowadays, reducing the effect of winter is much easier. Copenhagen and other cities have a fleet of snow sweepers that are dedicated to the bicycle infrastructure. Salting preemptively and sweeping as soon as the snow falls.

Most cities divide up their streets into categories, and Copenhagen is no exception. There are A, B, and C streets based on maintenance in the winter. Above them, however, is the bicycle infrastructure network. If you compare a map of Copenhagen's on-street protected bike infrastructure and one showing the city infrastructure that gets cleared of snow first, you'd be looking at the same map. The City's goal that all main cycle tracks must be cleared of snow by 8:00 a.m. is a necessity. If a few hundred thousand people walk out of their homes and are faced with 20–30 cen-

timeters (8–12 inches) of snow, most will call into work and say they can't make it or head for a bus stop or train/metro station. There aren't many public-transport networks that can accommodate a couple hundred thousand new passengers from a Tuesday to a Wednesday. A great number of people will be late for work—or not show up at all, which is bad for the economy. Therefore, Herculean efforts are made to ensure black asphalt.

A city like Copenhagen has to do it in order to accommodate the sheer numbers of cyclists. But also to continue making cycling a competitive, reliable transport form—which is why emerging bicycle cities have to do it from the get-go. According to the City of Copenhagen, 75 percent

An elderly cyclist in Italy's best city for cycling, Ferrara.

of the city's cycling citizens continue all winter. It doesn't matter how cold it gets in a city, there are ways to tackle it in order to enable those who want to cycle, to cycle.

MYTH 4: WE NEVER USED TO CYCLE HERE

Ah, yes. That old chestnut. A veritable classic. I've heard this from regular citizens and colleagues alike, in cities like Singapore, Vancouver, Los Angeles, Oslo, you name it. From the annals of history, surprising things appear, like this quote from an 1897 newspaper article: "There is no part of the world where cycling is in greater favor than in Southern California, and nowhere on the American continent are conditions so favorable the year-round for wheeling."

In the following years, Los Angeles enjoyed a 20 percent modal share for bikes. Public transport, too, was exceptional.

Who Framed Roger Rabbit remains one of the greatest urbanist films ever to come out of Hollywood. Eddie Valiant bums a ride on the back of a streetcar and the kid sitting there doing the same says: "Hey, mister. Ain't you got a car?" To which Eddie Valiant replies: "Who needs a car in L.A.? We have the best public-transportation system in the world." We all know the narrative about what happened to L.A. later. As Judge Doom says to Eddie later in the film:

"You lack vision, but I see a place where people get on and off the freeway. On and off, off and on all day, all night. Soon, where Toon Town once stood will be a string of gas stations, inexpensive motels, restaurants that serve rapidly prepared food. Tire salons, automobile dealerships, and wonderful, wonderful billboards reaching as far as the eye can see. My God, it'll be beautiful."

Yep. We know how that story ended—but the beginning was spectacular. In Los Angeles and in places like Singapore. After hearing two young urban planners who hail from that city say, "Nobody ever cycled in Singapore," I put out the word and archive photos started trickling in from a reader of our blog. Citizens cycling in Singapore. In the 1940s and even into the 1980s. Right there in color, sepia, and black and white. As normal as you like.

Brazil is another example. While the larger cities scratch their heads about how to design for bicycles, there are a number of smaller cities that never stopped cycling.

The list of cities goes on. What I've discovered is that it's possible to turn a blind eye to the obvious even in the same country, never mind short-term urban memory loss. I was working in Brno, Czech Republic, and was told by a local that the country never really cycled. This surprised me. "What about Pardubice? I just came from there." The group I was speaking to looked confused. I was talking about a city they knew, but I had to explain to them that Pardubice is crisscrossed by bike lanes and boasts a decent double-digit modal share for bikes. It's only 156 kilometers (97 miles) from Brno to Pardubice, and both are in the same country. I've had the same experience in Italy, having to explain about the city of Ferrara, with around 30 percent modal share, and Bolzano up there in the "uncyclable" mountains, which is modernizing its traffic with bikes.

Brazil is another example. While the larger cities scratch their heads about how to design for bicycles, there are a number of smaller cities that never stopped cycling. Ubatuba and Lorena both have around 85,000 citizens, and 55 percent of them in each city ride a bike daily. Aracajú has a population of 640,000 and has 100 kilometers of cycle tracks and 40,000 daily cyclists. Then there are Rio Branco, Praia Grande, Zona Oeste in Rio de Janeiro, and Montes Claros. The latter has a modal share of 65 percent, from what I've heard. Rio de Janeiro, like every Brazilian city, had a proud bicycle history. Do you see the pattern? Blinders off, people. Look past the trees and see the forest.

MYTH 5: THE DANES AND DUTCH HAVE ALWAYS DONE IT. IT'S THEIR CULTURE.

I've always had an awkward relationship with the phrase *bicycle culture*. One of the first slogans I developed for Copenhagenize Design Company was "Building Better Bicycle Cultures." It sounded good. Rolled off the tongue. An anthropologist friend took issue with it, however. He said that cultures evolve—they aren't built or constructed. Fair point. The phrase suffers from the same problem at the word *cyclist*. It conjures up subcultural images as opposed to a mainstream appeal.

While I accept that a culture evolves, I am adamant that bicycle culture doesn't really exist in the context that many people think about when hearing it or saying it. It's just efficient transport on bicycles on a network of protected infrastructure. Sure, I use the phrase *vacuum-cleaner culture*—but I do so ironically.

There is nothing unique about the transport habits of the Danes and the Dutch when everyone pretty much everywhere has been doing it for a long time. Indeed, the phrase *bicycle culture* is far more popular in the rest of the world. We can translate it into Danish—*cykelkultur*—but mostly when referring to what the rest of the world calls it when they look at us. Nor do we refer to *pedes-trian culture* when describing how people walk up and down our network of pedestrian streets in the heart of Copenhagen. In fact, many people didn't think we were pedestrians until not that long ago.

On September 2, 1962, the backbone through the heart of the city center, Strøget, became a pedestrian street. A bold move in the heady days of blossoming car culture. The idea was nothing new. The author, Johannes V. Jensen, wrote an op-ed back in 1913 about traffic on the iconic street after the introduction of omnibuses as public transport: "I find the increasing traffic on Strøget extremely dangerous. It should have been banned ages ago. These omnibuses wouldn't be tolerated anywhere else in the world. In Seville, where there are similar narrow, winding streets, all traffic is banned. In China it's been like that for centuries. All vehicles, including bicycles, should be banned from Strøget. It's the only promenade we have in the city. It isn't pretty, it needs more trees, but the people have made their choice and it should be allowed to exist in peace."

Another factor is prosperity. There is little standing in the way of Danes getting a car if they want one.

As the City moved forward with the plans to pedestrianize the street, inspired by the research done by Jan Gehl, there were protests from . . . guess who . . . motorists. One rallying cry was allegedly, "We are not Italians!" Meaning that Danes didn't want to walk around the city when they had cars. Never mind the fact that they had been doing just that in the capital for the previous millennium. The project was completed despite the protests, and lo and behold, the Danes of Copenhagen discovered their legs.

A couple doubling on a bike in Tokyo.

The rest is history. A fine network of pedestrian streets crisscross the medieval city center, and most Danish towns and cities have at least one pedestrian-only stretch in their center. Call it *culture* if you must, I don't mind. But infrastructure influenced behavior—it's as simple as that.

MYTH 6: DANES RIDE BIKES BECAUSE CARS ARE SO EXPENSIVE AND THEY CAN'T AFFORD THEM.

When you peer at Denmark and Copenhagen from afar and see all the bikes and also learn that there is a 150 percent tax on cars, you'll be forgiven for thinking those two factors are intertwined. You would be wrong, though. The reality in today's Denmark is that even with the 150 percent tax—which is the maximum on new cars—buying a car is accessible to the average Dane. In addition, the price of a driving license is,

on average, US$2,000. And yet licenses are still acquired and car sales set records each year over the past four years in Denmark, although mostly in the provinces and not the cities.

I have a 15-year-old son whose gaze is firmly set on adulthood. He has vaguely mentioned getting a driving license at some point after he turns 18, but a car? It simply doesn't register on his radar. There are backpacking trips to take, apartments to rent, parties to go to. The State pays for you to attend university or any postsecondary education, so tick *that* expense off your list and add beer. It's generally the same for his friends in our neighborhood. If I look at my friends who are my age and have families, most of them bought their first car in their late thirties. Perhaps because they could, but also to get to their summer cottages in the countryside of Denmark or Sweden. Speaking for my circle of friends, we

Left: *Creative way to double on a bike.*

Right: *Copenhagener arriving home with the weekly shopping in a cargo bike. Now known as "quaxing."*

still ride our bikes to work during the week. Elsewhere in Denmark, outside of the large cities, a young man who turns 18 has both *driver's license* and *car* at the top of his list. If that kid can get a car at that age, the price is hardly prohibitive.

Another factor is prosperity. The tax has been rendered quite irrelevant, what with increasing Danish wages since the 1980s. It is cheaper to buy a car today than it was during the oil crises in the 1970s. The same goes for gas prices. There is little standing in the way of Danes getting a car if they want one.

The tax is comprised of these elements: sales and registration, ownership tax, insurance tax, and a fuel tax. A few years ago, the tax was up to 180 percent but was later reduced to 150 percent. When the tax was at 180 percent, the Danish state earned 24 billion kroner a year (US$4.1 billion) and that fell, as Danes became wealthier, to just 14 billion kroner (US$2.4 billion). This morning in 2017, quite literally, I awoke to the news that the current right-leaning minority government has further reduced the tax to 85 percent on certain mid-sized models, although they're keeping the 150 percent on more-expensive cars. We have been throwing money out the window for a couple of decades, but now we're effectively shoveling it onto a bonfire.

MYTH 7: WE DON'T HAVE SPACE FOR BIKES

You didn't have space for cars in your city, either, but boy oh boy, look at you now! It is a classic comment that with all the cars in this or that city, there is no room for bikes. If that is the baseline, then yes, it will be hard. But we shouldn't be trying to squeeze bikes into our cities and onto our streets. The goal is reallocating urban transport space to other transport forms and, in the process, reducing the number of motorized vehicles.

A street is that space between building façades. All of it. We can do anything we want with it. Widen the sidewalks, plant trees, put in cycle tracks, narrow the width of the car lanes, put in a tram or a bus lane—you name it. People who just look at a street and see an immovable structure are not helpful to the cause of improving city life. In the medieval city center in Copenhagen and in countless cities around Europe, they've figured it out. One-way streets for cars and contraflow for bikes. Or bicycle streets, on which cars are allowed but have to follow the tempo of the cyclists. The urban space is ours to do with as we please. If you don't see cycling as a solution, you are part of the problem.

MYTH 8: I HAVE TO BUILD INFRASTRUCTURE FOR THOSE FEW PEOPLE CYCLING NOW?!

This is something I've heard from many politicians I meet through my work. You kind of get their point, however misguided it may be. The vice mayor of Saint Petersburg said it a few years ago, attempting to eliminate all talk of bicycle infrastructure by declaring that on his twice-daily journey up and down Nevsky Avenue, he saw only a few cyclists. Then bicycle advocates went out and did a bike count and registered 600 cyclists—which, of course, surprised the politicians.

I love the statistic that 67 percent of motorists in Copenhagen want more bicycle infrastructure.

If, while surveying a river or a harbor, you don't see anyone swimming, does that mean you don't need a bridge? No, of course not. We must plan our cities for the people that could be cycling, were

it safe enough. It's not about the avid, hard-core cyclists who would ride anyway. It's less about the people who are cycling now. It's about the massive potential of those who are ready in any city.

There was little space in which to drive cars back in the 1910s and 1920s. Through intense lobbying, Big Auto made that space available and enabled generations to drive the cars they subsequently bought. All we need to do is the same for cycling. Make the space available and an impressive number of people will ride. Every city has at least 25 percent of the population who will take to the "wheel," as it once was called, if infrastructure and traffic-calming are implemented. Two million private bicycles have been sold in Paris since the city's bike-share system, Vélib', hit the streets in 2007. This is positive induced demand.

If you don't see anyone swimming, does that mean you don't need a bridge?

I love the statistic that 67 percent of motorists in Copenhagen want more bicycle infrastructure. Why? Because we've shown them and they get it. They can do the math visually. If a motorist is sitting at a red light with five cars in front of them and 100 cyclists at the red light on the cycle track next to them, they can see it. "If those five schmucks were on bikes, I'd be the first car at the red light . . . " It's rarely "me" with motorists, it's "them"—but they get it. In short, if you build it, they will come. Time and time again.

MYTH 9: WE HAVE SPRAWL!

Many North American cities are, indeed, sprawled far and wide, thanks to several decades of flawed planning (although figuring out that it was flawed took a while), but I often get people commenting on the fact that American cities are way too big to ride in, compared to European cities. Again, it's not about everyone riding a bicycle everywhere all the time. It's about working on the low-hanging fruit first. Fifty percent of Americans live within five miles of their workplaces, so there's a place to start. It's important to connect public transport with bicycles, whether it is combining bikes and trains or providing safe infrastructure to and from stations outside of city centers.

In Copenhagen, roughly 50 percent of the bicycle infrastructure had been removed in the two decades of redesigning the streets for cars.

Copenhagen has sprawl. The third-largest urban sprawl in Europe, actually. People can commute for a hour and a half or more by car to get to the city, as in many other places. Intermodality is the key. Riding your bicycle to the local train station and combining travel modes helps increase bicycle share.

The main point here is that few people are going to ride long distances. More than a century of experience would dictate this. Sure, as quoted previously, many "found the bicycle a convenient form of transport for distances up to, say, ten miles." We know from years of data in Denmark and the Netherlands that the vast majority cycle up to seven kilometers (four miles). In fact, only 7 percent of the few hundred thousand cyclists in Copenhagen each day ride farther than that. It's related to anthropology. Humans prefer 30 minutes as the maximum time they want to transport themselves under their own power. Many medieval cities, Copenhagen included, take about 20–30 minutes to cross on foot.

Let's design our cities such that we'll get results first and then start focusing on expanding upon the success. "We have sprawl!" is not a useful argument. It's an uninformed excuse.

MYTH 10: YOU CAN'T DO THAT ON A BIKE

In regions where the only cyclists left on the streets are dressed up in lycra uniforms, it's fair enough if others assume that a bicycle's load capacity is limited to a water bottle, on-board computer, and an energy bar. But short-term memory loss applies here, too.

I don't even know where to start with this one. Since 2006, I have taken over 20,000 photos of urban cycling in close to 70 cities around the world. The quicker question would be "What can't you do on a bike?"

A few years ago, I was hanging out with some friends and discussing my ongoing photo series. For fun, they started challenging me. "I bet you don't have a photo of someone cycling with a bass." I took out my phone and found it. "I bet you don't have a photo of someone playing an instrument on a bike." Yep. "Someone who's missing limbs?" Yep. "A mom or dad with the kid on their shoulders?" Yep. On we went. I failed to produce a photo of a cat on a bike, but pulled up a hundred-odd photos of dogs of all sizes. As I'll discuss in the cyclelogistics chapter, the ceiling for what can be moved by bike is high.

The Internet is as fantastic as it is merciless. Back in January 2015, an unsuspecting and rather hapless politician in Auckland, New Zealand, named Dick Quax was involved in a lively Twitter discussion in which a citizen was suggesting that a local shopping mall should have better transportation options. Dick Quax responded with a few tweets claiming that: "no one in the entire Western world uses the train for their shopping trips." / "the very idea that people lug home their weekly supermarket shopping on the train is fanciful."/ "…I ride my bike to get my weekly shopping—yeah right." The rest is history.

Welcome to involuntary immortality, Mr. Quax. The Internet responded to your functional fixedness as only the Internet can. Photos started appearing on Twitter and the hashtag soon followed: #quaxing. While the initial discussion was about public transport, it quickly morphed into shopping and transporting goods on foot and by bicycle as well. I know some people who do their weekly shopping by bike, but most—like me—visit the supermarket almost daily. Numerous studies have shown that cyclists spend more on average than motorists do. Anyway, a New Zealand Twitter user, NonMotorist, made *quaxing* official with this definition:

quax [v.] — to shop, in the Western world, by means of walking, cycling, or public transit.
quaxer [n.] — one who quaxes.
quaxable [adj.] — something with which one may quax.

Gotta love it. It was the cycling citizens around the world who really latched onto this and gave it legs. Go forth and explore the hashtag. Remember, however, that the fine art of transporting all manner of things on bikes is as old as the bicycle itself.

Part of the infrastructure network that Ljubljana, Slovenia, copy/pasted from Copenhagen in the early 1970s.

MYTH 11: IT TOOK COPENHAGEN AND AMSTERDAM OVER 40 YEARS. IT'LL TAKE US THAT LONG, TOO.

Citizens working for better cities don't often utter this myth. They want change to come quickly. This line is usually reserved for politicians who are afraid of commitment, don't understand the potential, or really just don't care.

Has it taken 40-odd years? Yes. Why? Simply because there was no hurry. What started in the 1970s with the oil crises and accelerated through the 1980s and 1990s in Denmark, the Netherlands, and scattered individual cities was a steady, pragmatic process. The rest of the world didn't notice. The Danes and the Dutch didn't notice their indifference. They just soldiered on. Designing, building, measuring, testing, fixing. There wasn't any real hurry, because while they were on the right track, they didn't really know how far they were headed. In Copenhagen, roughly half of the bicycle infrastructure had been removed in the two decades of redesigning the streets for cars. The task at hand was to slowly rebuild it and adapt to a new car-centric reality. There were few Danes or Dutch being invited to conferences to talk about their work. There were no publishers emailing people like me to write books about bicycle urbanism. The work was done quietly in municipal offices, without much fanfare or external attention.

As user rates on the expanding infrastructure started to rise, the induced demand led to a further expansion of the network and the extent of infrastructure. Nowadays, bold political goals are laid out in our performance-based culture in order to keep people interested and get politicians elected or reelected.

Any other city on the planet could replicate the success of Copenhagen or Amsterdam in 40 years, absolutely. What we're seeing, however, is cities that are moving much faster now that the blueprints for success are readily available to copy and paste. To find one of the earliest examples of copy/pasted, best-practice infrastructure, we have to look to Ljubljana, the capital of Slovenia.

When I was working in the city in 2011, I was riding with the city's passionate and tireless bicycle officer at the time, Janez Bertoncelj. We were on a site visit to a new intersection to review some bicycle infrastructure issues. Heading out of the city center, I looked down and realized that we were cycling on some excellent infrastructure and commented on it. Bertoncelj shrugged and explained that it dated from the 1960s or 1970s.

It turns out that about 50 years ago, Ljubljana had started to look at increasing bicycle traffic while keeping cyclists safe. The renowned Slovenian architect Edvard Ravnikar played a role in this cycle-track development. Ravnikar led a new generation of Slovenian architects and was inspired by the Scandinavian architectural style. He wrote an article or two about the benefits of bicycle infrastructure, which was evidently instrumental in what happened next. A team of planners and engineers headed to Copenhagen.

There is no chicken or egg. There is only infrastructure.

Despite plummeting cycling rates in the Danish capital, there were still stretches of cycle track to be found. This was at the peak of the Cold War, and though the curtain around Yugoslavia was made of beads rather than iron, it is still impressive that such a study trip was made during that era.

After studying Copenhagen's bicycle infrastructure, the team returned to Ljubljana and got to work implementing 40 kilometers (25 miles) of Copenhagen-quality cycle tracks. Cycling levels rose from 2 percent to 10 percent in a year. Read that sentence again. That's a 400 percent increase in a year. In the country's third-largest city, Celje, there are still protected cycle tracks dating from the same era—also directly inspired by Copenhagen via Ljubljana. Cycling levels in the capital remained right there for the next four decades because no more infrastructure was planned or built. In recent years, Ljubljana has been at it again, looking at the bicycle as a solution for transport. They now have 73 kilometers (45 miles) of cycle tracks and 133 kilometers (83 miles) of bike lanes to serve their 280,000 citizens.

There were very few bicycles left in cities like Dublin, Paris, Barcelona, Seville, Bordeaux, Buenos Aires, and Minneapolis just a decade ago. Now these cities, and others, are accelerating towards a future in which the bicycle is a normal and respected transport form once again. As Ljubljana learned, there is no chicken or egg. There is only infrastructure.

Cyclist in Ljubljana, Slovenia.

定期利用

Secure bicycle parking facility under Minami-Ikebukuro Park and near Ikebukuro Station in Tokyo.

CHAPTER 10

ARCHITECTURE

The details are not the details.
They make the design.

Charles Eames

It is of vital importance to identify our shared strengths and weaknesses on our bicycle urbanism journey, but also to pay heed to the various allies who are often, in fact, our antagonists. Traffic engineering is one, but so is architecture. To many people, this may seem odd. Isn't architecture much the same as urban planning? Unfortunately, the divide is greater than it should be. The obsession with pretty buildings—inherent in architecture—all too often doesn't extend to an understanding of the space around a building.

There I was, in Trondheim. Norway's leading bicycle city for many years, despite climate and topography. Around 8 percent modal share. I was keynoting at a conference at the Clarion Hotel & Congress Trondheim. Built in 2012 with Space Group as the architects. I like the building. Beautifully designed, in my opinion. I spent a lot of time regarding the structure and the many details, both inside and out. And then I saw it. Outside the main entrance was a small bike rack with four spots. It wasn't pretty, but it was being used. Imagine designing a spectacular building and then having someone slap a cheap bike rack next to the front entrance. The architect might be rather annoyed, although I think that they should instead kick themselves for forgetting bicycle parking at the entrance. It should have been designed into the big picture from the beginning. Instead, the architects now have at the main entrance a symbol for how they neglected transport facilities in their design.

Ivy (*Hedera*) has a great name in Danish—*arkitektens trøst*, or "the architect's consolation." Good Danish irony to describe how ivy can cover up bad architecture. In the case of

Bike racks placed far from the popular destinations on Regnbuepladsen, Copenhagen.
© Steven Achiam/GHB Landscape Architects

this Trondheim hotel, the bike rack is the consolation and, unlike ivy, it also serves a practical purpose. It was placed there for a reason: people were parking their bikes there. You can see in the photo that more racks would be a good idea. I wandered around the building a bit, looking to see if the architects reluctantly threw in some bike parking somewhere else, but I couldn't find any. All too often, architects seem so enamored with their big shiny thing that they forget the people who will be coming to and from the building. If this were Phoenix or some other city where the bicycle is still struggling to establish roots, fine. But this is a city with an 8 percent modal share for cycling, which only makes it more embarrassing.

Hey, Danish projects can stumble, too, like the Inner Harbor Bridge. But also in more subtle ways that you don't notice right away. In the redesign of Vartov Square (now renamed Regnbuepladsen, or Rainbow Square) next to City Hall in Copenhagen, a great public space was created as a part of total redesign of the entire Vester Voldgade street. The bike racks, however, were placed next to the cycle track and on the opposite side of the square from the destinations, including a popular café. I ride past this spot every weekday, and while some people do use the racks, many others just park their bikes with a kickstand closer to the buildings. Closer to where they actually want to be.

The architects seem to have thought that the obvious spot to park is next to the cycle track, but cyclists prefer to park closer to their destinations and always have. A building without bike parking designed into it from the beginning is unfinished architecture.

We've seen some classic magpie architecture from Norman Foster with his SkyCycle lark. We could hope it was a one-off, but alas, it seems to be a thing. Architectural competitions are great. A flurry of designs emerge from Photoshopland that allow you to gauge the current mood, trends, and ideas, but we can also see how so many architects are more interested in the structure than the function.

It's a modern lifeline across a river in a world city, not a coffee cup.

One example was an open competition for a new bicycle and pedestrian bridge in London, across the Thames from Nine Elms to Pimlico, called the NEP Bridge competition. The competition brief stipulated that: " . . . it must be inspiring, elegant, and functional in its design and perfect in its execution," and it must also "provide a safe and attractive link for pedestrians and cyclists crossing the river, encouraging movement between the two banks."

Looking through the many shortlisted designs through a bicycle urbanism filter was a bit depressing. Let's just say that squiggletecture seems to be a new movement in architecture. Straight, logical lines to provide an easy trajectory for cyclists were thrown out the window on most of the renderings. Ramps seem to be popular.

What is a bridge? Isn't it just a vital mobility link from one side of a body of water to another? Isn't that really the baseline for every decent bridge in history? Look at a map of Paris or any other city with bridges. They are straight. From one shore to the other. Providing no-nonsense A-to-B access for the people using it.

Most of the designs for the NEP Bridge look like they were designed by people who don't ride a bicycle in a city, let alone people who walk often. Most are designs for meandering tourists licking ice cream on a Sunday afternoon. People with nowhere to go and nowhere to be. They're not designs for a city in constant motion and for citizens moving purposefully about. And consider the ramps . . . the ramps. Round and round we go, slowly descending to the river bank like a flower petal on a summer breeze. Perhaps ramps are a subliminal product of decades of car-centric planning. Is there a little voice embedded in the minds of designers and architects that says, "Hey . . . if you have to get up or down from an elevation, use a winding ramp. After all, that's what they do in parking garages and on motorways." Adobe Illustrator's improved Draw a Curve function was apparently a big hit. Okay, bling your badass bridge all you want, just don't force people to alter their urban trajectory because you learned a new trick in Illustrator.

Many designs in the competition just curve for no particular reason, with no regard for getting people where they want to go. Instead, there seems to be a distinct focus on increasing travel times by creating a mobility obstacle course.

A number of designs just discarded the idea of ramps altogether and rolled their dice on... stairs. A big, fancy, modern bridge across the river of a major world city, and you have to navigate stairs to get there. Although some designs featured elevators to further slow you down, and one chucked in escalators for bikes.

If you want to create a bicycle and pedestrian bridge in the first quarter of this new century, can we agree that stairs and elevators should not be your point of departure?

Architectural competitions can be exciting. The ones that combine architecture with urban space and/or transport, however, reveal a disconnect between architecture and the mobility needs of the citizens. The competition brief,

above, should have been reworded: " . . . it must be functional in its design, perfect in its execution, and also inspiring and elegant." It's a modern lifeline across a river in a world city, not a coffee cup.

Where many architects lack any real understanding of urban mobility and the role of the bicycle in our cities, developers seem to be lagging even farther behind. Fair enough, in many cities there is outdated legislation that forces developers to provide a certain number of parking spots to accompany new buildings. Also, to be fair, a number of developers I have spoken to would rather cut the number of parking spots and instead create extra units or retail space.

Change is slow in coming, but here is one bright star in the developer's night. In Malmö, Sweden, just across The Sound (Øresund) from Copenhagen, Hauschild + Siegel Architects designed the OhBoy Bicycle House. It is an apartment building with 55 units as well as a hotel with 32 rooms. The building has exactly one car parking spot—the disabled parking spot required by Swedish law.

The entire building is designed for cycling residents. The doors and the elevators are wider than normal in order to accommodate cargo bikes. Residents can, in principle, roll their bikes into the building, up the elevator, and right into their apartments. Even right up to the fridge so they can transfer their groceries from the bike.

So brilliant—but also so incredibly simple. Hauschild + Siegel and the City of Malmö are ahead of the curve, but we will see more developments like this appearing in cities around the world. Designing for bicycles *and* for urban living.

Top: A much-needed bike rack placed outside the front entrance of the Clarion Hotel & Congress Trondheim.
Bottom: The OhBoy Bicycle House development in Malmö, Sweden. Car-free living in a modern city.
© Hauschild + Siegel Architects

CHAPTER 11

DESIRE LINES AND UNDERSTANDING BEHAVIOR

You can observe a lot by watching.

Yogi Berra

Yep. You've heard it before. You might even have said it or at least thought it. *Those damned cyclists.* As bicycles return to our cities, many urban dwellers are trying to figure out cyclists, those urban autists. By and large, the primary focus is on behavior, but with an overwhelmingly negative focus that clouds all the positive aspects of having a cycling population in a city. We are conservative herd animals, governed by laws and moral codes. It is easy to look at a low-income neighborhood with a high crime rate and list possible rea-

sons for people breaking laws. Lack of opportunity, few jobs, a faulty education system, policymakers who fail to work on improving the social fabric, a system that neglects the poor, and so on.

Run a red light on a bicycle and there will be no attempt to understand the act. It is labeled as wrong, and that's the end of it. Obey the rules, you scofflaws! This is counterproductive. We should instead be questioning whether or not the car-centric traffic rules actually make sense for cyclists, and studying their behavior in order

Cyclist on a desire line trajectory across an intersection in Copenhagen.

to understand *why* they deviate from the rules. At the moment, so many cities are struggling to figure out where cyclists should be. They're often allowed to share sidewalks and use the roadway. They are not afforded their own system or their own space in which to move. They are just shoved rudely into an existing strict system, and this only serves to antagonize everyone, including cyclists. Surprisingly, given the fact that the bicycle has been a part of our urban lives for 130-odd years, I haven't had any success in finding useful examples of behavioral studies of cyclists. It appears that, for decades, the bicycle was so normalized that we didn't bother looking at it, and then, after it largely disappeared from our cities, we couldn't even see it anymore.

Even in Copenhagen we can hear the same comments about cyclist behavior as everywhere else. There is a great deal of vague and often inaccurate perception of cyclist behavior, but there is a huge black hole in the studies of it and also data collection. Personal perception of anything is fine for the individual doing the perceiving but quite useless when you're trying to understand, map, and address a given problem.

This lack of knowledge led me, together with my team, to pioneer what I call the Desire Line Analysis Tool. I decided it was time to begin analyzing and, hopefully, understanding cyclist behavior. If no one could give me data about it, I'd have to start gathering the data myself.

As with many aspects of bicycle urbanism, this lack of knowledge compels us to look elsewhere for inspiration. The American sociologist Howard S. Becker was instrumental in changing sociologists' ideas about deviant behavior, starting with his book *Outsiders* in 1963. Deviance theory, in the Beckerian analysis, has to look at what

causes an individual or a group to be considered an insider or an outsider.

The bulk of Copenhagenize Design Company's projects are urban planning, transport planning, and urban design. I find it much more helpful to place sociology and anthropology at the top of the pyramid in order to understand the citizens and their behavioral choices first, before planning for them.

Personal perception of anything is fine for the individual doing the perceiving but quite useless when you're trying to understand, map, and address a given problem.

In 2012, I stuck a camera out the window on a Wednesday in April and filmed a Copenhagen intersection for twelve hours in order to record the choreography of an urban intersection. I chose the intersection outside my apartment on the corner of Godthåbsvej and Nordre Fasanvej because it was easy but also because this intersection is really a transport space. Nordre Fasanvej is a crosstown street, and Godthåbsvej leads people to and from the city center. It is a densely populated neighborhood, but at this intersection there are few popular destinations. People move through it in all directions. The design is the same as most other intersections in the world—car-centric—but there are cycle tracks leading to and from it. After filming, I handed the footage to an anthropologist, Agnete Suhr, and tasked her with studying how the cyclists and other users were using the space. We would map, down to the centimeter, the exact desire line of every single cyclist passing through the intersection, register how many cyclists broke a Danish traffic law, and study the interaction of cyclists and other traffic users. Direct human observation, nothing less.

I am convinced that *desire line* is one of the

Photo from the author's hotel room of The Common, in Halifax, Canada's oldest urban park, with green lines showing the existing pathways and red lines showing the desire lines through the fresh snow.

Left: *A cyclist following a desire line up to a highway in São Paulo, Brazil.*
Right: *Cyclists have carved a desire line in Dublin next to a pathway.*

most beautiful expressions in urban planning. Also referred to as "desire path," it describes how citizens—or wandering animals—will choose the most direct route, regardless of efforts to control their movements with barriers. The winding streets of old European cities may seem illogical compared to planned grid cities, for example, but many were originally formed by farmers shepherding livestock, or they were old rural pathways and buildings were erected around them later.

Desire lines butt heads with the immovable structure of traffic engineering, and attempts to control these urban desires are visible in cities everywhere. Bollards, fences, and railings have been erected in the hope that pedestrians and cyclists can be forced to follow predetermined routes—most of which avoid messing with the flow of car traffic. As ever, humans react to

design and will find ways around such barriers.

From a hotel room in Halifax, Canada, a few years back, I looked out at Canada's oldest urban park. Halifax Common dates from 1763 and while a large section of the original space has been developed, it is still the city's main park. Snow fell during the night. The next morning, I looked up a map of the existing pathways, but then I saw two straight trails through the snow forming elsewhere as citizens walked and even cycled in the morning commuter rush from the neighborhoods to the city center. There was also a transit strike in the city that day, adding to the footfall through the park. Two desire lines, straight as arrows carved through the snow. It snowed again the next night and there I was, like a puppy dog in the window, watching the desire lines form in exactly the same places. A modern city would take note and plan accordingly based on these lines. Another example is in the Mile End neighborhood of Montreal. There has been a railway here since 1876, part of the transcontinental railway that united Canada. Nowadays, there are densely populated neighborhoods on both sides of the tracks. The Canadian Pacific Railway has been reluctant to hear the calls from the citizens and the Borough of Le Plateau for level crossings. They are content with people having to make massive detours to get across the divide. There are a number of obvious locations for desire lines, and the citizens continue to insist on getting access. Holes are regularly cut in the fences on both sides. Canadian Pacific plays cat-and-mouse, fixing the holes when they discover them, sometimes on the same day. They patrol the tracks and hand out fines when they catch "trespassers." The citizens, meanwhile, even have a Facebook group to keep each other informed about new holes, and they show no signs of stopping creating access to their desire lines.

The citizens of our cities send us a constant flow of messages about how they want to use the urban space, and it is our job to watch, listen, and redesign, based on their movements. It is easy to brush off desire lines as a defiance of authority, but this is more important than that. This is urban democracy in motion.

Back at the intersection outside my apartment, in the course of 12 hours we recorded 16,631 cyclists passing through the space in every direction. Each trajectory was dutifully recorded and was allocated a letter. Gradually, patterns began to emerge. The first task was counting and gathering basic data about the number of users in the intersection. Then we started to map out behavior.

One of the first numbers I wanted was how many people broke a traffic law. We realized early on that it wasn't as clear-cut as we had expected, but an amazing 93 percent of the cyclists did everything by the book. We categorized them as Conformists. I had asked some colleagues, including the traffic and environment mayor at the time, Morten Kabell, who worked hard to improve conditions for cycling, to guess how many people deviated from the traffic laws. Most people guessed 30–50 percent. Hearing that the actual number was only 7 percent came as a shock to everyone. Personal perception was trumped by data. When we looked closely at the 7 percent, we saw that we could divide them further into two groups.

It is easy to brush off desire lines as a defiance of authority, but this is more important than that. This is urban democracy in motion.

Sure, a purist might say you can't "bend" a law. A law is a law is a law. But if our point of departure is that car-centric laws are not conducive to other transport forms, then we need to think differently. As we stared at the cycling citizens, we studied how they were breaking the rules. It wasn't black and white. We created a new category we called Momentumists. True, they were breaking a traffic law by riding through a pedestrian crossing or turning right on red, but the way they did so was slow and considerate toward other traffic users. The nature of the machine is that you don't want to stop rolling and you will do what you can to keep up your momentum. The final group we called Recklists. They smashed through the rulebook, with little regard for anyone else. Leaving the cycle track to turn left like a car or blowing through a red light. They made up just 1 percent of the 16,631 cyclists, and most of them were bike messengers—who are hardly representative of regular citizens anywhere in the world.

Since 2012, Copenhagenize Design Company has directly observed 106,000 cyclists in numerous intersections.

We observed just a little bit more closely, and wonderful, fascinating behavioral details emerged in the Momentumist camp. A pattern became clear, and we noticed their body language as they tried to maintain their momentum by, for example, snaking through the pedestrian crossings in a left turn.

We don't need to be anthropologists to assume that if people do something "illegal" or socially unacceptable, they as humans might physically shrink themselves or make themselves less noticeable to the rest of the "herd." When we are embarrassed, we shrink or cover our faces or employ other body-linguistic techniques to draw attention away. The opposite proved to be true in this particular intersection. A guy rolled through the pedestrian crossing. He was standing up out

of his saddle and rolling very slowly. He increased his body size to make himself more visible to others. Many people doing this kind of thing, when we zoomed in closer, had a subtle smile and a goofy, apologetic look on their face and were glancing around, but not at anyone in particular. This whole set of behaviors would indicate that they were being very considerate of other traffic users. As soon as they hit a "legal zone" again, they would resume their habitual posture and head off to their destination. This is something we've seen in all the desire-line analyses we've done since this inaugural study, and it is fascinating.

There are a number of variations on the theme. Cyclists sometimes rise up from their saddle, but they also sometimes turn their bike into a kick scooter, swinging a leg off and propelling themselves with their foot. "I'm not really a cyclist, anymore, see?" Until they hit the cycle track on the other side and then start cycling again. But they keep their momentum going, which is the primary goal.

Assuming that cyclists have a desire to break the law is a weak postulate that lacks a basic understanding of human nature. Homo sapiens are a conservative flock. We don't move around a city looking for opportunities to break the law. We just want to live a good life, free of hardship. Get a good job, fall in love, stay healthy. But we will react to bad design—or to no design at all.

Another detail that emerged involved "first movers"—those who influenced the behavior of others. Not surprisingly, the stop line for bikes on the cycle track is designed for cyclists to stop. Once in a while, a cyclist will slowly roll past it in order to gain some psychological real estate on their A-to-B journey. If the first cyclist at the red light stopped at the line, the rest who rolled

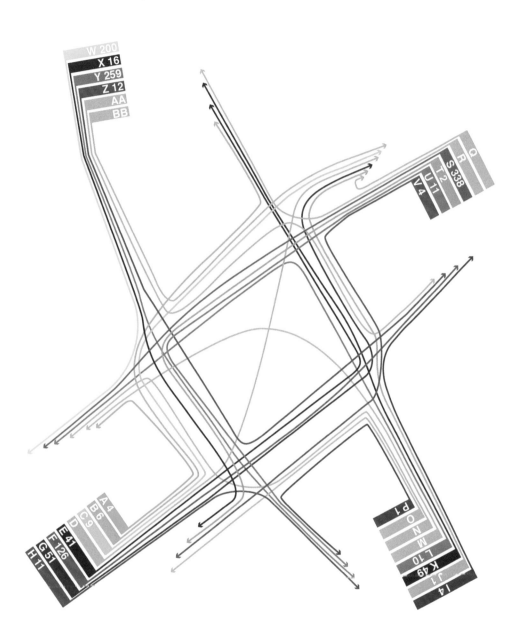

Example of Copenhagenize Design Company's work in
mapping the desire lines through an intersection.

Example of a cyclist changing his physical form to make himself more visible to other traffic users on the street during a marathon event.

up afterwards would wait behind. If that first cyclist rolled past the line to wait closer to the corner, the following cyclists would do the same. The first mover influenced the behavior of the people behind him or her.

This direct-observation approach is so interesting, useful, and rewarding. In most surveys, people get called up and are asked some questions. A useful technique, albeit flawed. In a survey about whether you use a seatbelt when driving, for example, an overwhelming majority will answer yes. Because that is the right answer and the one society would expect from us. This is a *declared preference*. Despite the majority declaring

that they wear seatbelts, though, there are still large numbers who get ticketed for not wearing one, revealing that they perhaps were liberal with the truth when answering the survey question. By just letting people get on with their lives and observing them doing so, we are working exclusively with *revealed preferences*. When the only information we had about cyclist behavior was mainly a long line of non-cyclists' personal perceptions, being able to inject some serious data and observations into the conversation became incredibly important.

Since 2012, Copenhagenize Design Company has directly observed 106,000 cyclists in numerous intersections. Eighty thousand of these were in Copenhagen, but we have also done analyses in Paris, Barcelona, Amsterdam, and Montreal in order to see how the cycling homo sapiens react to different infrastructure typologies.

Among those 80,000 Copenhageners, only 5 percent of the observed cyclists violated the traffic laws. There were more at some locations due to urban planning flaws, and by identifying this we can suggest improvements to the infrastructure. At Søtorvet, the intersection leading to Nørrebrogade—the busiest bicycle street in the world—the corners are landscaped with wide swaths of sidewalk. There are more Momentumists at this location than at the other intersections we have observed. Cyclists heading home from the city see a direct A-to-B route before them, one that is sparsely used by pedestrians. Instead of proceeding to the corner to wait for the light in order to turn right, many cut across the sidewalk.

The advantages are clear. You maintain your momentum, and while cutting across the space you have a clear view of the oncoming cyclists and can adapt your speed in order to merge. Whereas we notice a distinct change in body language when an individual enters an "illegal zone," it is different here. Cyclists don't alter their posture apologetically. Cutting across the sidewalk at this location is considered to be normal and acceptable mobility behavior. A redesign of the bicycle infrastructure at this location would be wise. It would legitimize the behavior of many of our citizens as they head home in the afternoon.

We studied ten intersections in the morning rush hour for the City of Amsterdam, working together with the University of Amsterdam. Congestion on the bicycle infrastructure was a problem, as the crowded space caused cyclists to avoid it and to try to maintain their momentum, bending or breaking traffic laws in the process. The City has now redesigned some of the intersections, and it will be interesting to go back and see how things have improved. After the first analysis, we recorded 15 percent of the cyclists as Momentumists or Recklists. More than in Copenhagen but still shockingly low compared with the perception of cyclist behavior when we asked Amsterdammers to guess what the number would be. Data changes the conversation.

It would appear that, as herd animals, cyclists in the morning rush are less likely to break out of the herd and do things considered socially unacceptable.

The process of direct observation of all these cyclists begins with getting the raw numbers recorded, and then we start observing behavior. During the first analysis in 2012, one of my staff, Pedro Madruga, an environmental engineer, decided to dig a bit deeper in order to see if we could mine even more data. Among other things, he divided the cyclists across a timeline, and one thing in particular surprised us. We could see what time of day the majority of the Momentumists and Recklists were deviating from the traffic laws. Once Pedro had the numbers ready, all of us at the office guessed what time of day the

The subtle, poetic elegance of casual signalling in Copenhagen.

majority would bend or break a traffic law. We were all convinced that it was during the morning rush hour, which in Copenhagen is high-volume and intense, as well as being compressed into a narrow time frame between 7:45 and 9:00 a.m.

Most Copenhageners seem to arrive at work at 8:00, 8:30, or 9:00 a.m., with the peak coming at 9:00 a.m. We all assumed that the morning would be when people would take liberties with the laws, due to the sheer volume in the allocated cycling space on the busy cycle tracks. We were wrong. Most of the deviant behavior occurs in the afternoon rush hour, which spreads out over a longer period of time than it does in the morning.

It would appear that, as herd animals, cyclists in the morning rush are less likely to break out of the herd and do things considered socially unacceptable. We're elbow to elbow with each other, so any deviant behavior is more likely to be noticed, and therefore we stick to the rulebook. In the afternoon period, though, the herd spreads out a little more thinly. In the morning there are only two common destinations—work or school—whereas in the afternoon there are many. People head home early to pick up kids, or they work later. There are supermarket visits, sports and recreation activities, social calls. The point is that cyclists cycle back from the city with more space around them and fewer "eyes on the street," giving them the feeling that nobody will notice if they are more flexible with the rulebook. You don't pick your nose on a crowded, standing-room-only train. You wait until you have a bit more space around you. With all that said, the deviant acts were minor and rather undramatic.

Copenhageners are not environmental warriors with a superior conscience who cycle, recycle, and eat organic food as they peer down at you from their moral pedestal.

By and large, after staring at 106,000 cyclists in five cities, we have determined that the vast majority have the same wish as everyone else: to just move about the city by the book. A small percentage will gently massage the rules in order to keep their momentum. Only a fraction of these will deviate in ways that most would consider to be unacceptable. Cyclists want to conform, but it is up to us to design infrastructure that allows them to do so. We have the best-behaved cyclists in the world in Copenhagen because of the intuitive, well-designed, and uniform bicycle infrastructure network that prioritizes them and appreciates them.

With that said, I have a number of spots on my daily commute where I become a deviant myself—and I'm fine with that. I will slow to a crawl on the cycle track at two T-intersections on my route, stopping only if pedestrians are crossing, but otherwise I roll through the light. The Copenhagen police refuse to allow T-intersections to become yield zones instead of being regulated by traffic lights, so I react to their lack of professional knowledge of urban planning and their stick-in-the-mud attitude by ignoring them. I'll turn right on red in a couple of locations—again slowing to a crawl while doing so—because I want to free up space for the cyclists heading straight by removing myself from the equation, and also because I want to maintain my momentum.

There is no longer any doubt that infrastructure is the only way to grow cycling levels in a city. If that infrastructure is designed well and prioritizes cycling, then so much the better. I often compare this to garbage. Denmark fares well on global lists for recycling garbage and I, like many citizens in the cities especially, am informed about the importance of recycling as much as possible. I'm also a busy man and the father of two kids. I would not recycle as much as I do if it were difficult. My city has provided me and my neighbors with the infrastructure that makes it rather effortless to recycle. In our apartment we have small containers for metal, hard plastic, batteries, cardboard, paper, and glass. Out in our back courtyard, large corresponding containers are in place near the bike sheds. No laborious detours, just an easy and efficient A-to-B that works well in my daily life, where time is of the essence.

Another example is the Danish bottle-deposit system, which was set up in 1942. Many countries have a deposit system, but I find this one to be quite exceptional. It provides citizens with an easy and highly profitable system for recycling. Similarly, Danes buy more organic food per capita than the citizens of any other nation. The reason is simply that the food-production industry recognized early on that organic food would grow exponentially in popularity. Instead of slapping on an idealistic markup on the goods, they kept the prices reasonable, which makes it easy and affordable for regular citizens to make the right choices at the supermarket.

So if we have been saying the same things for nearly a century without any resulting behavior change, perhaps it's time to change our perception about our perception of cycling.

The point? Copenhageners are not environmental warriors with a superior conscience who cycle, recycle, and eat organic food as they peer down at you from their moral pedestal. Nah. They are regular, conservative homo sapiens who have been given the necessary infrastructure to make doing things that are good for society easy and effortless. This isn't nudging people to change their behavior. This is taking them by the hand, with a smile, and leading them down the collective path.

We can battle the skewed perception of cyclist behavior through data, and we will continue to do so. In the debate here in Copenhagen, when faced with such personal perceptions, I often point out another aspect. People have complained about cyclist behavior since the day the bicycle was invented. I have researched articles, op-eds, and letters to the editor in Danish newspapers dating as far back as the turn of the twentieth century. *Whiners gonna whine* is hardly a new concept.

One of Denmark's most loved satirical cartoonists and writers, Robert Storm Rasmussen, known as Storm P., published a satirical essay in a 1935 book in which he made fun of cyclist behavior—or rather the public perception of it. Like most people in Copenhagen in the mid-1930s, he was a cyclist himself. He included a drawing of a man pointing almost imperceptibly to the left with one finger.

The caption read, "In Copenhagen, if you are going to turn, you extend your arm straight down and stick one finger out to the left. This tells everyone in the traffic which way you're NOT turning." The whole essay is funny and representative of cycling in Copenhagen—or really any city where cycling is mainstream. Little has changed since the 1930s. So if we have been saying the same things for nearly a century without any resulting behavior change, perhaps it's time to change our perception about our perception of cycling. We've clearly been looking at it all wrong for a very long time, without trying to understand it.

I'm not quite finished with behavior. In my work I am relentless in my focus on getting The 99% to ride bicycles for transport, and I find it interesting that some cities have made more progress than others. Infrastructure is key, absolutely, but fruit seems to hang lower in some cities than in others.

BEHAVIORAL CHALLENGES

In the 1970s, when Copenhagen started on the journey to reestablish the bicycle on the urban landscape, there were no noticeable cycling subcultures present at that point of departure. Women were cycling in smaller numbers than men, but there were no bike messenger tribes or lycra-clad "avid cyclists" to influence our mainstream bicycle culture. We made the jump directly to the mainstream and the democratization of urban cycling for every citizen. What happened was that there was a growth in the number of subcultures, and this continues to this day. Mainstream urban cycling encouraged a rich diversity.

In some re-emerging bicycle cities, this is how the development of urban cycling has been panning out. In the absence of any strong subcultures, the first movers are just regular citizens looking to optimize their A-to-B journey by shaving valuable minutes off their travel time. In Paris, for example, most of the people who started using the Vélib' bike-share system arrived from the Metro or from trains. To this day, the majority of the people you see cycling about the city are the same as those you would see on public transport.

As in Copenhagen, the blossoming mainstream bicycle life in Paris has spawned a growing interest in subcultures, adding to the rich fabric of a bicycle-friendly city. If we compare Paris to other cities in the same league, elsewhere there is a strong, often dominating, presence from cycling subcultures, be it the messenger crowd in cities like New York or the racing crowd in many cities. Most of them would continue to ride bicycles even without this current and intense period of interest in urban cycling and without the growing network of bicycle infrastructure.

Decades of a narrow projection of cycling's image has caused the general population in many of these cities to regard cycling as a fringe activity, and they often associate riding a bicycle with "uniforms" and clubs or tribes, as opposed to being something for everyone.

The reemergence of the bicycle on the urban landscape has brought new cyclists onto the streets, and many of them are influenced by the preexisting subcultures, be it "gear" or attitude. Their role models are clearly defined, whether they adhere to them or not. By taking to the bicycle they become, in the eyes of the general population, members of the subculture. Often against their will. It would appear that the general population has hungered after other role models. Subcultural influence on the mainstream is nothing new, of course. Subculture influences mainstream culture every day of the week, but there are few examples of a fringe tribe completely dominating the mainstream. Most of us have licked stamps and sent letters, but very few of us are members of a stamp-collecting club.

The question is to what extent are subcultural cycling groups limiting the growth of urban cycling with their predominant fringe attitude. How can we separate cycling's image from its subcultures and normalize it? That's the challenge.

I've seen behavioral campaigns start to pop up wherein cyclists are being told to "behave." All cyclists. Unfortunately, the predominant nature of cycling's subcultures makes it hard to transform urban cycling and sell the concept of the bicycle as a normal part of traffic to the skeptics. Many people only see the aggressive attitude of the fringe groups and judge cycling based on the way these individuals ride in the city.

When you produce behavioral campaigns for cyclists, the issue is defining your target group. Whom are you speaking to? Can you really throw everyone on a bicycle into the same box? The mother with her child on the back of the bike, together with an adrenaline-driven "urban warrior"? No, you can't. Campaigns aimed at "all" cyclists risk alienating the new cyclists who really are the key to redemocratizing cycling. The most fertile buds on the rose bush.

If this is our goal, then it may be necessary to distance the image of urban cycling from the subcultures in order to show the general population that the bicycle belongs and that those are just regular citizens who are using it as a transport tool. Without a doubt, this may be a painful step, given the small, tight-knit character of the cycling community in many places. When the common good is in play, however, it is a necessary step. When I voice these principles on, say, Twitter, I get the usual responses.

"We're ALL cyclists! Don't be divisive!" Well, dude (and, sorry, it usually is a dude), I'm not a card-carrying member of your club and I never will be. Nor will the massive majority. Ever.

Producing behavioral campaigns focused on cyclists only serves to continue the marginalization of cycling and just hammers home the misconception that urban cycling is not something for everyone and is still just an outsider.

Pointing fingers at cyclists' behavior serves no good purpose if you don't point those fingers at the other traffic users at the same time. Behavioral campaigns aimed at everyone remove this focus on cyclists and also serve to place the bicycle on an equal footing in the public psyche.

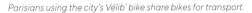
Parisians using the city's Vélib' bike share bikes for transport.

But if pointing fingers is your thing, then point them at the most dangerous and destructive elements in cities and towns: motorists and the automobiles they drive. Even if you are addressing a subculture, it gets tough. Subcultures have their own codes and language—and cycling is no exception, whether it's fixies or spandex-clad racers. They are proud of being different and have often defined themselves by their unique identity in the cityscape. Their external environment—car culture, etc.—has in many ways dictated their perceived (and sometimes real) attitudes, styles, roles.

You don't get very far when you tell them to behave. And the new cyclists, with a lack of alternative role models, will perhaps feel like you're speaking to them. You'll either strengthen their links to the underground or you'll push them away completely. Treating cyclists as equals is more beneficial than highlighting that they are strange or *aparté*, especially when you're dealing with so many new cyclists who perhaps don't wish to be "underground."

There's an important sociological angle worth considering. When an underground group sees their chosen culture going mainstream, it often breeds resentment. "I've been doing this for years, now everyone's doing it!" It's not helpful for mainstreaming urban cycling. Here's a quote I harvested from a New York newspaper article:

"There is definitely a downside to biking when bikes become a fashion fad . . . If you unleash a herd of teetering, wobbly fashionistas into city streets without any real knowledge of how to ride a bike in traffic, accidents can (and likely will) happen."

Experience is important, sure. But this is a "purist" attacking other people riding bicycles.

You know what? The people who are new to the wild ride at the amusement park hold on tightest. "Wobbly" doesn't need to be dangerous. "Style Over Speed" may be one of the greatest traffic-safety slogans in the history of cycling. It may be irritating to the purists who now have to ride crazier to avoid new obstacles on their previously sacred urban landscape. But really, who cares? Such is democracy and democratization.

Producing behavioral campaigns focused on cyclists only serves to continue the marginalization of cycling and just hammers home the misconception that urban cycling is not for everyone .

Segments of the underground are revolting against the mainstream. Just like they did over 100 years ago when the rich saw their prized toy—the bicycle—go mainstream. They mocked, ridiculed, spat upon the laborers and women on bicycles. History is repeating itself, it seems. All the more reason to stick to our guns and continue to work towards giving the bicycle back to the people. It worked the first time. It'll work again.

The only thing that will get us homo sapiens to do something—anything—is a lot of other people who resemble us doing it. If people peer into a big, societal mirror and see like-minded fellow citizens staring back, they'll be more primed for behavior change.

Cyclist using a footrest at a red light. It reads: "Hi, cyclist! Rest your foot here and thank you for cycling."

CHAPTER 12

A SECRET CYCLING LANGUAGE

> **The purpose of psychology is to give us a completely different idea of the things we know best.**
>
> Paul Valéry

We have to see in order to understand. Observing cyclist behavior, especially when so few people have been cycling on any useful scale, is paramount. After so many years of seeing it, I can't unsee it. Not just the fascinating observations of the Desire Line Analyses but the subtle, poetic details all around me.

I've been observing what I call the Secret Language of Copenhagen Cycling for many years. It was first brought to my attention on a bike tour with a delegation from Portland back in 2008. I led

them on a couple of tours of the bicycle-urbanism highlights in the city. One of the delegates, on day two, said to me as we cycled through the city that he found it strange that Copenhageners didn't shoulder-check when passing a cyclist ahead of them. "Of course they do!" was my response. I had never thought about it before. He said he had been looking at this for two days.

We were slowly catching up to a young woman who, in turn, was about to pass a cyclist in front of her. "Watch her," I said, and we did. I saw it, but he didn't. Not right away. It was a smooth passing procedure. Her bicycle tilted slightly as she pulled over to the left of the cycle track and accelerated slightly as she passed the other cyclist. After she reached an acceptable distance, she slid back into line on the right side and continued on her way.

"See?" I asked. "See what?" he replied. I explained that she had cocked her head to the left before passing. We cycled along and watched others doing the same, and then he got it. My colleague was looking for a full, demonstrative turn of the head, when in fact it was an experienced and subtle movement that was the key. First of all, when cycling along cycle tracks, you only have to deal with other cyclists, except at intersections. Cars are off to the left in their own lane. When you cycle in tightly packed formations every day of your life in Copenhagen, you develop the ability to require only a quick glance. It is a habit that forms gradually, but automatically.

The desire to park as close as possible to your destination is universal. The flexible nature of bikes makes it considerably easier, compared to cars.

After that revelation, I continued to study the details. The slight cock of the head increases a bit in the morning rush hour, when the cycle tracks are more congested, but it remains subtle. What I also noticed is that there seems to be an acquired ability to hear other bikes. I test it

regularly to this day. When passing, or watching other people ahead of me passing, I often notice how the heads of those being overtaken cock ever so slightly. There is no rule for when to do so, but it seems to be when the front wheel of the bicycle on the left is just about to pass the back wheel of the one on the right. Sometimes I'll change gears or just clear my throat a bit to see if these sounds elicit a response.

Sure, many bikes in Copenhagen are rusty or squeaky, but it would appear that our cycling citizens have tuned their hearing to know when another bike is coming up, thanks to everyday experience of cycling in large groups.

I have further observed that many cyclists will signal a turn or a stop when there are bikes behind them, but fewer will do so if there aren't. It is a combination of auditory awareness and, on occasion, a quick glance backwards. I noticed this behavior in myself first. I was only signaling my directional intentions when there was another traffic user ahead or if there were bikes or cars behind me, and then I observed that this is a broadly shared habit.

While cycling, I'll do regular over-the-shoulder glances as though just keeping tabs on the bike traffic, and many others do the same. While I have been observing this for years and in great detail, I wasn't the first to notice it. Here's another passage from the 1936 novel *Gudrun* by Johannes V. Jensen: "If one is bumped by a car, the whole school is bumped. It's a nerve one has in the elbow, a flock function, which Copenhageners have learned so well that it is second nature."

I saw more evidence of Jensen's observation when a Canadian friend was visiting Copenhagen and we were cycling around the city. Chris Turner is a writer and no stranger to integrating smoothly

A railing and footrest for cyclists at an intersection in Almetyevsk, Tatarstan, similar to those around Copenhagen. © City of Almetyevsk

into cities around the world. He was following me on the cycle track through the city. I was glancing backwards regularly and, when the coast was clear and no cyclists were coming up from behind, I would swing out onto the left side, giving him space to ride up next to me to continue our conversation. But he didn't. He stayed in the same position behind me. I even waved my hand to signal to him to come up alongside, but he just kept the same distance and speed. I realized all this in retrospect, but at the time, I was just getting irritated with him. I shifted back onto the right side of the cycle track and accelerated, and, sure enough, he just followed my tempo.

The City announced that they wanted to spoil their cyclists by given them a designed solution based on their existing habit of leaning on light poles and other urban furniture.

Later, at a bar, it all hit me. I explained to him my earlier irritation at how he didn't recognize my visual clues and how he probably hadn't learned this secret language. We laughed it off. He said that cyclists aren't allowed to ride two abreast where he's from, so it didn't even occur to him.

I continue to test this with others I cycle around the city with, Copenhageners and visitors alike. For locals and Dutch friends, it's a no-

brainer. Others need to learn the subtle behavioral intricacies. As I studied it, it only became more beautiful, whether I was the one instigating it or the one following the leader.

One cyclist checks to see if the coast is clear and slips elegantly to the left and slows ever so slightly. The other accelerates smoothly until we are alongside each other. This continues until we either approach a cyclist to pass or are about to be passed. As a general rule, the cyclist on the left assumes the responsibility to keep an eye on bikes approaching from behind, but this isn't carved in stone. One of two things then happens, in either case. One cyclist will speed up or slow down slightly. The other will notice and balance it by doing the opposite. The faster cyclist will glide to the right and the slowing cyclist will give them space. When there is space again, one or the other will swing out to the left, and on it goes. It is all so impossibly subtle and smooth, this elegant cycling ballet, and not a word needs to be spoken.

While Storm P. was poking fun at the perception of Copenhagen cyclists with his satirical drawing, he was, in a way, close to reality. A stop or a turn is often signaled with a dreamy wave of the hand, so cool and casual that you want to frame it and hang it on a wall. The pursed-lip safety crowd probably toss and turn at night about how there are no fully extended arms for turning or rigid 90-degree angles for stopping. I don't see the problem. Even when a cyclist ahead slows almost imperceptibly, I observe cyclists register this and prepare to slow or to pass.

All the signs are there for us to see—and those of us who cycle daily in cities like Copenhagen or Amsterdam see them. The desire to park as close as possible to your destination is universal.

The flexible nature of bikes makes it considerably easier, compared to cars. It is not possible to accommodate this desire in every location, but it is important to use this desire as a starting point. When planning parking for bikes, start at Mile Zero—the destination. Or Inch Zero, perhaps— bike parking right outside the door. Then work your way backwards from there based on feasibility. All too often, bike parking is stuck out of the way by design or only appears as an afterthought.

I see bicycle magnets forming every day. In the densely populated parts of the city where I seem to gravitate to when filling my belly or quenching my thirst, space for parking your bike is limited. A city bylaw dictates that bikes cannot use the roadway for parking, but that becomes a mere suggestion outside cafés, restaurants, or nightspots. For example, one time there was an empty parking spot outside a bar in the Vesterbro neighborhood. I parked my bike in it and sat at the window of the bar to watch a bicycle magnet form. It never fails. Before long, after I "legitimize" parking in that location, other citizens join the party. This repeats itself ad infinitum every day of the week and, more often than not, I'm the one who starts the ball rolling. I even have a cheeky hashtag for it: #ParkWhereYouWant. In many of these neighborhoods there is insufficient space for sidewalks, let alone bike parking, so I feel just fine in reallocating some urban space from cars

Parked bikes next to a no parking sign show that the demand for parking is high.

and advertising the fact on social media. The City understands the nature of bike-parking psychology and has tested parking zones as a solution, as opposed to putting up bike racks. Almost every bike has a kickstand—how can you not have one in a bicycle-friendly city where the bike is your fifth limb? They legitimized parking outside various destinations by simply painting a zone. This new concept had a slow start until the City placed a couple of bait bikes to show people that parking was possible, and then they started to work. It's not always possible to provide the perfect solution for on-street bike parking, but it is paramount to think long and hard about the user psychology in order to arrive at a suitable solution.

It's clear that urban cycling allows us to interact with the urban landscape, even physically. Everywhere in Copenhagen, where there is a light pole next to or at least near the stop line for bikes, a section of the metal is rubbed smooth. The bicycle urbanism version of Buddha's tummy. Day in and day out, cyclists who stop at that spot will lean against the pole so as not to get out of the saddle. Leaning up against your city is romantic and practical.

Even just resting your foot wherever you can is a simple benefit at a red light, be it a permanent or temporary solution. In 2012, I designed some handles that could be easily attached to light poles next to the stop lines for cyclists. I

Light poles near the stop lines for bikes are rubbed smooth in the middle from cyclists leaning against them all day long.

enlisted a welder to cut handlebars in half and weld on the necessary bits for attaching them. We put them in six locations in Copenhagen for a ten-day period. We called them Love Handles. An intern went out to observe how long it would take for cyclists to notice and use them. "Not very long" was basically the answer he came back with. Cyclists used them from day one to support themselves while waiting for the light to turn green. We observed an added value. Cyclists would use them to propel themselves forward off the light to make it easier to start rolling until sufficient momentum was achieved. I put one up in Amsterdam afterwards, and it stayed there for two years.

The City of Copenhagen took this simple act of leaning up against the city to the next level. They have installed a couple dozen railings and footrests around the city, always at carefully chosen locations so as not to impede pedestrian access. Cyclists can hold onto the railing, use the footrest, or both. The City announced that they wanted to spoil their cyclists by giving them a designed solution based on their existing habit of leaning on light poles and other urban furniture. The concept has proven to have a positive behavioral effect as well. Cyclists, in their constant quest to maintain momentum, will sometimes crawl slowly past the stop line while watching the lights, anticipating their imminent change

The City of Copenhagen successfully piloted parking zones for bikes without any bike racks.

The author recorded the formation of a bicycle magnet, using his own bike as bait in a car parking spot outside a Copenhagen bar.

of color. Being spoiled with a railing or footrest while they wait has reduced the frequency. This idea has spread far and wide. I have seen them in a number of cities around the world.

Bikes are unique human-powered machines. They move people to and fro effectively and efficiently. Equating them with motorized vehicles, however, is a mistake. They are driven by momentum, and planning for bicycles needs to address that fact as well as the inherent psychology of the urban cyclist.

It's clear that urban cycling allows us to interact with the urban landscape, even physically.

In the United States, the "Idaho stop" for bikes is a welcome move towards understanding cyclists. By a law first implemented in Idaho in 1982 (mainly to free up the courts from minor traffic offenses), cyclists can treat stop signs as yield signs in order to maintain their momentum.

In most parts of the world, turning right after stopping at a red light is not allowed for any traffic users—and it shouldn't be allowed anywhere for motor vehicles. At the time of writing, it is now legal in France and Belgium and on the way in Denmark. I rode all over Paris a few months ago and quickly learned to spot the small signs indicating that it was legal. This also applies to many T-intersections, so bikes can turn right or roll

Aerial shot of a cyclist signaling a right turn in Copenhagen.

through. Prioritizing cycling, giving them a head start in the traffic as well as respecting their momentum. In the chapter on innovation, I'll highlight other simple tech solutions in the same vein.

The point is that there is so much under the surface that we haven't noticed—and if we haven't noticed, we can't hope to understand. It is time to begin. Let's look around our cities. Observation is power. Citizens see more clearly than engineers and planners as they move through the public space. *Their* space. We must follow *their* lead.

CHAPTER 13

A2BISM

A great part of courage is the courage of having done the thing before.

Ralph Waldo Emerson

I know exactly what you want. It's the same thing that I want. Indeed, it's what every homo sapien who has ever lived wants: a direct line from A to B when we're transporting ourselves. Humans are like rivers carving through a landscape—we will always find the easiest route. This is the most basic principle in transport planning. I call it *A2Bism.*

The history of traffic engineering can be summed up concisely. For most of the 7,000-odd years we have be cohabiting in urban centers, we were rational. For millennia we provided our primary transport forms—pedestrians and horses or donkeys—with the fastest A-to-B routes. By 1900, the bicycle had appeared in amazing numbers. Public transport in the form of trams and omnibuses had also appeared on our streets. Still, we were rational. Direct A-to-B lines. By 1920, cars had shown up in our cities and yet we still maintained our rationality.

Then around 1950, what had begun in the thirties and forties in the United States washed

Cyclist at night in Copenhagen.

A SHORT HISTORY OF TRAFFIC ENGINEERING

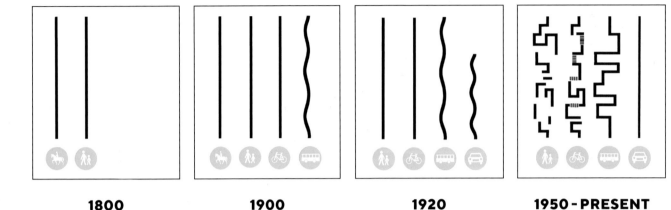

1800   **1900**   **1920**   **1950 – PRESENT**

Top: *A short history of traffic engineering.*

Right: *The Copenhagenize Traffic Planning Guide.*

over the world like a tsunami. American traffic-engineering standards and principles. To this day in most places, the automobile has been handed exclusive rights to go fast from A to B, at the expense of everyone else just trying to get around a city.

The quickest and simplest traffic planning guide for a life-sized city isn't difficult to produce. Give the three transport forms on the left a high level of A2Bism, and make driving a car difficult, inaccessible, and expensive. Make it less competitive in travel times. All the campaigns in the world for *Ride a bike! It's good for you! Save a polar bear on your bike today!* are completely irrelevant and a colossal waste of money unless we are doing that fourth line.

Cyclists, pedestrians, and public-transport users are by nature intermodal. Personally, if my tire is flat in the morning, I chuck the bike into the bike shop and walk to the metro to get to work. With 600 shops serving 600,000 people—I have 50 of them within a five-minute bike ride—it is the easiest option. It only costs about $8, on

average, to have a flat tire fixed. The bike is the quickest way to get around, but public transport, combined with walking, is a respectable option. Switching among the three is easy and intuitive.

Motorists are the last traffic-user group to change their behavior. It's hard to escape the metal-and-glass bubble that they invested money in and that has cut them off from the city through which they drive. In many places, having your car break down is virtually an acceptable excuse for missing work.

We know that A2Bism is a key factor in making cycling desirable. In their biannual Bicycle Account, the City of Copenhagen has been asking the citizens since the 1990s to specify their main reason for riding a bike in the city. The numbers never change: 56 percent say that it is quick; 19 percent say that they like getting some exercise (not fitness cycling, just riding to work to help them get that 30 minutes of exercise that the doctor said they should); 6 percent say it's because it is inexpensive; and only 1 percent say they ride to *save the planet* (that is, environmental reasons).

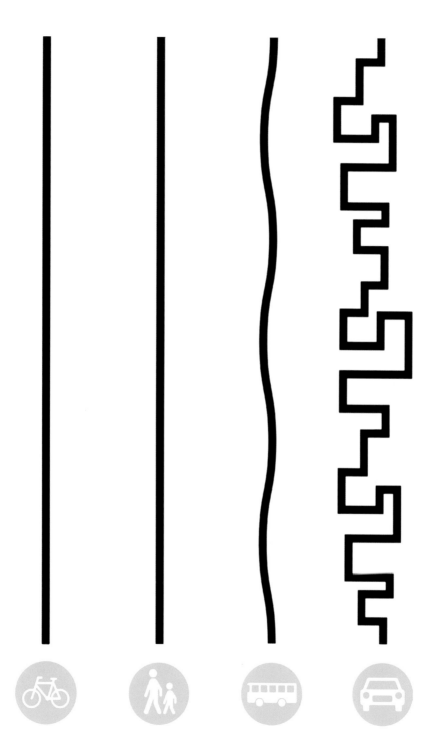

If you make the bicycle the fastest way from A to B in a city—any city in the world regardless of climate or topography—you are halfway to the goal. Everything is 20 minutes away in Copenhagen, even if it's actually longer. That's what it feels like.

I was interviewed for the German edition of *Greenpeace* magazine in 2017. The journalist had lined up a great show for me. She was intent on testing travel times in Copenhagen. We started in the Nørrebro neighborhood, near Åboulevarden and Blågårdsgade, and the destination was the Copenhagenize Design Company offices on Paper Island, south of the city center.

First up was car-share. It took 37 minutes to drive the 4.8 km (about 3 miles), park, and walk to my office entrance. And this was in the late morning. The drive back to the point of departure took 40 minutes. What a nightmare. A totally restrictive, stressing experience. From the same departure location, I walked to the Forum metro station, traveled three stops to Christianshavn, and walked the last mile to the office. That took 32 minutes and was quite pleasant, even with some light rain. Finally, the *pièce de résistance*. I hopped on my bike and it took 13 minutes to get there and 14 to get back.

By and large, the City of Copenhagen understands desire lines as well as A2Bism. At the intersection called Søtorvet, where the world's busiest bicycle street, Nørrebrogade, enters the city center, something strange evolved. For centuries, the street was the primary artery for getting to the capital from the northwest. The all-roads-lead-to-Rome principle has applied in Copenhagen for a very long time. But recently the City noticed that something new was happening at this intersection: many cyclists were turning off the cycle track and traversing a sec-tion of sidewalk to get to a parallel street, Vendersgade. Instead of putting up barriers to stop this—cycling on the sidewalk is illegal in Denmark—they set out to find out the reason. The first guess was that people were trying to get out of the incredibly intense morning rush hour for bikes, but the actual reason turned out to be a a bit more than that.

> If you make the bicycle the fastest way from A to B in a city — any city in the world regardless of climate or topography — you are halfway to the goal.

Ørestad, the new development to the south of the city, is a popular destination, with new university buildings and many workplaces. People were taking a little shortcut to escape the rush hour, yes, but also to circumnavigate the city center and head over to Ørestad. For a century this had never happened before at this location, but a new mobility pattern had emerged. The City observed and respected this behavior and made a temporary bike lane across the sidewalk to see if it would work. It did. Less than a year later, permanent infrastructure was put in. By legitimizing the behavior of a handful of citizens, the City carved out a new route that has proven to be incredibly popular. No time-consuming survey or long meetings, just human observation leading to improved facilities.

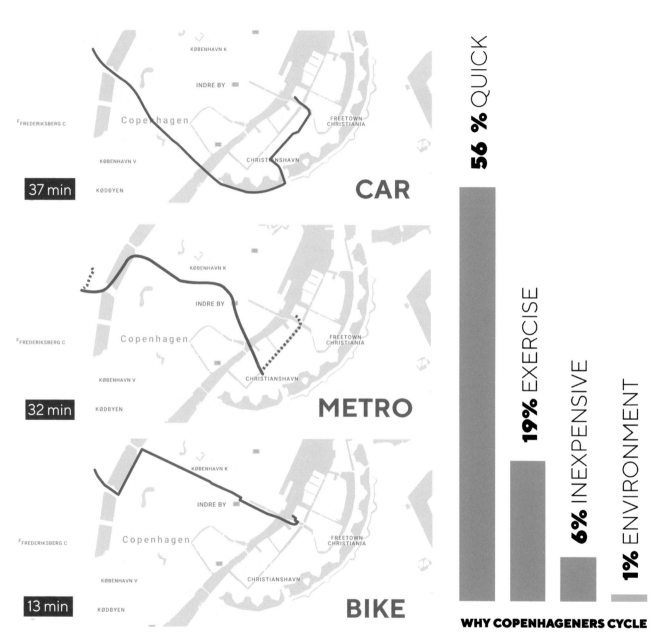

37 min | CAR

32 min | METRO

13 min | BIKE

56 % QUICK

19% EXERCISE

6% INEXPENSIVE

1% ENVIRONMENT

WHY COPENHAGENERS CYCLE

Right: The reasons why Copenhageners choose the bicycle as transport.

Left: The author's travel times through Copenhagen in a car, by the metro, and by bike.

On a much larger scale, A2Bism's greatest experiment in Copenhagen unfolded inadvertently between 2012 and 2013. From one year to the next, the modal share for bicycles, measured by how people arrive at work or school in the city, exploded from 36 percent to 45 percent—a leap of 9 percentage points. That has never happened anywhere. Ever. Seriously.

Copenhageners, being rational homo sapiens with places to go and people to see, chose other transport forms.

The modal share for cars also fell from 27 percent to 23 percent. The average trip length in Copenhagen rose 35 percent from 3.2 kilometers to 4.2 kilometers in that year. That means that the oft-quoted statistic about how Copenhageners cycle 1.2 million kilometers a day needs to be upgraded to more than 2 million kilometers per day. Okay, okay. But what does it all mean? When the data came out, journalists began scrambling for answers. Two researchers at the Danish Technical University were "surprised." They were quoted in the Danish press as saying things like, "Uh . . . the City's new bridges and traffic calming on certain streets seem to have worked. Giving cyclists carrots encouraged cycling."

The detail they forgot was that the new cycling bridges weren't quite finished yet, nor was the traffic calming on Amagerbrogade. The Nørrebrogade stretch is from 2008. Cycling rose on that street by 15 percent, but that was before 2012, obviously. Basically, there hadn't been many carrots dangling in this city for a few years at that point. What did happen was that 17 huge construction sites fell out of the sky all at once—stations being built for the new Metro ring. That's not something that happens every day. In addition, most of central Copenhagen—between 2012 and 2013—was under further construction because of the upgrading of district heating pipes beneath many streets that had to be ripped up.

Driving was rendered incredibly difficult. Copenhageners, being rational homo sapiens with places to go and people to see, chose other transport forms. The use of public transport increased, too, but the bicycle was clearly the chariot of choice. It was the greatest urban

**10. Why do you choose
to bicycle to work?**

▨ Being *green*

▨ Avoiding traffic

▨ Saving money

▨ Excercise

✔ Other

**11. What holds you back
from commuting more often?**

Opposite Left: *Heading to the
Central Station by bike.*
Opposite Right: *Family arriving at
Copenhagen Airport by bike.*
Left: *A question in an American
survey about cycling that misses
the point.*

experiment anywhere in the world, and it proves the entire A2Bism premise. Mark my words, however. When the Metro construction is finished in 2019, we will see a sharp drop in cycling levels, back to the standard levels we've plateaued at for the past few years. You read it here first.

Unless, of course, the City of Copenhagen has the *cojones* to embrace this experiment and use it to finally make the leap back to the future. Expanding and widening the cycle tracks. Re-allocating space from diminishing car traffic to bicycles and public transport. If they don't, this rich petri-dish experiment will just rot and be forgotten.

Desire lines are happily married to A2Bism even on a micro-scale. The photo of the small ramp shows how you are technically expected to continue onward for about 100 meters, turn right, and then loop back in order to get to the harbor. Cyclists and pedestrians were observed taking this obvious shortcut, lifting their bikes down. (Again, it serves no democratic or planning purpose to erect barriers.) So a ramp and some stairs were put in after the fact. Not a comfortable ramp but just enough to make it more pleasant and accessible. For bikes or parents with baby carriages. This is still an idea that needs to

catch on in some parts of the world. There was a survey about cycling habits that was posted on a website called Ecology Action in 2010. The single most important reason wasn't even on the list. "Quick and convenient."

Richard Masoner from the Cyclelicio.us blog wrote about this survey when it came out, and I agree: "No wonder we fail so miserably at cycling promotion. Do car advertisements speak blandly to the raw, number-crunching, analytical bottom line? Or do they appeal to your desire for the visceral, go-fast, fantastic feeling of freedom and sexual prowess?"

On the *Ecology Action—Bike2Work* website that hosted this poll, I found this list and added my own comments:
Why Bike Commute?
» *It's good for your health.
(Nice… but I want to get there quick.)*
» *Saves you money on gasoline, vehicle maintenance, parking fees, and parking tickets.
(I don't care…I want to get there quick.)*
» *Reduces air, water, and noise pollution associated with driving.
(Sweet… but I want to get there quick.)*
» *Reduces automobile traffic.
(Good… but I want to get there quick.)*

Left Page: Three photos that show the transition from a bike lane across a sidewalk to permanent infrastructure based on the desire lines of cyclists in Copenhagen.

Right Page Top Left: Bicycle seatbelts on the train between Denmark and Sweden.

Right Page Top Right: *A2Bism messaging from the City of Sydney. ©Gerry Gaffney*

Right Page Bottom: A small ramp put in to legitimize a user-defined desire line.

» *It's good for the community by making our streets safer, quieter, and cleaner. (Yeah, yeah, sounds nice… but I still just want to get there quick.)*

Once you discover the freedom, convenience, and fitness benefits of biking to work, you'll wonder why you didn't start riding sooner. Bicycling can be a convenient, dependable, and virtually free mode of transportation. And bicycling burns about 500 calories an hour, so you can commute and stay fit at the same time.

From a marketing perspective this is really dreadful copy. It isn't selling anything, let alone cycling. And yet this is the standard fare on so many "advocacy" websites all over the world—

but I'll get into that later. The point is that we need to understand that A2Bism is an absolute truth for homo sapiens. It's hardwired into our brains. Make the bicycle the fastest transport form by building infrastructure, prioritizing cycling, and respecting the psychology.

THINKING INTERMODAL

As ever, it's not just about the bike. It's about creating an urban framework that makes the bicycle a natural and intuitive choice, either alone or combined with public transport. There are different approaches to this. In the Netherlands, the national railway (NS) is not a big fan

The massive rise in passenger numbers after DSB made it free to take bikes on their S-Train network.

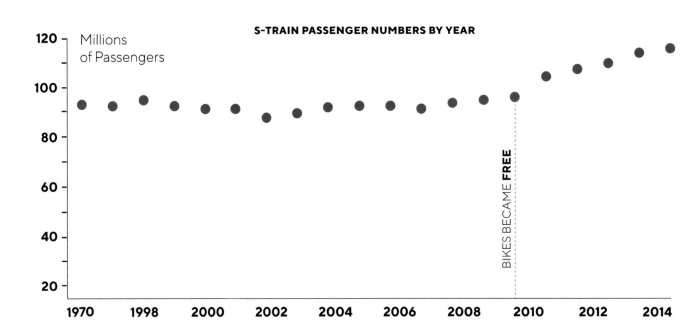

of bikes on trains, although it is an easy process for passengers to bring one. Their unique bike-share system, OV-Fiets, is available at most train stations, and the A-to-A concept allows people to grab a bike, use it, and drop it off at the station when they leave. They have a train network with high volumes of passengers in their small country, which is also saturated with bicycles.

From 2014 to 2017, Copenhagenize Design Company was a partner on a European Union project called BiTiBi—Bike Train Bike. The project was tasked with inspiring citizens to ride a bike to the station and combine it with a train journey. It involved pilot projects in Belgium, Catalonia, Italy, and the United Kingdom that improved parking facilities for bikes and also tested bike-share programs available at the stations. I was in charge of getting the logo made and producing posters and materials for the project. It was important to avoid the typical messaging about saving polar bears by riding your bike and to focus instead on *faster, easier,* and *cooler* as keywords. A poster campaign from one of the project's partners, Merseyside Rail, highlighted the ease of use and convenience of their Bike & Go bike-share.

In Denmark, Danish State Railways (DSB) has been transporting passengers with bikes almost since the bicycle was invented. Greater Copenhagen is served by the S-Train network—S-tog in Danish—and for many years passengers had to buy a reasonably priced bike ticket. In 2010, DSB decided to make bikes free on all their red S-Trains that transport people to and from the city from the far reaches of our urban sprawl. It was a bold move, but far from being an example of corporate social responsibility, it was simply a clever business model. They assumed correctly and rationally that bikes don't travel alone, so by making it free, there were good odds of increasing the number of paying passengers. Boy, did they nail it.

What started with inventive campaigns advertising the fact that bike tickets on the S-Trains would be eliminated—like placing a makeshift tunnel resembling a mock train compartment on the cycle track, complete with hot air heaters to warm cyclists, however briefly, on a cold December day—ended rather well for them.

When the Metro construction is finished in 2019, we will see a sharp drop in cycling levels, back to the standard levels we plateaued with for the past few years.

Actually, "rather well" would be an understatement. The number of passengers taking a bike on board rose from 2.1 million to 9 million. A total, whopping passenger increase of more than 300 percent. And it continues to rise.

The loss of income from ditching the bicycle ticket has been paid off several times over with the increased passenger numbers. It is estimated that almost 10 percent of passengers now take a bike with them.

Indeed, when asked in a survey, 91 percent of passengers were positive about the possibility of taking bikes on the trains; 27 percent of the cyclists on board responded that they wouldn't have traveled by train if they couldn't take their bikes with them; 8 percent even said that they travel more by train now that taking a bike is free.

In May 2009, before it was free, 188,000 bikes were taken on the S-Train network. A year later, after the bike ticket was eliminated, 630,000 bikes were taken on board, and those numbers are rising, too. In order to meet the demand, DSB redesigned the compartments on all their trains and created so-called Flex Zones with fold-up seats and bike racks beneath each seat. They adjusted the seating on all trains so that every single one now has a capacity for 60 bicycles.

The redesign also included a comprehensive reworking of pictograms and the implementation of a one-way system to ease conflicts when bikes are rolled on or off the train. The spacious bicycle compartments are located in the middle of the trains, since DSB research showed that the seating in the middle of the train was less popular with passengers. Continuing with their work to encourage bicycles on trains, DSB has toyed with the idea of putting bicycle pumps on board trains, but so far they have gone with bicycle foot pumps integrated with advertising facilities outside their stations.

With all that said, most stations in the suburbs are also fitted with ample bike parking as well as secure facilities for a subscription fee. On the trains that operate between Denmark and Sweden, there are even lovely little bike seat belts in the bike compartment. Whatever the situation, whether you park at the station or take your bike with you, it should be an easy way to travel.

Interestingly, bikes on buses have been through a few pilot projects in Copenhagen. Buses have space for two baby carriages at a time, and on some routes the bus company added bikes to the mix. Very few people use this, however. The Copenhagen Metro still charges for bikes and doesn't allow them during rush hour, but as with the buses, they cover an area and distances that are easy to cycle.

The bicycle must be integrated at every step of people's daily lives if a city is to be truly bicycle-friendly. Think bicycle-first.

Worldwide, there is a broad spectrum of ways that rail operators deal with bikes. Some are far ahead of the curve, including regional operators in Germany, the United Kingdom, and Catalonia, while others lag far behind. A pragmatic approach, coupled with a cool business decision, has paid off for DSB. The bicycle must be integrated at every step of people's daily lives if a city is to be truly bicycle-friendly. Thinking bicycle-first in urban planning and intermodality ensures prioritizing the bicycle as transport.

Left: *Mock train compartment with heaters for cyclists to pass through, promoting DSB's new policy of making bikes free on their S-Train network.*
Center: *Campaign by Merseyside Rail's Bike & Go bike share system in Liverpool.*
Bottom Left: *Copenhagenize Design Company poster for the European Union BiTiBi project.*
Bottom Right: *A typical bicycle compartment on an S-Train in Greater Copenhagen.*

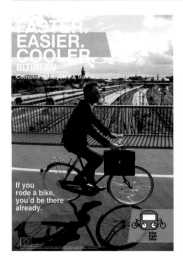

Pyöräilijöitä tänään

206

Cycling with friends in Helsinki.

CHAPTER 14

THE ART OF GATHERING DATA

> You can have data without information, but you cannot have information without data.

Daniel Keys Moran

From my professional point of view as the CEO of an urban-planning company, living in a city that is unrivaled in the world regarding the amount of data it gathers is both a blessing and a curse. Actually, it's like an addiction. While my company harvests its own garden of data, the City of Copenhagen feeds us with an inexhaustible variety. When we have to use the City's data in comparison with other cities' data, it is always a letdown. "That's all you have?!" Followed by a sigh. Copenhagen has developed a strong municipal culture of collecting data over many years— collecting it and also learning how to interpret it and how to use it going forward in planning. Not to mention using it to convince skeptics. The City has a website onto which they make all the data freely available. It is currently only in Danish, but the list is long. You can see pretty much every-thing: where things like fountains, kindergartens, or garbage cans are located, which zones street vendors can operate in, where chargers for elec-tric vehicles can be found, or where the city has current urban-planning projects underway.

Most relevant for my work is the cycling data. There are the maps showing the infrastructure for bikes, and you can see all the spots where bikes were counted. Furthermore, you can click on them to see a PDF with information about when the count was done and all the details that were recorded. It's El Dorado meets Nirvana.

In late 2016, Copenhagen could reveal that the number of bikes crossing into the city center exceeded the number of cars for the first time since 1970.

The city has over 20 sensors under the asphalt and does regular counts at around 200 locations across the city. It is pleasing to know that many cities are getting their data-collection game face on. Amsterdam has just as many sensors under the cycle tracks as does Copenhagen, but so do other cities, like Oslo and Warsaw.

The first serious example of data being used to convince authorities about the necessity of bicycle infrastructure dates back to 1909.

Around the turn of the last century, the streets along the Lakes in Copenhagen were the busiest in the entire nation for bicycle traffic. The conditions for cyclists, however, left much to be desired. The swarms of cyclists only had the narrow edge of a riding path to use. Back then, the horse-riding crowd hailed from bourgeois circles and enjoyed a jolly good trot on their dedicated paths.

The Danish Cyclists' Federation, founded in 1905, started lobbying for a cycle track on the route, but the city's equestrian elite refused to relinquish space. In a case of early nimbyism, these influential citizens from the upper classes felt ownership and wished to protect their privileged infrastructure, so the City was loath to rock the boat. Other equestrian paths in the city had previously been reallocated to cyclists, starting in 1892 with the first dedicated bicycle infrastructure in the world on Esplanaden, so perhaps the elite were tiring of having their riding space reduced. Nevertheless, data won the day. Indeed, it beats mere perception and guessing any day of the week, anywhere.

In many ways, motorists are the new equestrian elite. As André Gorz has written: "Mass motoring effects an absolute triumph of bourgeois ideology on the level of daily life. It gives and supports in everyone the illusion that each individual can seek his or her own benefit at the expense of everyone else."

A colleague went spelunking in the archive caves of Helsinki and found another interesting historical reference to data collection. He found maps from bicycle counts in 1937 showing not only the best-practice infrastructure network, but also the amazing volume of cyclists. The thickest red lines indicate 10,000 cyclists. Another example that we've all been here before.

In 2010, my staff and I were discussing what a list of the most bicycle-friendly cities in the world would look like. We couldn't find anything out there, which was frustrating. In a flash of inspiration, we decided to make that list, and the Copenhagenize Bicycle-Friendly Cities Index was born: www.thecopenhagenizeindex.com. It's a biannual index that ranks cities based on 14 parameters—all of them data-based. We were surprised by the overwhelming response when we published the first index in 2011. We can discuss whether or not there are too many indices out there, covering every possible subject, but by all accounts the Copenhagenize Index was something that many people were waiting for. Each time we publish it, the interest in it increases. Mayors tweet about it, city councils discuss it, newspapers slap it on the front page.

Bike vs. Car. Traffic volume at select locations in Copenhagen.
Data: City of Copenhagen

You can check out the website for the latest list, but what we find most interesting about the entire process is how, since 2011, cities have been trying to improve their data in the interest of making sure that they are fairly represented. In increasing numbers, we receive emails from staff in cities around the world that include the latest data. There is no lobbying involved. They just want to make sure we include them. For whatever it's worth, the Copenhagenize Index has spurred cities to focus on data just a little bit more than they used to.

Most cities are much better at collecting data now than ever before. Indeed, my team and I work with client cities such as Long Beach, California, on the subject of learning how to harvest data about cycling and how to use it going forward. Copenhagen started to get serious about it around 1970, just as Amsterdam had done in the mid-fifties. In 1990, Den-

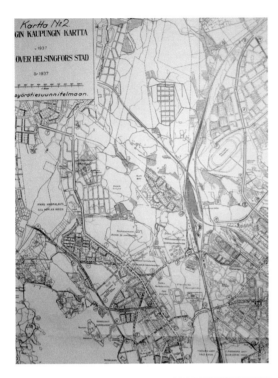

Old maps of Helsinki with red ink showing infrastructure and bicycle counts in 1937. The thickest red lines denote at least 10,000 cyclists counted. Photo: Marek Salermo

mark in general began to gather data in much more detail. In late 2016, Copenhagen could reveal that the number of bikes crossing into the city center—past the Lake Ring—exceeded the number of cars for the first time since 1970. It's a development that's hard not to get excited about, even though the number of cars crossing the municipal border is still stable.

On a similar note, the City uses its data tradition to hand influence to our citizens in the form of a website and an app called "Giv et praj" (or "Give us a shout" in English) that lets citizens report issues live from the front lines of the urban jungle. Maybe there is a garbage can that hasn't been emptied, a pothole in a cycle track, or a sign that is broken or missing. You can pin it on the map, and the City is exceptional at keeping you updated about the status of your request. If they deem it worthy of attention, they have a good track record of sending out people to fix it within a reasonable time frame. A growing number of similar apps are appearing in cities. Among them, YouPin in Bangkok and See-Click-Fix in New York.

Counting cyclists and other traffic users, and building comprehensive, long-term data sets is incredibly important. So is measuring the costs/benefits and returns on investments in having a cycling population and building infrastructure for them. We know why we're doing what we're doing. It's just a pragmatic approach to moving people around a city in effective ways. But does it pay off? If so, how long does it take? Is it worth it? Does it help? Knowing the answers to these questions makes it easier to understand the efforts and investments and to use that knowledge in planning more infrastructure, as well as drastically shortening the inevitable conversations with skeptics.

Luckily, Copenhagen has its finger on this pulse as well. Since the mid-nineties, the City has published a biannual Bicycle Account — *Cykelregnskab* in Danish—wherein they measure cyclists' sense of safety and satisfaction with the various conditions for cycling in the city.

In 2009, the City commissioned a study by an engineering firm, COWI, with the title *Samfundsøkonomiske analyser af cykeltiltag—metode og cases* (or *Socio-economic Analyses of Cycling Projects—Methods and Cases*). It's a fascinating document. For example, they calculated the socio-economic results of Bryggebroen, the first bicycle/pedestrian bridge over the harbor, which opened in 2006. The first new link over Copenhagen Harbor in seven centuries.

They determined that building the bridge had a cost/benefit return of 7.6 percent and a profit of 33 million kroner (about US$5.2 million in 2017). In comparison, the proposed road and rail link from Denmark to Germany, Femern Belt, will give Denmark a cost/benefit return of 6.8 percent, and the best solution for upgrading the rail line between Copenhagen and Ringsted would yield a benefit of 5.8 percent.

The intersection where Gyldenløvesgade meets the Lakes was long the blackest of black spots in the nation for cyclists. Improving the conditions with new infrastructure and recalibrating the light signals to improve safety for cyclists gave us a socio-economic profit of 59 million kroner (about US$9.3 million) and a benefit of 33 percent.

Time and time again, the numbers come out in favor of investing in urban cycling as transport. Without any risk of exaggeration, it is the most cost-beneficial transport form we have ever invented.

The statistic that seems to capture the most imaginations is based on an updated calculation with its roots in the foregoing socio-economic analysis. Every time I ride a bicycle, I put 26 cents right back into society. Pure profit, man. This is because of the health benefits of urban cycling. I will live longer and I'll be less ill while I'm alive, so I'll be both more productive and less of a burden on the health system. In addition, if all goes well, when I do die I'll die quickly, so my fellow taxpayers don't have to foot the bill for caring for me due to the bad lifestyle choices I made during my life. That is, I (hopefully) won't need the extensive care required if I am obese or suffer from type 2 diabetes or heart disease. In addition, it is rare that I lose time in traffic when I'm on a bicycle, so society benefits from my getting a full workday in.

> Every time someone drives a car 1 km, we pay out 89 cents. We just throw it in a big black hole and never see it again.

On the other hand, every time someone drives a car one kilometer, we pay out 89 cents. We just throw it in a big black hole and never see it again. We have been desperately trying to claw some of that loss back by means of the tax on new cars I mentioned earlier. But in vain. If I were to calculate how much that negative number would be in countries without a tax on new cars, I don't think I would want to see the result.

Between 2006 and 2016, the City of Copenhagen invested 2 billion kroner (about US$317 million) in bicycle infrastructure and facilities. The cycling citizens of the city save us 1.7 billion

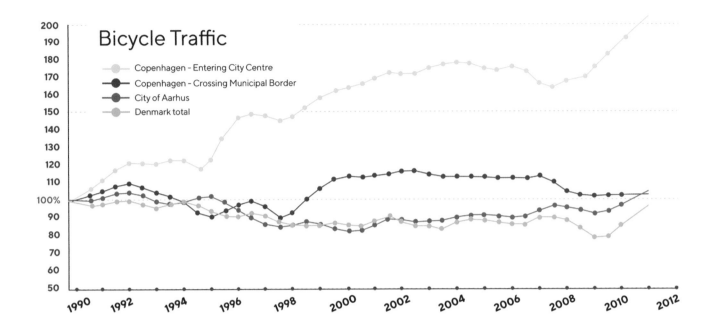

Bicycle Traffic

- ○ Copenhagen – Entering City Centre
- ● Copenhagen – Crossing Municipal Border
- ● City of Aarhus
- ● Denmark total

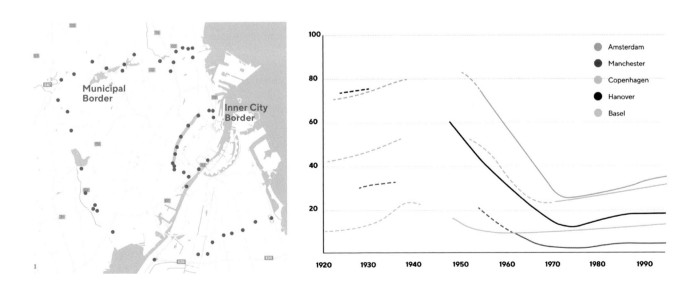

kroner (about US$270 million) *each year* because of the health benefits. I am notoriously bad at math, but even I can figure out that spending US$317 million in a decade is no big deal when we're saving US$270 million every year. Every time we build one kilometer of cycle track, we get our investment back in under five years. What an astonishing business model.

On the ground, we should also consider the massive cost of wear and tear caused by motor vehicles on our roads. A car is estimated to be 16,000 times more destructive to asphalt than bikes are. Even with the finer, more expensive asphalt on cycle tracks, there is still a huge difference.

Professor Lars Bo Andersen from the University of Southern Denmark is one of the most published academics in the world on the subject of the health benefits of having a cycling population. His extensive research has produced a great number of statistics that have to be considered when we're planning our cities for bicycle traffic.

He says that with the current levels of cycling to work in Denmark, we prevent around 10,000 new cases of cancer, heart disease, and type 2 diabetes—and 2,500 premature deaths—every single year. He has calculated that a child who rides a bike just one kilometer to school is noticeably healthier than a child who walks to school, let alone one who is driven in a car. His research results are consistently confirmed by international studies.

A 2017 study from the University of Glasgow found that cycling to work reduces the risk of cancer by 45 percent, the risk of heart disease by 46 percent, and the risk of premature death caused by those illnesses by 41 percent. And remember, the health benefits of daily cycling are 20 times greater than any risk.

Opposite Top: The growth of bicycle traffic in Copenhagen compared to Aarhus and national levels.
Opposite Bottom Left: The locations where the City of Copenhagen does permanent traffic counts along the municipal border and around the city center.
Opposite Bottom Right: Graph showing cycling levels in select cities. The dotted lines are estimates. The gap is World War II. The solid lines show when cities started serious data gathering.
Left: Cyclists waiting for a ship to pass before they cross Bryggebroen.

People! Are you *getting* all this? We are, quite simply, in possession of a spectacular medicine. One that can both prevent diseases and cure them. The bicycle is a veritable wonder drug. That we are not in a state of constant bicycle infrastructure construction in every city in the world is, frankly, beyond me.

Once in a while the issue of "bikes should pay" rises to the surface like bubbles of methane in Lake Kivu. Of the half a billion citizens in the European Union alone, close to 100 million of them say they regularly ride a bicycle for transport. None of them are inconvenienced by bicycle licenses, least of all the Netherlands or Denmark—the two countries with the highest levels of cycling.

Between 2006 and 2016, the City of Copenhagen has invested $317 million USD in bicycle infrastructure and facilities.

There have been cities elsewhere that have considered bicycle licensing or registration and did some math about what the administrative costs would be. None of them have found that licensing bicycles was cost-efficient. Sometimes we hear calls for a symbolic "appeasement fee": cyclists paying a fee to get the motorists et al. to shut up—for a while. No matter how you twist and turn it, there is little indication that a license or registration fee would be cost-efficient. So yeah, good luck with your ridiculous bicycle tax, Oregon.

Here are some things to consider from my ragged little bag of opinions: First, imagine the logistical nightmare of registering tens of millions of bicycles. You would need to pay to develop or adapt a computer system to register them, and you would need to hire people to run the system to issue registrations and pay for producing licenses.

Consider the aforementioned impact on the roads. The average car, in 2005, weighed 1,650 kilograms (3,582 pounds). My best guess as to the average weight of a bicycle is about 13 kilograms (30 pounds). Based on those numbers, a bicycle weighs 0.8 percent of a car.

I clearly don't have a degree in rocket science, but even I can figure out that the weight impact on asphalt by bicycles is marginal—16,000 times less than motor vehicles, as I mentioned. Let's say that a car registration costs $100, just to pick a number. Based on that figure, a bike registration should then cost 80 cents. But hang on. Then we'll have to subtract from those 80 cents. A car's environmental impact is considerable, but a bicycle has none. Let's say a 50 percent reduction in the 80-cents fee for zero environmental impact, just to pick a number. And I'm being extremely kind.

Okay. Now we're down to 40 cents per bike. But we need to put cash into the administration fees for running the system. Let's knock off 35 cents—the rest of the fees will have to come from somewhere else—but that leaves us with a nickel. Five cents. That seems fair.

Wait a minute. We're not quite done. According the health benefits I wrote about above, society is saving a bundle due to my preferred transport choice. For every kilometer I cycle, I'm putting 26 cents back into the public coffers. I've calculated that by cycling 12 kilometers to and from work, plus all the trips to the supermarket, cafés, school, shops, etc., I'm contributing roughly $830 a year, give or take.

I am all for most of that going back into the system. It makes me proud to be able to contribute positively to the society in which I live, through my transport choices. But hey, paying people to cycle is a thing. In Denmark I can get a tax break of 32 cents per kilometer if my cycling commute to work is 24 kilometers or more. As I write this, there is a proposal to lower that distance to 12 kilometers, which would put me, personally, in the zone. That means I would get $998.40 a year back for riding my bike. Keep your nickel and send me $998.35 and we'll call it quits. Thanks. Love your work.

If a successful businessman or woman bought a city and started looking hard at how to turn it into a profitable business and began by focusing on transport, you would see a drastic reduction in the number of cars in that city. There wouldn't be money allocated to issuing bike licenses or registration. The money would go instead to bicycle infrastructure and traffic calming, as well as public transport.

If, however, a city or state does implement a program of bike registration, they should go the whole nine yards and start a shoe tax for those pesky pedestrians sponging off our public funds.

1 km
+26c   FOR SOCIETY   1 km
-89c

The cost-benefit of cycling one kilometer by bike
and the lost-benefit of driving a car that distance.
Data: City of Copenhagen

The morning rush hour on the world's busiest bicycle street, Nørrebrogade in Copenhagen, with over 40,000 cyclists a day. And this is just one light cycle.

THE
TOO

All right then. Let's roll up our sleeves and open the toolbox in order to figure out how to get the bicycle back as transport in our towns and cities. There is a wealth of experience and knowledge from the past century as well as the last few decades. Let's explore what we have and how to use it.

Room for everyone on Nørrebrogade, including a human-powered wedding procession.
© Lorenz Siegel

CHAPTER 15

BEST PRACTICE DESIGN AND INFRASTRUCTURE

Quality is not an act, it is a habit.

Aristotle

If, as I have said, the bicycle is the most important and powerful tool in our urban toolbox for making cities better, it's high time that we took a long, hard look at the blueprints. Our greatest advantage is that we possess them. There is no need to reinvent the wheel when this particular wheel is round and has been rolling for more than a century.

A street is the space between the façades of the buildings on it. That is the space with which we have to work. All too often, people look at the street as the place where we have put cars and promptly eliminate it from further consideration, thereafter declaring: "We don't have any space!" This is an undemocratic approach. As my friend Jason Roberts from Better Block Foundation puts it, "You have to shrink the scale." Our urban short-term memory loss applies here, too. Sidewalks in New York and many cities were wonderfully wide and welcoming in the decades before the automobile started chipping away at them. Our streets have morphed several times through the centuries. For example, Roman

175

streets were concave, to act as drainage canals when it rained. With car-centric traffic engineering, they are now convex, allowing the water to flow into the gutters—towards homes and buildings—and away from the cars traveling on them.

You may have seen guides to infrastructure design before. What I will present here is the definitive guide to best-practice infrastructure for cycling in cities. I have seen and studied infrastructure standards—or the lack thereof—in dozens of countries. What a crazy, ragtag collection of ideas! I want to make it clear that overcomplication is unnecessary and to present tried-and-tested designs that form the backbone of Danish bicycle planning.

There are only four basic designs in Danish bicycle planning. One of these four fits every street in the Danish Kingdom and, indeed, every street in every city in the world.

In a way, my colleagues and I have the easiest job in the world. If a city asks me to design infrastructure on a street, I ask two questions. First, how many cars are there in a 24-hour period? Second, what is the posted speed limit for those cars? Based on the answers to those two questions, I will choose one of four designs.

Four. There are only four basic designs in Danish bicycle planning. One of these four fits every street in the Danish Kingdom and, indeed, every street in every city in the world. Nothing less. I find it fascinating how our design traditions eventually filtered down into our bicycle infrastructure, where we boiled them down, simpli-

fied them, and ended up with a tidy and intuitive package.

The journey had a rocky start, from the world's first dedicated path for cyclists in 1892 in Copenhagen and the 1896 law allowing cyclists to use the outer edge of riding paths elsewhere. Bikes were dominant as a transport form, but there were few rules to govern them. In fact, there were few rules for traffic in general, at least until the first Danish traffic law was established in 1923 and revised in 1932. Bicycle users in the 1920s were "irritating" to motorists. Cyclists often rode in rows and crossed the streets when it pleased them to do so, using the streets like seven centuries of city citizens had done before them—just on two wheels. Traffic behavior was a new phenomenon now that cars started multiplying. It was in 1924 that red reflectors were made mandatory on the back of bicycles, but tackling the growing number of accidents involving cars was tricky. Giving each traffic user group a section of the streets was the way forward.

In December 1928, Denmark's Cycle and Auto Industry Association and the Danish Cyclists' Federation tried to call attention to the problem of traffic crashes—contacting all the authorities they could, from the government to the local parish councils. By the mid 1920s, the construction of bicycle infrastructure had become such a hot topic that it was discussed at the annual general meeting (AGM) of the Association of County Councils in July 1929. Separating traffic was a compelling necessity, even though it cost money and demanded space, stated Vice Chairman Henningsen of the National Tax Council (Landsoverskatterådet) in his speech at the AGM. His main message was that cycle tracks should be of high quality, because otherwise cyclists would just use the road. But which solution was best and least expensive?

Cycle tracks physically separated by curbs or grassy strips, bike lanes on the side of the road and separated with painted lines, or cycle tracks

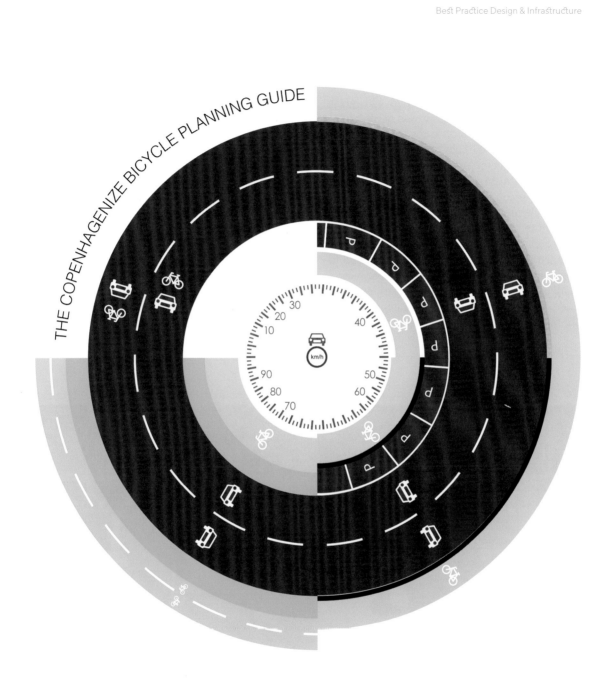

THE COPENHAGENIZE BICYCLE PLANNING GUIDE

DANISHBESTPRACTICE:10–30KM/HNOSEPARATION.40KM/HPAINTEDLANES.
50–60KM/HCURBSEPARATEDLANES.70–130KM/HFULLYSEPARATEDBYA
MEDIAN.BICYCLEINFRASTRUCTUREISPLACEDONTHERIGHTSIDEOFPARKED
CARS.BI-DIRECTIONALONLYOFF-STREET.THANKYOU.

parallel to the roads and separated with grass, trees, or ditches? Or perhaps it was necessary to build fully separated bicycle roads? There were many opinions on the subject around the country.

County Inspector Troelsen from Aalborg, in a speech at the AGM about bicycle stripes, claimed that on the country roads of Northern Jutland the bicycle users didn't mind cycling on the narrow painted lanes on the shoulder of the roads. The county road administration had therefore widened the asphalt on the sides of the road to allow for one meter on either side for bicycles.

Aalborg had built physically separated cycle tracks along the roads leading to the town center, but they were little used. "Building physically sep-

arated cycle tracks along our country roads is, in my opinion, the wrong approach," stated Inspector Troelsen. They were also more expensive to build, which appeared to be the primary hurdle.

Elsewhere, Holbæk County supported cycle tracks parallel to roads. They also painted lanes to separate bicycles from cars, as was popular in Germany at the time. They were a cheaper solution in case the roads needed widening, and many roads did back then, because of increasing traffic.

Dedicated bicycle roads were widespread in densely populated areas in the Netherlands, but such areas were rare in rural Denmark. The Dutch had a bicycle tax for financing a national network of cycle tracks. A similar tax was dis-

A street in Montreal showing that there is ample space for a cycle track.

cussed in Denmark, too. Taxing the rubber used in bicycle tires was proposed as a means of paying for cycle tracks, but it never ended up happening.

All of this was a response to the rising number of bicycles and motor vehicles, not to mention horse-drawn wagons, all of which needed some structure and fast. In 1933, 1.5 million Danes rode bikes daily, which was 44 percent of the population. The cities were first movers, as per usual, but it was a slower process in the countryside. In 1930, there were only 88 kilometers (55 miles) of bike lanes on country roads in the nation. That rose to 342 kilometers (213 miles) just three years later, but this only meant that 4 percent of rural roads had infrastructure.

It was in the late 1930s that the goal of keeping cyclists safe with infrastructure really gained purchase. The quick and dirty solution was painting a lane on the side of the road, but this did little to protect cyclists. Even then, the Dutch were on the same page. As the head of municipal planning for The Hague put it at the International Road Congress in that city in 1938: "The usual reserved stripes for cyclists that only separate them from the road with a line, can only be regarded as a surrogate solution."

Physically separated cycle tracks weren't popular among planners and engineers in Denmark in the 1930s because the price was prohibitive. Nevertheless, the 1930s saw a massive growth in research of the best solutions for bicycle infrastructure, and many standards were established. Various designs were tested, and the pros and cons dutifully recorded. Many different surfacing solutions were prototyped, such as gravel, bitukalk (a mix of bitumen and chalk), cast asphalt, and cement. The need for infrastructure was determined if there were more than 100 cyclists

per hour or at least 100 motor vehicles per hour.

They went into the hills as well. In early examples of direct observation being used to aid bicycle infrastructure planning, research was done on roads with steep inclines, including one of the country's steepest, with a 10.7 percent grade. They watched to see when cyclists could power up the hill or had to get off and walk. The official recommendation was that bike lanes or cycle tracks should be created for grades between 2.5 percent and 4 percent, depending on the length of the hill.

When the speed limit hits 50 or 60 km/h, it's time for hard separation.

The many results were published by the Danish Road Laboratory's Road Committee in 1938 and 1944, so the various road directorates around the country could start working with tested standards.* In the following decades there was a great deal of fine-tuning of these standards—and that continues to this day. Generations of planners have boiled down the designs to something beautiful, simple, and useful.

First, let's look at the two questions I need to ask. The car volume and the posted speed limit for those cars are the determinants for which type of infrastructure is preferred. The first type of infrastructure is none at all. I live in a densely populated neighborhood at the intersection of two busy streets, but the residential streets behind my apartment are low-volume and traffic-calmed with continuous sidewalks that force cars to slow down. I cycle effortlessly

*The historical references were translated freely from an article by Mette Schønberg, former head of Denmark's Road and Bridge Museum, in Danske Vejhistorisk Selskabs magazine *Trafik & Veje,* September 2009.

here and so do my kids. Traffic calming that forces motorists to drive more slowly is physical. The street is designed to keep speed down and people safe. In many cities in the United States, on the other hand, posting lower speed limits on streets designed for high speed means absolutely nothing.

Second, when the speed limit hits 40 km/h (25 mph) or the volume of cars rises, painting a lane is an acceptable solution. It is important to note that the lane will run alongside the sidewalk and will be a minimum of 2.3 meters (7.5 feet) wide, running one way on both sides of the street. It must be said that a number of municipalities, especially in and around Copenhagen, will upgrade to the next level because that will ensure a higher level of safety and a sharper increase in the number of cyclists.

Third, when the speed limit hits 50 or 60 km/h (30–37 mph), it's time for hard separation. Since 1915 in Copenhagen, this has been the curb-separated cycle track that physically protects cyclists from motorized vehicles. It is raised to mid-curb height and also keeps cyclists separated from pedestrians on the other side. This is the gold standard in a city like Copenhagen. Indeed, there are 375 kilometers (233 miles) of curb-separated cycle tracks in the city of Copenhagen and only 33 kilometers (21 miles) of the aforementioned painted lanes. Again, the minimum width is 2.3 meters (7.5 feet) and it should run along the sidewalk, like the painted lanes. Always and forever. On cycle tracks with a higher volume of cyclists, then the cycle track is widened to accommodate them. The unwritten standard for cycle-track width is that you and I can cycle together, having a conversation, and a cargo bike can pass us.

When the speed limit for cars hits 70 km/h (43 mph) or higher, such as highway speeds, there is only one goal: getting cyclists as far away as possible from the motorized traffic. You don't mix bikes with cars going that fast. You find the

space and you create as big a buffer as possible. It is in this category that we allow for bidirectional infrastructure. In Denmark, on-street, bidirectional lanes were found to be substandard back in the 1930s, but they lingered here and there until about 20 years ago, when they were effectively removed from the arsenal. Such bidirectional bike lanes simply aren't safe enough. When placed in off-street contexts with no contact with cars, however, they are suitable. Like on the Green Path system crossing Copenhagen.

The usual reserved stripes for cyclists, that only separate them from the road with a line, can only be regarded as a surrogate solution.

The highways leading to Copenhagen feature wide bidirectional bike paths on both sides, shielded by trees and at least one meter (three feet) of grass median, as do parks and stretches of roadway along, for example, Copenhagen Harbor. Even in the countryside, space is found, where possible.

When you design something—anything—you have to test whether it serves its intended function. If you think about it, these designs have been through the most rigorous design test phase in history. Hundreds of millions of cyclists have used them for many decades in Denmark and many other countries. An impressive network of cycle tracks was once found in what seems today to be unlikely places. Many British cities readily adopted the designs, as did German cities. Flaws were identified. Improvements were made. I know I keep going on about how we've been doing this for a very long time and how best-

Top Left: *Cycle track in the suburbs along the #16 highway north of Copenhagen.*

Top Right: *In rare instances, painted lanes are used in Copenhagen but they are still a minimum of 2.3 meters wide and parallel to the sidewalk. © Lorenz Siegel*

Bottom: *Morning traffic along the #16 highway heading towards Copenhagen.*

practice has been thoroughly established. It is of utmost importance to know that cities wanting to improve conditions for bicycles and increase cycling levels have a much shorter journey if they want it.

Traffic-engineering standards for motorized vehicles are largely similar all over the world. Most are flawed, sure, but everyone has agreed upon them. If I travel to any point on the map and want to play soccer or tennis, I won't have to first learn the intricacies of the field or the court. They are the same everywhere. All sorts of people from all sorts of cultures have agreed what a soccer field or tennis court should look like. The designs have been tested and deemed best-practice. The standards are carved in stone. Shouldn't it be like this for bicycle infrastructure as well?

I have noticed that large, proud countries suffer from a "not invented here" mentality. Adopting ideas from small countries like Denmark or the Netherlands? Nah. We can do it ourselves. Through this curious peacocking, time is lost doing work that has already been done. Designs that were tossed out decades ago are developed from scratch. New designs that should never see the light of day are presented as "cutting edge" and "innovative." Hey, bloodletting was once considered a cutting-edge and then mainstream medical treatment for a variety of diseases. That doesn't mean it worked.

So, four types of infrastructure. I could mic-drop it right there, but I bet you might have some supplementary questions.

BUS STOPS

The preferred design of bicycle infrastructure past a bus stop in Copenhagen is creating an island for bus passengers. In this situation, cyclists are allowed to continue without stop-ping and bus passengers wait until the coast is clear. Moving to this design has drastically reduced bus passenger / cyclist conflicts. With that said, there are still bus stops where there is limited space. In these cases, cyclists are obliged to stop to allow bus passengers to embark or disembark. Even when space is limited, the protected cycle track continues parallel to the sidewalk, and while passengers are expected to mix with braking cyclists, the real danger of bus–cyclist interactions is avoided. When Winnipeg, Canada, starts to figure it out, you know it must be—and should be—*a thing*.

OTHER SOLUTIONS FOR PROTECTED INFRASTRUCTURE

The gold standard is curb-separated cycle tracks. They may seem expensive, but they're rock-bottom-cheap if you compare them to roads for cars, what with the minimal wear and tear and the fact that the return on investment is quick. A city should be planning for the future, so this is the best solution. My team and I will always recommend this design for our client cities. When faced with financial reality, there are other solutions that we will recommend:

» Modular-concrete curb separation, which allows water drainage and requires no full street rebuild, but still gives real vertical protection;
» Modular-plastic curbs or planters (some of which feature funky built-in footrests);
» Bollards or buoys, which provide good visual separation and help somewhat in keeping cars in their own lane, though they are also easily run over;
» So-called armadillos, which have proved to be effective in cities like Barcelona and Mexico City, especially when they provide a hard edge towards the cars.

Preferred best-practice solution in Copenhagen for a cycle track passing a bus stop. © Lorenz Siegel

WHAT ABOUT CONTRA-FLOW?

There are few great contra-flow solutions running through the heart of the Danish capital. On some streets with low speeds, bikes use the travel lane and a cycle track runs in the opposite direction. On others, cycle tracks feature on both sides. In all cases, high-quality bike traffic lights are in place to manage safety at the intersection.

WHAT ABOUT SHARED SPACE?

I'm rather enamored with the shared-space philosophy, and always have been. While it is a great solution for small towns and residential neighborhoods where traffic calming and street design are in place, it is not entirely suitable for transport in a larger city with great numbers of people moving to and fro. Certainly not now or in the near future in cities still under the boot of the automobile. Copenhagen's pedestrian street network is a fantastic addition to our city. Parallel to the famous Strøget, the city has a shared-space street called Kompagnistrædet (or Strædet, for short). Our offices were at one end for a time. I sailed down the empty street in the morning but avoided it like the plague in the afternoon. While cars and bikes are permitted to use the street, cycling down it was an exercise in trying not to fall off my bike when riding at a

snail's pace. I love the street, absolutely, but it is just a destination rather than a transport corridor. In the United States, I have heard shared space touted as a solution, but by people clearly unwilling to spend money or who don't understand urban cycling as a transport form. In such cases, shared space is a surrogate, much like the dreadful sharrow.

BUT ISN'T ANY BIKE LANE BETTER THAN NOTHING?

A dry, stale rice cake is better than no food at all if you're stuck the desert, yes. We can agree on that. And like I've said, a chair with two legs will let you rest a bit. But neither is a sustainable solution. By choosing ready-to-implement designs that have been tested and proven to be effective, the chances of success are, quite simply, greater. You don't choose half-baked versions of the other products you acquire, do you?

I would rather ride on a 2- to 3-meter-wide (7- to 10-foot-wide) bidirectional bike lane through a city than be forced to run with the bulls on a street without any infrastructure at all. I get it. But we are planning our cities for the next century, and we need to get it right from the start.

You don't choose half-baked versions of the other products you acquire, do you?

We also need to understand that our choices now will impact our choices later. Montreal started building a (fragmented) network of bidirectional cycle tracks in the late 1980s. It largely ignores the naturally existing desire lines of

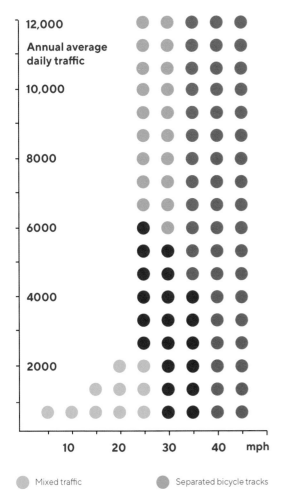

12,000

Annual average
daily traffic

10,000

8000

6000

4000

2000

10   20   30   40   mph

● Mixed traffic   ● Separated bicycle tracks

● Painted bicycle lanes   ● Bicycle track with buffer

*Opposite: Contra-flow cycle track against the flow of traffic.
Another cycle track is on the opposite side, allowing cyclists
to ride with the flow. © Lorenz Siegel*
Top: *The simplified standards for which type of infrastructure
to put in based on car traffic volume and the speed limit for cars.*
Bottom: *In cities like Barcelona, hard separation between bikes
and cars is achieved by solid blocks bolted into the asphalt.*

the city and sends cyclists on time-consuming detours. Now there is a focus on unidirectional infrastructure, and it's proving tricky to connect up the two types.

You might have heard of the American organization NACTO—the National Association of City Transportation Officials. NACTO was developed as a response to AASHTO—the American Association of State Highway and Transportation Officials. The epic acronym battle aside, the latter are the engineers, unmoveable in their professional faith and infamously oblivious to bicycles as transport. The former, NACTO, focuses more on planning and creating better conditions for transport in cities. The ballet dancer versus the sumo wrestler. While I like what NACTO is trying to do and I understand their quest in light of the stone-faced opposition, they have misunderstood best-practice. On their website and in their design guides, for example, they promote bike lanes in between the door zone and moving traffic and painted lanes that cross car-travel lanes to allow cars to turn right. Not to mention bidirectional cycle tracks. Much of their inspiration comes from Denmark and the Netherlands—and yet they fail to nail it, or even to provide details for building such treatments. I would prefer a clear and defined approach that features solutions that will get results and form the foundation for the future in a city.

On their website and in their published material they cite best-practice and claim that their inspiration stems from the Netherlands and Britain, but they still happily recommend making bike lanes narrower. It is an example of American bicycle-planning that implements solutions that are not meant to entice people to join cycling for transport, but rather are based on the assumption that "there aren't enough cyclists now, so they don't need to pass each other."

We are planning our cities for the next century, and we need to get it right from the start.

Battling engineering standards with visions and solutions based on design is a noble cause. It is a necessary and welcome development. A similar approach is taking place in Oslo, Norway. When speaking at a transport conference in Trondheim, I gave my usual keynote with focus on design and best-practice. I was followed by Rune Gjøs, the head of Oslo's Bicycle Office—Sykkelprosjektet—and a third speaker. All of us were speaking the same language about infrastructure. In the Q&A afterwards, an audience member, frustrated and not a little indignant, stood up and asked why Norway didn't just implement the Danish standards.

A woman from the National Road Directorate, Statens Vegvesen, was tasked with responding to the query. She, too, spoke with an irritated tone, coupled with condescension, and explained that Norway can't just adopt standards from other countries—she made it sound frivolous—and that the Norwegian standards were there for a reason. She lumped Denmark into an "other countries" category like it was Zimbabwe and not a neighboring nation. Trondheim experimented with protected, curb-separated cycle

tracks in the 1990s, and Oslo even had its first cycle track back in 1941, but the National Road Directorate later eliminated them from their car-centric standards.

Oslo decided to react by creating what they call the Oslo Standard. It's a comprehensive guide to infrastructure that the City of Oslo wants to put into place and that conflicts directly with the archaic national standards. It's as political as it is practical, but it's a bold move in the struggle to improve city life.

Previous attempts to explore how to change the standards in Norway were made back in 2012 by the Norwegian Ministry of Transport, which wanted to figure out how Norwegian cities could increase cycling levels. Their usual channel of communication has the Road Directorate on the other end, but the administration was tired of the same-old, same-old answers. They decided to ask someone else. Copenhagenize Design Company, partnering with Civitas, was hired. Five Norwegian cities were selected for comparison with five Swedish and five Danish cities. The methodology behind the Copenhagenize Index was used to explore the differences between the cities. The short version of the results was—surprise, surprise—that the Norwegian cities lacked infrastructure.

PLAN A NETWORK

As you have probably figured out by now, all this infrastructure has to be part of a cohesive, coherent, and well-designed network. We can agree that a train line that forces you to get off and then walk two kilometers to a station on another train line in order to continue your journey is not a good rail network. The same applies to a bicycle network. Far too many cities are

Top Left: *A quiet residential street with low car traffic volume and no protected infrastructure for bikes.* © Lorenz Siegel

Renderings: *Copenhagenize Design Company renderings for our client city, Detroit. Courtesy: City of Detroit*

taking baby steps. Trying out one bike lane on one street to see how things go. It's completely irrelevant. Some other cities claim to have a network, like Berlin and Barcelona, but it there are only bizarre infrastructure designs in vague lines on a map. Luckily, more and more cities are getting the fact that networks are vital.

An early example is Rio de Janeiro. The city was to host the first Earth Summit in 1992 and, almost as an afterthought, decided to create a cycle track out of a car lane along the iconic Copacabana Beach— a symbolic gesture, since the world was coming to talk climate. After the world left, the next neighborhood, Ipanema, which had seen the cycle track in action, extended it down their own beachfront. Then Leblon followed suit. Rio is still very much a work in progress, but I can now get picked up at the national airport by friends on bikes and can ride the whole 15 kilometers to Leblon on a network of bicycle infrastructure. Which is pretty cool, even if the quality of the cycle tracks isn't up to par.

A city in the heart of the Russian oilfields, with hard winters, decides to *copenhagenize* in two short years, and the sixth largest oil company in Russia helps finance the visionary project.

In our work designing the bicycle network for the City of Detroit, creating a network of unidi-rectional cycle tracks intuitively criss-crossing the downtown core was the key. Throughout the process, we did have to compete with designs from consulting firms that were trying to push for bidirectional cycle tracks through the downtown core. Working in tandem with the City's passionate team, which was keen on turning the Motor City into the Mobility City, was professionally rewarding and personally inspiring. Detroit now has the framework for redefining itself as a modern transport city.

Calgary, Alberta, had planned a series of pilot projects—seven over seven years—featuring bits and pieces of bike lanes. The City realized that it would be far more effective to pilot the whole network all at once instead of taking baby steps. The results so far are positive, which should come as no surprise. Copenhagenize Design Company was also on the team designing the bicycle and pedestrian strategy for the City of Winnipeg, and I am looking forward to following the developments there as they begin work on their network.

You'll recall my story about Ljubljana, Slovenia, being ahead of the copy/paste curve in the early seventies. If you liked that tale, you'll love this one: In 2015, when the City of Almetyevsk, in Tatarstan, Russia, contacted me with the declared goal of becoming Copenhagen in two years, I was skeptical. I am quite familiar with the state of cycling infrastructure in Russian cities. On a global scale, Russia either struggles with it or ignores it altogether. Most often there is a lack of real political will in recognizing the bicycle as a legitimate mode of transportation. In Almetyevsk, however, political will would prove to be the guiding strength. Ayrat Khayrullin is the young, ambitious mayor who acknowledged the importance of a holistic bicycle strategy that values world-class facilities, constructive communication strategies, and, above all, dedicated cycle tracks. From the get-go, Khayrullin expressed an unwavering desire to transform Almetyevsk into the most bicycle-friendly city in Russia, one where he would feel confident sending his young children off to school by bike.

In our preliminary meetings with the city, we quickly agreed on the process and the goals: 200 kilometers (124 miles) of bicycle infrastructure in a cohesive network of best-practice infrastructure. Nothing less. Khayrullin had done his homework. He knew, for example, that on-street, bidirectional cycle tracks were a substandard solution. He understood the importance of establishing a complete network and prioritizing cycling as a transport form. He was well versed in the health benefits of having a cycling population. All he needed was someone to design it. To create the gold-standard bicycle city in Russia.

The entire Copenhagenize Design Company team went to work—not only our staff in our main office in Copenhagen, but others in our offices in Brussels and Montreal as well. Time was short. At our meetings in the city in fall 2015, we were told that they wanted to get to work in spring 2016, when the snow melted. We divided up our work on the bicycle strategy into stages in order to give the City a chance to plan and prepare their engineering department for the work. Their challenge was to figure out how to best use the roadworks season—from April to September—to create the first 50 kilometers (31 miles) of hard infrastructure. The core network along the city's main streets.

АЛЬМÉТЬЕВСК? Yes, Almetyevsk. Let's create some context for this place. It's a city of 155,000 people located smack-dab in the middle of Tatarstan—a semi-independent republic in the Russian Federation. Our colleagues in Russia inform us, grudgingly, that Tatarstan is a place where things just get done in an urban-development context. The capital city, Kazan, is the only Russian city to have built a subway system after the collapse of the Soviet Union, although they have done very little for bicycles as transport. As Almetyevsk is projected to grow by 30,000 new residents (many of them young workers and families) by 2030, the administration is looking to improve overall livability and attractiveness. Mayor Ayrat Khayrullin is keen to attract new residents with a life-sized city, as well as to improve the quality of life of the current residents.

He understood the importance of establishing a complete network and prioritizing cycling as a transport form. All he needed was someone to design it.

The city's built form is characterised by an arterial ring road framing the residential, cultural, and commercial center along a grid-like street network, with Soviet-era roads so wide that they make Salt Lake City's streets look like the back alleys of Amsterdam. The city center measures eight kilometers from east to west, four kilometers from north to south. In other words, the city's relatively small footprint, with its dense network of medium- and high-rise residential housing coupled with wide roads,

Photos from Copenhagenize Design Company client city, Almetyevsk, featuring newly paved cycle tracks, a garbage can for cyclists, and a bicycle parade. Photos: City of Almetyevsk

presents plenty of opportunities to accommodate the bicycle as a mode of transport.

When we first arrived in the city, we were amazed at how many pedestrians there were—something you don't often see in Russian cities. In addition, a thriving trolley bus system is a main transport form. As we know, these two elements are prerequisites when designing for bikes. All the great bicycle cities in the world have excellent public transport and a strong pedestrian culture.

A place where the young and old, rich and poor, can cycle alongside one another on a safe and connected network of best-practice bicycle infrastructure.

The financing of this phase of the project was a unique public–private partnership. Tatarstan's national oil company, TatNeft, bought into the idea early on, and their enthusiastic backing—both moral and financial—was key to the project's success. Their headquarters are in Almetyevsk as well. It only makes the storytelling better. A city in the heart of the Russian oilfields, with hard winters, decides to *copenhagenize* in two short years, and the sixth-largest oil company in Russia helps finance the visionary project.

Like some Russian cities, Almetyevsk had dabbled in bike infrastructure, but, as is often the case, half-steps and compromises have only led to conflicts. The City was quite open in admitting the shortcomings of their existing infrastructure. The shared pedestrian/bike spaces often resulted in confusion and conflicts, while the cycle tracks contained within a new development district didn't connect to the greater city network. In fact, conflicts between pedestrians and cyclists in 2014 heightened the public discussion around the role of cyclists in Almetyevsk, prompting the mayor and his colleagues to look abroad for experienced help, rather than simply crack down on cyclist behavior.

After multiple site visits for consultation, documentation, and data collection, we returned to Copenhagen to begin our analysis. Taking a detailed look at the city, with tried-and-true methodologies, we built up a thorough understanding of the city, developing an understanding of the strengths, weaknesses, opportunities, and threats facing the development of a connected network of bicycle infrastructure. We analyzed the connectivity of the network, the destinations and origins, intermodal linkages, road typologies, and, beyond all that, gradually building up an understanding of how best-practice bicycle infrastructure could fit into the city streets of Almetyevsk. Perhaps one of the more transformative events of the whole process was welcoming the mayor and a small team to Copenhagen for a private master class. Through workshops, talks, guest speakers, and bicycle tours, we opened their eyes to how best-practice infrastructure really functions. Nothing beats watching wide-eyed traffic engineers and planners wake up to the potential of the bicycle.

With a strong baseline understanding of Almetyevsk and a freshly inspired project team in the city, we developed a vision for a not-so-distant future Almetyevsk: "A place where the young and old, rich and poor, can cycle alongside one another on a safe and connected network of best-practice bicycle infrastructure." Some more quantifiable goals will help in guiding this vision forward into the future:

» There will be 50 kilometers (31 miles) of protected bicycle network built within the first year.
» Almetyevsk's bicycle modal share will reach 10 percent within the next five years.
» Twenty percent of schoolchildren will be cycling to school within five years.
» Cycling will be just as popular among women as men.
» Cycling in Almetyevsk will be safer than ever before.
» Winter maintenance will be prioritized.

Working off our baseline insights study and a guiding vision, we worked alongside a project team in Almetyevsk to develop the city's first Bicycle Strategy, one that guided the city forward in laying out 50 kilometers (31 miles) of bicycle infrastructure in 2016. Laying out an appropriate first-phase network and addressing smaller design details appropriate for each identified street typology. Details such as bus-stop treatments, major and minor intersection treatments, and appropriate bicycle-parking solutions were explained. Complementing the physical infrastructure, our strategy also laid out soft-infrastructure strategies, turning towards communication campaigns to encourage cycling, school and workplace programming, public events, and future engagement campaigns aiming to get people on their bikes for the first time, a critical step in expanding ridership.

Construction on the project began in late May 2016, coinciding with Russia's annual bicycle parade day and a ribbon-cutting ceremony. Upon our arrival in the city on that visit, we did numerous site visits and saw how the foundations were already laid for several kilometers of bicycle infrastructure. It was an amazing sight.

The next day, however, was unforgettable. Over 1,000 residents on bikes came out for a bicycle parade through the city. We stopped at a location on the main thoroughfare, Lenina Street, where an asphalt machine was waiting. Together with Mayor Ayrat Khayrullin and former heavyweight boxing world champion—and current member of the national parliament—Nikolai Valuev, I shoveled cement into the foundation for the first bicycle sign, spread asphalt on the first stretch of cycle track, and watched as young activists pressed a large red button to start the paving machines. Billboard campaigns for the City's vision hung above locations where the infrastructure would soon be rolled out—a part of the City's comprehensive communication campaign.

There were hurdles to overcome along the way. While political leadership was key, traffic engineers still needed convincing.

Implementing bicycle infrastructure and facilities in Russia had its challenges. There is nothing in Russian road standards about best-practice bike infrastructure (but there will be now), as the city engineers kept mentioning at the beginning, before political leadership took the reins once and for all. The quality asphalt required for cycle tracks existed, but nevertheless the City conducted a series of outdoor tests to make sure they had selected the right kind (they had). Along a piloting stretch of road, the director of transportation in Almetyevsk showed us the different materials, surface treatments, and signage they were trying out. They hadn't had any luck finding a supplier of bicycle traffic signals in Russia. So what did they do? They made their own, using vinyl stickers and traditional signals. They made bicycle railings and footrests and tilted garbage cans for cyclists as well. Taking their lessons from our Copenhagen master class, the director and his staff had begun experimenting and, as a result, pushing the boundaries of the status quo on Russian roads.

There were hurdles to overcome along the way. While political leadership was key, traffic engineers still needed convincing. In order to perform studies about density, connectivity, space syntax analyses, etc., Copenhagenize Design Company needed local data, but Russian cities do not have the same data-gathering culture as, for example, Scandinavian cities. In addition, a lot of the existing data was classified as secret—echoes of the Cold War persist. Nevertheless, the challenges were overcome. At the end of the day, the City of Almetyevsk turned out to be the most amazing client. We would receive emails from the street, where asphalt machines were rumbling along, to double-check about how to proceed—followed by photos the next day showing what had been done. That kind of client relationship is like nothing we've ever dreamed of. Every night since May we knew that when we woke up in the morning, more meters of fresh asphalt in the form of best-practice cycle track

would be cooling off in the dry Almetyevsk air—and the quality of life in the city had improved.

Mayor Ayrat Khayrullin hasn't restricted himself to bicycle infrastructure either. In 2015, together with Kazan design agency Evolution, he created Shamsinur—an urban park that has become an amazing destination for the citizens. In 2016, a massive lake park with a sandy beach opened in the city as well.

"There are only two problems in Russia: fools and roads." We just might have finally solved the latter.

By establishing themselves as first movers within Russia (and beyond), Almetyevsk has garnered attention from policy makers who may be weary of looking outside the Federation for best-practice. By seriously investing in a network of dedicated bicycle infrastructure, Almetyevsk has firmly positioned itself as the gold standard for a bicycle-friendly city in Russia, simply by learning from over 100 years of best-practice infrastructure in Denmark. Knowledge transfer at its finest. And it doesn't stop here. The City looks forward to building a total of more than 200 kilometers (124 miles) of infrastructure that will connect all neighborhoods and beyond.

There is a centuries-old saying in Russian that everyone knows: "There are only two problems in Russia: fools and roads." Copenhagenize Design Company and the City of Almetyevsk just might have finally solved the latter. It is a wild

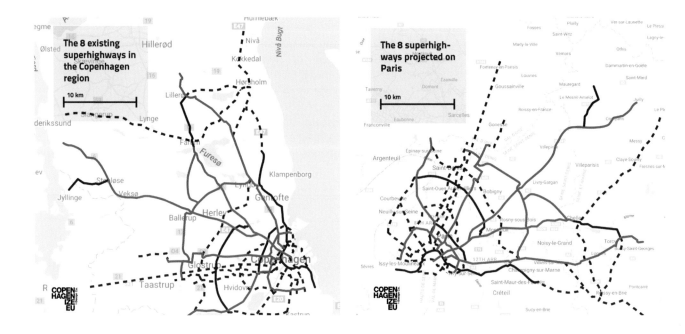

ride that continues into 2017 and beyond. Quite possibly the most exciting urban design project in the world at the moment. If you build it, they will come. In the most unlikely places. And in Almetyevsk, they are coming by bike.

THE BICYCLE DESERVES A SUPERHIGHWAY

Many cities are expanding on their growing urban network for bikes by developing infrastructure that leads farther out. The Copenhagen Capital Region is building a bicycle superhighway network that extends out into the suburbs. Five hundred kilometers (300 miles) are planned, and the first 200 kilometers (124 miles) are already financed.

Many of the municipalities are on board, but they still need inspiration, nudging, or even shoving. My team developed an idea catalogue featuring ideas that municipalities can choose from. Original ideas but also many that have been harvested from the global narrative. It took some convincing, but the Danish Road Directorate finally agreed to specialized signage, logos, and wayfinding as part of the continued development.

Strasbourg, for decades France's leading bicycle city, is another example. They are designing a comprehensive network to complement their existing infrastructure. Three ring roads and ten superhighways leading in and out of the

Opposite Left: *The existing bicycle superhighway routes in Greater Copenhagen (orange) and the proposed routes (black).*
Opposite Right: *The Greater Copenhagen network superimposed on a map of Paris.*
Top: *Wayfinding pictogram letting cyclists know they are on a bicycle superhighway route in Copenhagen. © James Thoem*

city. I designed the logo and visual identity for the City, choosing graphics that have more of a public-transport feel to them, instead of clichéd bike imagery. That's what a network for bicycles should feel like: public transport.

All in all, a good street is one where no one gets killed and users actually get healthy by using it.

I worked on three projects for the Irish National Transport Authority focused on improv-

ing conditions for cyclists in Dublin. One of them was exploring the possibility of a bicycle super-highway along the River Dodder. Some cities are jumping the gun and going straight for the sexy, headline-grabbing bicycle superhighway con-cept first but neglecting to build the hardwired infrastructure in the city center that should form the foundation for all expansion.

All in all, a good street is one where no one gets killed and users actually get healthy by using it. That should be the goal for every city. We know how to do it. It's all been invented. Excuses ring more and more hollow for every day that passes.

CHAPTER 16

PRIORITIZING CYCLING

>> **You take delight not in a city's seven or seventy wonders, but in the answer it gives to a question of yours.**

Italo Calvino

Yeah, so, we have the blueprints. We can design and build the macro infrastructure. It's right there for the taking. But before we drop the mic and exit stage left, there are a number of important elements to consider. By definition, cycle tracks do prioritize cycling, of course, but let's get into the details about what else we can and should be doing.

Setting goals is important, so let me put this one out there: if you look around your city and don't see urban cyclists yawning, you're probably doing something wrong. Nothing says "mainstream bicycle city" like citizens rolling along and yawning. I see it every day in Copenhagen. I see it in cities in the Netherlands and in cities that are taking the task seriously. I never yawn when cycling in cities that make me think too much, or worry, or even fear. For all the urban-planning talk and professional considerations, let's make yawning cyclists our goal.

In my perfect world, anyone working on bicycle infrastructure or planning should be handed a

If you don't see cyclists yawning in your city, you're doing something wrong.

20ᵗʰ CENTURY: HOW MANY CARS CAN WE MOVE DOWN THE STREET?

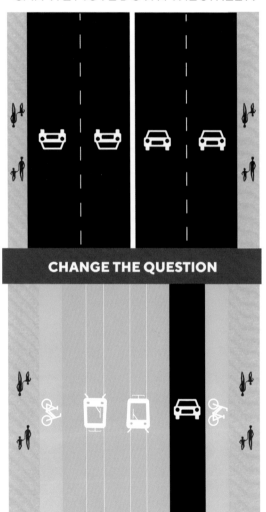

CHANGE THE QUESTION

21ˢᵗ CENTURY: HOW MANY PEOPLE CAN WE MOVE DOWN THE STREET?

It's time to change the question about transport in our cities. The model on the bottom has ten times the capacity for moving people down a street than the last-century model at the top.

bicycle and told to ride it in their city for a month. The first step in bicycle urbanism is to think bicycle first, and that would certainly force the issue in the minds of the inexperienced or skeptical. We have been thinking car first for decades, and that worked out pretty well for motorists and the engineers who cater to them. Now it's time to switch it up. It's time to change the question.

> At the end of the day, it seems that policymakers exercising top-down leadership are the catalysts for real change.

There are many questions we need to change now that we're looking at our cities differently for the first time in more than a century, but there is one question regarding transport that needs to be changed first. For decades we have only really asked one question of our traffic engineers: "How many cars can we fit down this street?" Having explored the traffic-engineering curriculum in a number of countries, I can't even see that any other questions have ever been posed. We know that a car lane, when flowing smoothly, can move a measly 1,300 vehicles per hour, at best. There's your answer right there. But the question itself is loaded. The wording of it seems simple enough, but really, the desired answer would explain how capacity can be increased, flow improved, congestion reduced. Sadly, there is no real answer to this.

If we could somehow calculate how much money has been spent, globally or even just nationally, on roads, highways, asphalt, studies, and research, etc., over, let's say, the past 75 years, I think we would collectively throw up in our mouths. While I would love to know that number, I probably don't need to know it. Add to that equation the lives lost or ruined in car crashes and the injuries suffered—about 1.2 million people a year around the world. Every year. You get my point.

So let's change the question. Let's ask instead how many *people* we can move down a street. Using all the transport options at our disposal. All that cool stuff we've invented. Trains, trams, buses, and bicycles. In the illustration, based on capacity standards, the design on the bottom has ten times more capacity for moving people down a street than does the design on the top—a design that we just inherited from a previous century without thinking about it. With urbanization accelerating rapidly everywhere, we must do the rational math and place our focus and investment on a combination of transport forms that can move a whole bunch of people through our cities. There is a new puzzle to solve. New answers to be sought. Let's reverse the pyramid, placing other useful professions first before getting down to the construction.

GET POLITICAL LEADERS ON BOARD

When I look around the world at the growing list of cities that are once again taking the bicycle seriously, I can identify one primary factor: political leadership. Advocates and activists continue to do their part, pushing from the bottom

upward. At the end of the day, though, it seems that policymakers exercising top-down leadership are the catalysts for real change. On the one hand, it is positive that an increasing number of politicians are getting on board. On the other hand, it could be depressing that progress seems to hit a bottleneck in city halls.

It is hardly a news flash that investment prioritizes cycling as transport. Politics is complex, and while some politicians are going all in, others, despite wanting to move forward, are limited by budget constraints or their political systems. My rational brain always finds it odd that the cost of building bicycle infrastructure and facilities is considered high. It is rare that the price is compared to the price of roads or highways for cars or public transport such as trams, metros, or trains. The misconception that a city has to build infrastructure for the people cycling now, as opposed to the 20–25 percent of the population that could be cycling, still reigns supreme. For the price of 5–10 kilometers of six-lane highway, my team and I could copenhagenize an entire city in five years. When you compare the cost, cycling always comes out on top. It is inexpensive and has an amazing cost/benefit return and ROI.

So let's change the question. Let's ask instead how many *people* we can move down a street. Using all the transport options at our disposal.

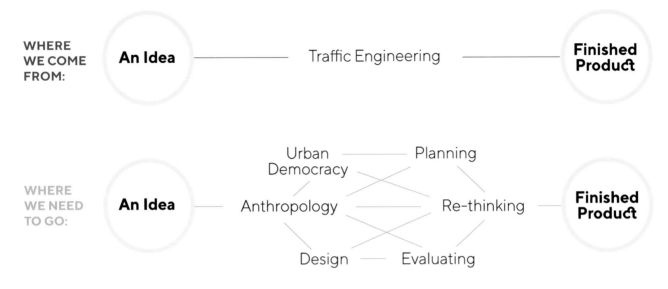

WHERE WE COME FROM: An Idea —— Traffic Engineering —— **Finished Product**

WHERE WE NEED TO GO: An Idea —— Urban Democracy — Planning / Anthropology — Re-thinking / Design — Evaluating —— **Finished Product**

Top: *Instead of using only traffic engineering to plan transport, we need to use a variety of schools of thought.*

Opposite: *A street in the heart of Copenhagen.*

There are many ways of measuring a city's commitment. Actual cash spent is one thing, but another great indicator is how much a city is spending per capita. For example, since 2004 the City of Copenhagen has invested €39.60 per person per year (about US$46) on improving the bicycle network. Feel free to have a grain of salt handy when politicians announce that they are spending x dollars over the next y years. Calculate how much the amount is per person before you get excited—or angry.

The politicians who are prioritizing cycling effectively may notice something curious happening to their careers. I've joked that nobody ever remembers politicians who build highways. Internationally, there are really only two. American president Dwight D. Eisenhower is one such politician. He championed the Interstate Highway System in the United States and was inspired by the other politician, Adolf Hitler, who built Germany's Reichsautobahn (later just *"Autobahn"*)

system. As political legacies go, this might not be a club you would wish to be a member of.

What we see now is that politicians, primarily in municipalities, are enjoying a personal brand boost when they take matters to the next level, whether it is urban cycling or modern city development. Klaus Bondam served as mayor of the Technical and Environmental Administration in the City of Copenhagen between 2005 and 2010. He came to power as one part of a dynamic duo, the other being Lord Mayor Ritt Bjerregaard. Social issues like housing were important to them, but Bondam saw early on that cycling for transport, such an integral part of life in Copenhagen, could be improved. He changed the question from *How do we maintain our cycling levels?* to *How can we take them to the next level?* It was a curious new question. There was a respectable status quo in place. Cycling was a primary transport form—indeed, the main one for the citizens of the city. What was this "next level" that Bondam sought? Perhaps he didn't have the answers himself, but he found the money to set the wheels in motion. He was instrumental in creating the first cykelpakke—"bicycle package"—which earmarked €4 million (US$4.7 million) for improving the development, quality, comfort, and connectivity of the Copenhagen bicycle network. While the City had a budget for maintaining the infrastructure and adding to it, this extra injection of funds was exciting and it kickstarted many of the projects I'll explore in the chapter, "Design and Innovation." Because of his work in his own city for his own fellow citizens, Bondam is invited to speak around the world about his work and legacy.

Elsewhere, Enrique Peñalosa had a massive impact on improving the quality of life in Bogotá,

Colombia, when he was mayor between 1998 and 2000. In a transport context, he developed better public transport and constructed bicycle infrastructure with an impressive vision and drive. His brother, Gil Peñalosa, was appointed commissioner of parks, and both brothers are still asked to speak about their work. Enrique was again elected mayor in 2016, and Gil heads the *8 80 Cities* NGO out of Toronto.

Janette Sadikh-Khan, as commissioner for New York's department of transportation between 2007 and 2013 under Mayor Bloomberg, worked tirelessly to form the foundations of a bicycle-friendly city in the Big Apple. Luc Ferrandez was elected mayor of the Plateau borough in Montreal in 2009 for the political party Projét

Montréal and promptly transferred his ideas for a better city onto the streets of his neighborhood. Keep an eye on the new kids on the international block. Morten Kabell occupied the same mayoral post in Copenhagen as Klaus Bondam for four years until 2017 and he placed a massive focus on further improving urban cycling in his policy. He left politics after the municipal election in November 2017 and will continue working with bicycle urbanism. Mayor Ayrat Khayrullin from Almetyevsk is fast becoming the darling of Russian urban development, thanks to his vision for his city.

Choosing to be a visionary urbanist politician seems to be a cool gig with long-term benefits.

Perhaps the simplest way to prioritize cycling is to show that you're doing it. Show that you're doing something. One great indicator is seeing your leading politicians, whether the mayor or key councilors, ride bikes in their city. The best thing would be to see them cycling to work and meetings every day or as often as possible. There is no credibility in failing to invest in bikes as transport, but there is also little credibility in not getting out there and showing how it can be done. To support the citizens cycling now and to encourage those who are hesitant. Luckily, I have met a number of mayors all over the world who realize that this is a part of the game and of their responsibility. It's a no-brainer for politicians in

cities in Denmark and the Netherlands, and it is of utmost importance in emerging bicycle cities. I remember seeing a news clip from Philadelphia in 2009 about the city opening a crosstown bike lane. The reporter was interviewing the mayor at the time, Michael Nutter, who was preparing to ride it, about the project. The reporter was comically astonished. To the camera he said, "And he's wearing a suit! In a light drizzle!" As though he were about to base-jump off a cliff naked and holding an umbrella. Mayor Nutter, cool as you like, just shrugged and hopped on his bike.

Another mayor who stands out in my mind is Betsy Price from Fort Worth, Texas. The state cycling NGO, Bike Texas, encouraged her to use the city's bike-share system, and she took them up on it. Even more, she instituted rolling meetings on the bike paths along the river. If you wanted face time with her about an issue—any issue—you were welcome to find yourself a bike and go for a ride with her.

Choosing to be a visionary urbanist politician seems to be a really cool gig with long-term benefits, even after you leave politics. It's as though we want to hear stories about people with convictions and passion who bucked the trend and got work done in cities. We never seem to tire of it and we're hungry for more. Prioritizing cycling, it turns out, is good for the city—and your personal brand.

CURB THE PARASITES

In prioritizing cycling, we have to identify where, how but also who. When I was working in Ferrara, Italy, I was studying a map with a colleague who works for the City. He was filling me in about the various bicycle-friendly initiatives in place. For example, Ferrara doesn't have a congestion charge for its historic center—it has a congestion ban. Nonresidents are not allowed to enter by car, and trucks transporting goods must pay a fee. Eight cameras are installed around the city to photograph number plates. If you're caught in the city without a permit, you are fined €100. Ah, simplicity. Ferrara enjoys a bicycle modal share of around 30 percent.

My colleague was telling me about a main route through the city—outside the historic center—and the plans to tackle the motorists who use it. He called them parasites and kept using that word to describe the motorists. Finally, I had to ask why. He looked at me quizzically and said that it was simply the word they use in Italian urban planning. *Parasites.*

What a great word. The host organism is, of course, the city off which they feed. The streets outside my apartment as I write this on a Tuesday evening are relatively free of parasites. The ones that plague Copenhagen aren't nocturnal. They desert their host organism on migratory patterns, scurrying back to their nests in the afternoons, only to return to feed upon their host in the morning. To continue their infestation, causing all manner of illnesses that the host organism is unable to defend itself against: traffic pollution with its toxic emissions and noise pollution, a lower perception of safety for pedestrians and cyclists, traffic crashes that kill and maim, reduced property prices, and so on.

Parasites. It's a brilliant way to describe the motorists who roll down these streets, contributing nothing to the liveability of my neighborhood, hardly making a dent in the economic well-being of the shops and paying their taxes in other municipalities. They don't stop at my hairdresser, local hardware store, café, or supermar-

ket. They do all that closer to their homes. They just rumble on past, spouting the residue of their combusted fossil fuels behind them to the funky tunes on their radio while they check Facebook on their smartphones. It's an epidemic.

Forests and green spaces are often referred to as "lungs" in countries and cities. Cyclists are the transportational lungs of a city. I certainly don't mean that my body is used to convert carbon dioxide, but nevertheless it's true that the 63 percent of my fellow citizens who choose to ride a bicycle each day are a rolling metaphor for photosynthesis—as are all cyclists in any city. Photosynthesis—from the Greek φώτο- (photo-), "light," and σύνθεσις (synthesis), "putting together" or "composition." Using the energy from sunlight to do their magic.

Forests and green spaces are often referred to as *"lungs"* in countries and cities. Cyclists are the transportational lungs of a city.

In Copenhagen, as in many cities, when we talk about reducing traffic we hear the same arguments from—and about—people who live in the surrounding municipalities: "But we have to go to work in the city!" As though that negates all calls for reducing pollution and improving traffic safety from those of us who live in the city. It's tough being a major metropolitan center surrounded by suburbs. Sure, people need to get

Various examples of accommodating cyclists during roadworks and maintenance.
Bottom Right: *The measuring car from the Danish Road Directorate.*

to work and home again. Providing competitive transport alternatives is the way forward. As it is now, my taxes go to providing asphalt for people who use it twice a day and who contribute little. That simply doesn't make sense to me. Put those parasites onto trams and bicycles and you turn the parasitic relationship into a mutualistic one, by increasing their opportunity to contribute to the local life in the neighborhoods they pass through.

MAKE A CLEAN SWEEP

Do you want to know what my favorite car in the whole world is? It's yellow and cute and drives on a cycle track. This is a rare example of a car you really want to see on any bicycle network. The happy logos on the sides read: "Cycle Track Measurer—we measure for your sake." A small armada of such cars are deployed on a regular basis by the National Road Directorate around the nation, equipped with all manner of equipment that measures the quality of the infrastructure. The smallest cars fit perfectly on the cycle tracks. Two lasers measure how even the asphalt is, supplemented with photos taken every 10 meters. In addition, the equipment can register roots or grates that are sticking up. The data is converted into a comfort rating.

It doesn't make much sense to build bicycle infrastructure and then not keep it clear. To take care of this beautiful thing. In addition to the cute measurement car, a number of pint-sized maintenance vehicles are used to keep cycle tracks clear of debris or snow. The bicycles must roll on.

It is standard practice in Copenhagen not to block the cycle tracks at any time, whether there are road-works or construction on buildings. It simply doesn't happen. Prioritizing cycling is important, but here an understanding of transport psychology also comes into play. Bicycles are flexible chameleons. If cyclists are faced with a barrier, they will find a way to flow around it, be it on the sidewalk or popping out into the car

lane. In the interest of both mobility and safety, cyclists are always accommodated.

I see examples on a daily basis. If a large maintenance truck needs to occupy a space on the street for a while, the roadway will be used or it will straddle the curb but still provide space for cyclists to pass. Signage is required, informing the various traffic modes about the obstruction. In cases of more permanent obstructions like construction work or renovation of a building with scaffolding on the façade, the contractor and/or City will think bicycle traffic into their solution. Containers used for construction material storage or as offices for the workers are placed on the street. Any cables or wiring must be raised up and over the cycle track or under bike-friendly plastic ramps if they are led across the cycle track. When motor vehicle traffic volume is high, solid separation solutions are put into place. Many of these temporary solutions are better bike infrastructure than the permanent ones in many other cities.

This is a rare example of a car you really want to see on any bicycle network.

Whether temporary like a façade renovation or semi-permanent like metro construction sites, cyclists are given the opportunity to maintain their pursuit of A2Bism. Data from the City is taken into consideration. If the volume of pedestrian traffic is low, pedestrians are instructed to cross and use the opposite side. On occasion there are situations where cyclists must share the sidewalk with pedestrians or the roadway with motor vehicles for short stretches. That's when the standard Cyclists on Sidewalk or Cyclists on Roadway signs are deployed. Roadworks do have a distinct advantage, though. They allow bicycle users to lean against them while waiting for red lights.

Keeping the cycling citizens rolling is paramount. Year round. Winter, as you might expect, is the most challenging season, but Copenhagen has your back. The work starts before you even know that snow is forecast. I live on a busy street, and on a dark winter evening, if I hear the cycle track sweepers buzzing back and forth, I check the weather forecast and, sure enough, snow is on the way. They salt preventively before the flakes fall. When it starts to snow, they're back at it. Sweeping from the front and salting from the back. In heavy snowstorms, I have seen them zip back and forth six or seven times even before the first plows hit the car lanes.

Left: Farmers from rural areas come into the city to assist with snow clearance during snowstorms.
Center: One of the City's many cycle-track sweepers keeping the path clear.
Right: One of the City of Almetyevsk's snow sweepers in action in the first snowfall after the city constructed bicycle infrastructure. Photo: City of Almetyevsk

I really find it impressive. The dedication to keeping the cycle tracks clear but also the logistics involved. The City employs its own armada of sweepers, but when the going gets tough and the snow really intensifies, there is an arrangement—many decades old—with farmers from the rural areas outside Copenhagen. They come into the city and assist the snow-clearance work. If there is snow falling, it's getting cleared. At all hours.

If you let me hop back to best-practice infrastructure for a moment, snow clearance and maintenance are made easy when you have a raised, dedicated space to work with. A painted lane is rather ineffective in keeping snow from being pushed, sprayed, or splashed from a car

lane. Oslo is a city that is currently working hard to build bicycle infrastructure and raise their bicycle modal share. In 2016, they increased their budget for snow removal and tried to approach the Copenhagen standard. The prevalence of painted lanes running along the wrong side of parked cars proved to be the challenge. (They are currently working on upgrading their design to align with best-practice.) The bike lanes were nicely swept from early in the morning, but then motorists left for work and the lanes were covered in snow again from the cars crossing them. Rookie mistake.

Other cities have geared up for winter maintenance as the realization dawns that cycling is

a year-round commuter option. That darling of bicycle urbanism, Almetyevsk, proudly sent us photos of one of their new cycle-track sweepers at work when the first snow fell after construction.

PAY ATTENTION TO PARKING

While bicycles need the momentum generated by our muscles in order to move, they are frightfully inanimate after we walk away from them. Whether you are planning to build or have already built a cohesive and connected network of safe and logical cycling routes along the major streets in your city, and you've committed to maintaining them year-round and shown your residents that you value the bicycle as a powerful transport tool, then you have to ask yourself: What next? Parking, of course. Where will all of your cycling citizens place their chariots by their workplaces or at their homes? Or along their local shopping street? Logical measures for bicycle-parking capacity need to be taken seriously to make cycling work for people in large numbers.

In Copenhagen, when looking at a metro transit hub, for example, the City is expected to build parking capacity for 10 percent of daily ridership. So, if 15,000 people use that metro station daily, the City will build 1,500 bicycle parking spaces at that station. They are usually at or near full capacity. Compare that to many other cities in the world where you are lucky to find one or two measly bike racks that hold maybe 20 bikes. And this isn't even the best example of quality bike parking. While there is a plan for bike parking in Copenhagen, it falls short of the massive and impressive parking facilities at Dutch train stations. Even Antwerp, Belgium, has huge interior facilities for safe, long-term, weather-protected bike parking for thousands at their central sta-

tion—more spots than at Copenhagen Central Station. Even Washington, DC, invested in an architecturally splendid building dedicated to bike parking at their main station. It is bizarre how the Danes lag so far behind the Japanese, the Dutch, and others when it comes to bike parking at stations. There is no decent excuse, but it's worth mentioning that, in the Netherlands and Japan, taking bikes on trains is discouraged, whereas in Denmark and certainly the Copenhagen Capital Region, it is the modus operandi.

Where will all of your cycling citizens place their chariots by their workplaces or at their homes? Logical measures for bicycle-parking capacity need to be taken seriously to make cycling work for people in large numbers.

Still, I try to push the issue when I can. I designed, with the help of my team, a proposal for 7,500 bike parking spots in the dead air above the train tracks immediately behind Central Station in Copenhagen. Simply to slap some visuals on it and move the debate forward.

When you look around your neighborhood and see bikes attached to everything—trees, poles, fences—clearly there is a deficiency in bike park-

Top: Secure bicycle parking in a dedicated facility
outside the main train station in Washington, DC.
Bottom left: Bicycle parking outside a train station in Japan.
Bottom right: Bicycle parking at Groningen Central Station.

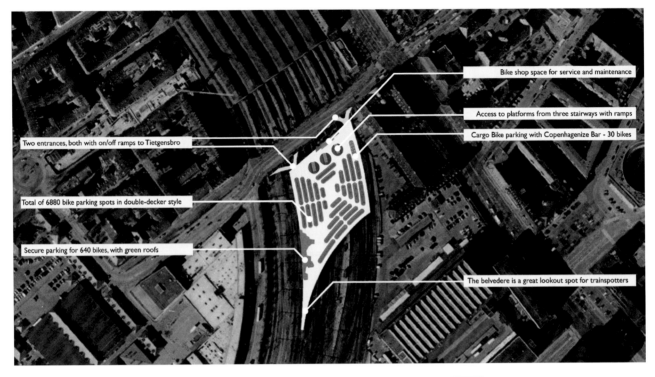

Bike shop space for service and maintenance

Access to platforms from three stairways with ramps

Cargo Bike parking with Copenhagenize Bar - 30 bikes

Two entrances, both with on/off ramps to Tietgensbro

Total of 6880 bike parking spots in double-decker style

Secure parking for 640 bikes, with green roofs

The belvedere is a great lookout spot for trainspotters

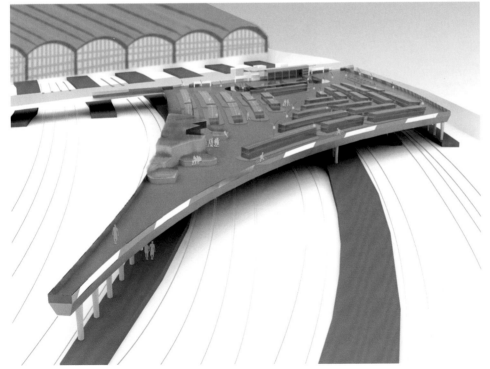

Copenhagenize Design Company's design for 7,500 bike parking spots behind Copenhagen Central Station. Design: the author and Steve Montebello

ing; the people are shouting at their local government to build good facilities. And it isn't even that space-intensive. One car parking space can hold more than 10 bikes with enough space to access them easily. If we only took out two car parking spaces for bike parking—or "bike corrals," as they are also called—on every city street, we would have over 20 new spots per street for bikes. Let's do the math. That's a start. Build it and they will use them.

MAKE INTERSECTIONS SAFER

If we want to build cities that are truly life-sized, that promote parents to get up in the morning and comfortably get their kids onto bikes and get about their days, we need to make sure that people are safe and feel safe. If you imagined walking to work, having to weave between cars and dodge trucks because you didn't have a curb-separated sidewalk, I'm not so sure you'd feel great about getting around on your own two feet. The same can be said about getting around on two wheels. And no place is more of a perceptual and real concern than an intersection. If we build good intersections we're more than halfway there. Every signalized intersection in Copenhagen has clear blue paint guiding bikes through this zone of potential conflict, with stop lines ahead of motorists to ensure they stay visible, and dedicated bicycle signals where they are needed. When we see a large number of cars wanting to make turns onto another major street, we protect these intersection corners with additional signals, concrete barriers, and painted crossings. When we force two-ton boxes of steel to slow down their turn and tighten their movements so that they can see and must wait for vulnerable cyclists and pedestrians, we make intersections safer for everyone. The Dutch have become internationally renowned for their protected intersections, and in the last few years this has begun to create a buzz in even North American cities. Salt Lake City has put one in, for example. People are talking about this once again in urban planning and transportation circles, but many don't realize that protected intersection plans have existed in an American context for decades.

Davis, California, had plotted out Dutch-style intersection designs in the seventies, but much of this work did not catch on nationwide.

Davis, California, had plotted out Dutch-style intersection designs in the seventies, but much of this work did not catch on nationwide due to a lack of political will and pushback from engineers. None of these designs are new. While many cities worldwide, at the mercy of short-sighted politics, bicker about testing out smart design incrementally, the cities of Northern Europe are trotting ahead with even more innovative solutions. Look at the Dutch city of Eindhoven, where they stopped scratching their heads about what to do about a large, chaotic roundabout and just elevated the cycle tracks above the roadway with their floating roundabout. It's a beautiful architectural marvel. If this doesn't entice bicycle use just for the sheer joy of getting to use this intersection on your commute, I don't know what does.

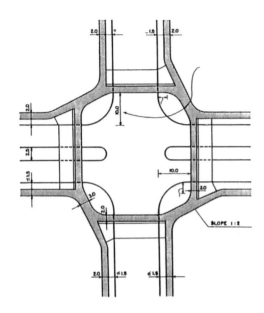

*Proposed protected intersection design from the early 1970s
in Davis, California based on Dutch designs.
Illustration: De Leuw, Cather & Company*

CONSIDER ELECTRIC BIKES CAREFULLY

There is one aspect of the bicycle boom that
engages my rational brain in a confusing dance.
Electric bicycles. If we are wishing to prioritize
cycling, do we include them? There has been a
thick cloud of hype surrounding e-bikes, most
of it stemming from the massive e-bike industry.
Where there is hype, there is often another side
to the issue that is being neglected, especially
when there is a huge follow-the-money back-
ground to it.

But in densely populated urban centers with bicycle traffic and pedestrians? Nah. Nobody wants more scooters.

E-bikes serve a purpose. Absolutely. They are
a great niche addition to the existing armada
of bicycles that have served citizens for 130-
odd years. They have the potential to increase
the mobility radius of cycling citizens—especially the elderly. All good. The first point of
interest to anyone working in urban mobility,
active transportation, or whatever they call it
where you're from should be the safety aspect.
The average speed of cycling citizens in Copenhagen and Amsterdam is around 15–16 km/h
(9–11 mph). Putting vehicles zipping along at
25 km/h (16 mph) or more into that equation
would not seem to be wise.

If you've been to Amsterdam, you know the
scourge of the scooters—fast-moving vehicles
that cause injury and death to the riders themselves and to others in their path. Adding more
scooters to the cycle tracks and bike lanes is
hardly beneficial to the development of better
traffic safety. Especially when these new electric scooters—which is what e-bikes are, essen-

tially—appear suddenly and silently, whereas at least the older gas-powered scooters make an infernal noise.

So e-bikes to increase the mobility radii for people "cycling" from greater distances are generally a good thing. But in densely populated urban centers with bicycle traffic and pedestrians? Nah. Unwise. Nobody wants more scooters. Unless they use the car lanes. Fortunately, there aren't many e-bikes in Amsterdam, or in Copenhagen, either. I only see a few here every week. You can spot them easily. They're the ones braking hard and abruptly at intersections. The City of Groningen has even taken the step to start building e-bike lanes parallel to existing bike lanes, in order to separate these two different forms of transport.

Apropos of Groningen, I spoke to a city planner there and he outed himself as an e-bike skeptic. He was concerned about the speed factor—about casting faster-moving vehicles into an existing flow. He mentioned that 11 percent of cyclist fatalities involved cyclists on e-bikes. They were going too fast and lost control, or motorists were surprised by a speed faster than that of the average cyclist. He was also concerned about the lack of interest in such matters. Twenty percent of e-bike crashes send the cyclist into intensive care. Only 6 percent of crashes on normal bikes end up in intensive. According to Statistics Netherlands, in 2016 629 people died in road accidents in the Netherlands, of whom 189 were cyclists and 28 were on e-bikes. Since 2014, at least 79 people have been killed in road accidents while using e-bikes, of whom 87 percent were over the age of 60. Similar stats are emerging in Denmark, where 10 percent of cyclist fatalities were on e-bikes. Going too fast, losing control, etc. A Swiss national study about e-bike safety cites "the most important findings: according to official statistics, e-bike accidents are more serious than bicycle accidents, and serious single-vehicle accidents are more frequent than serious collisions."

The point here is that there is clearly an issue. One that isn't mentioned in the Hype Cloud. The solution is a call for training courses for e-bikes. How long will that take? How many people will die or get seriously injured until it happens?

In October 2015, the head architect of the City of Copenhagen, Tina Saaby, stated that she had tried an e-bike for three months—and hated every moment. Motorized vehicles go against all the knowledge we have about how to create liveable cities. She referred to Jan Gehl's body of work about the necessity of slowing a city down to a human speed.

They are a great niche addition to the existing armada of bicycles that have served citizens for 130-odd years.

E-bikes inhabit a gray area. They are often labeled as "green." I would think that anything that needs to be hooked up to power plants should not be labeled as "green." Let alone the whole ethical issue of how we get lithium for the batteries. The e-bike industry is quick to slap the GREEN label on their products but, as always, a grain of salt is required.

Another point that is invisible in the Hype Cloud is the Chinese experience. They have had large numbers of e-bikes and e-scooters for over a decade. Almost every month, another Chinese city bans all forms of e-bikes, simply because of the alarming rise in accidents and deaths. We don't often fancy looking to China for inspiration, but in many cases we should. Beijing is now desperately trying to get its citizens back onto normal bikes instead of cars and electric-powered bicycles.

When you have a powerful industry looking to make some cash behind any product line, you have cause to be skeptical. Unlike the bicycle industry, the e-bike industry is pushing hard to make their products mainstream. A man named Hannes Neupert, founder and president of ExtraEnergy, an electric-vehicle lobbying organization based in Germany, has declared that "Electrification will kill the mechanical bicycle within a few years, like it has killed many other mechanical products. Bicycles . . . will remain as ~~histori~~cal items hanging on the wall." He isn't the first. Many e-bike websites feature similar claims. It's odd to see that there are clear battle lines drawn.

The average speed of cycling citizens in Copenhagen and Amsterdam is around 15–16 km/h. Putting vehicles zipping along at 25 km/h or more into that equation would not seem to be wise.

I first noticed e-bikes on my radar back in 2010. A rumor that pro bicycle racer Fabian Cancellara used an e-bike in a professional race went viral on the Internet. The rumor led to a frenzied flock of journalists around the world trying to find out if it was true. I remember saying at the office when the story hit that "within a week, a company name will emerge." Sure enough, journalists who were fed the rumor found out that, indeed, such a motor did exist but it was a couple of mil-

limeters too thick to fit into Cancellara's frame. He was then free from suspicion. The Austrian company that produced the motor was all over the press, however.

I have no idea if this company was behind it all. This is probably unlikely. I remain convinced, however, that it was one of the most brilliant guerrilla marketing campaigns I've ever seen, regardless of who started it. Since then, I've been wary of the massive e-bike industry—like any other massive industry—and their tactics.

Many people have an anecdote to tell me. About themselves or someone they know who now uses an e-bike. I know some stories myself. My main problem with anecdotes is that they are often presented as the complete story and the end of the conversation. Just because one person's dad or grandmother hopped onto an e-bike doesn't mean that everyone is doing so. But the neo-religious Hype Cloud fogs up the lens sometimes. Another grain of salt, please.

Sales are booming! This is the primary rallying cry heard by e-bike proponents and the industry. "Look at the sales numbers!" All sorts of stats are thrown around like confetti at a wedding. One million e-bikes sold in the Netherlands, where 28 percent of bike sales are e-bikes, they say. It is 9 percent in Denmark and rising. And so on.

When working in Bergen, Norway, I spoke with a guy working at a bike shop. He knew about my skepticism regarding the e-bike hype. He said they sold many of them but, he added with a wry smile, they never saw them again. They leave the shop, but never come back. "They're just standing unused in a garage somewhere," he added. Interesting. I started asking about e-bikes at other bike shops around Europe, and every time the answer was the same. They make a quick profit on the sale,

A grain of rational salt regarding electric bikes, please.

but many of the bikes are unused and therefore require no maintenance. Sales statistics are not usage statistics. The health benefits of cycling are well documented. We get it drilled into our heads here in Denmark that we need to exercise regularly and to get our pulse up. E-bikes reduce the health benefits of cycling by up to 70 percent. Then there is the issue of elitism. Expensive e-bikes are becoming the chariot of the privileged middle and upper class—quite possibly the laziest demographic in history. It is important that we keep a cool head regarding electric bicycles as we go forward.

*Cyclist using the handrail
at a red light in Copenhagen.*

CHAPTER 17

DESIGN & INNOVATION

Imagine having a city full of things that no other city had.

Bill Bryson

I will always boldly declare that everything we need in order to design a bicycle-friendly city has already been invented. All the macro-inventory is in place and ready to use. That doesn't mean we're done and dusted. We have an ocean of opportunity to tweak, adapt, or improve. Strangely, though, it was wasn't really happening. We were content with the status quo in mainstream bicycle cities and ignorant of the need for it in others—until 2006, when Klaus Bondam swung open the door to Copenhagen's mayoral office and started work. The bag of money he brought with him for cycling was more than a financial boost—it was a catalyst for innovation. It changed the question. City employees were handed an *espace libre* to think completely out of the box on a scale never before seen in Copenhagen or anywhere else since the 1930s. I was hired by the City on a variety of projects back then, and, man, I can tell you that the energy in the City's Bicycle Secretariat was electric. The greatest brainstorm in the history of urban cycling was underway. So what were the results? Let's run through the highlights.

THE GREEN WAVE

The old idea of coordinating light signals in order to improve traffic flow for cars has long been in place in a number of cities, but it was dusted off and recycled for bikes in 2006 and finally achieved its true potential. This adapted idea actually saw the light of day in 2004, but it was first implemented permanently in Copenhagen in connection with the massive redesign of Nørrebrogade, the main artery leading to the city center from the northwest. The street ceased to be a through-street for cars, and, instead, buses, bicycles, and pedestrians were placed at the top of the pyramid. There are many cross streets through the densely populated neighborhood, and cycling down the street was a constant stop-and-go.

> The Green Wave proved to be a massive success and was implemented on other main streets leading into the city.

The Green Wave is a direct treatment that respects the transport psychology of cyclists. The light signals were coordinated for 20 km/h (12 mph) along a 2.2-kilometer (1.2-mile) stretch. There were discussions about setting it at 25 km/h (16 mph) but that was deemed too fast. The average speed for cyclists in Copenhagen is just over 16 km/h (10 mph), so the slower cyclists can easily find four extra kilometers per hour (2.5 mph) in their legs. The most important thing was getting the speed demons to slow down. It was initially uncertain whether they would, but the simple principle of the Green Wave is that it appeals to everyone. Sacrificing some speed (and

the wrath of the majority) was an easy choice when you can sail comfortably into the city on a simple technological tailwind with having to stop or put your foot down. The wave is optimized toward the city in the mornings, and it reverses in the afternoon to get everyone home.

The Green Wave proved to be a massive success and was implemented on other main streets leading into the city. In the morning rush on Nørrebrogade, cyclists could save two and a half minutes on the route. The City counted an average of 70 percent fewer stops for cyclists on Østerbrogade, and travel times were reduced by 10 percent. The City couldn't measure any negative effect on bus traffic. The reports that I've read about it don't even mention cars—they're simply not relevant, apparently. When I cycle down one of the streets in the morning, I don't need to think about my speed. There are no on-board computers on the other bikes. The regular commuters on the route have it all figured out through daily routine. I just slip into the current and follow their flow. It is completely effortless.

The City has made some innovative adjustments in a few places. On a crosstown corridor with less bicycle traffic, Farimagsgade, they noticed that the Green Wave was less effective. One reason was that there is a long stretch between traffic lights, measuring about 500 meters (1640 feet). With the next traffic light so far ahead, the flow was interrupted. The slower cyclists would revert to their usual subconscious speed, and the faster cyclists would speed up to their personal comfort zone. Borrowing an idea from the City of Odense, the City of Copenhagen embedded small green LED lights in the asphalt on the left side of the cycle track for about 100 meters (328 feet) before the intersection. If you're cycling along and all the lights are green, you're good to go. You'll roll through the green light. If, however, when the lights start turning off one by one and you are not next to a green light, you will hit the red light. Cyclists speed up to catch

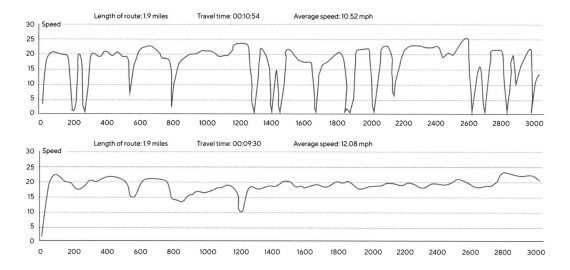

The flow of bicycle traffic improved greatly after the Green Wave was implemented on
Nørrebrogade. Above is before and below is after. Data: City of Copenhagen

the lights and make it through without having to stop. Simple and effective. Farther along, there are radar sensors that measure your cycling speed as a friendly reminder that you need 20 km/h (12 mph) to keep surfing the wave.

The City has been testing a kind of 2.0 version of the Green Wave, using sensors that read how many cyclists are approaching. If five or more people are traveling in an impromptu pack, their speed is measured and the light signal ahead will stay green just a bit longer in order to get them through. It's a simple democratic algorithm. Fewer than five won't cut it. There are, after all, other traffic users waiting to cross the intersection. Likewise, if there is a bus with 50–60 passengers in play, they will trump the five or more cyclists.

PRE-GREEN TRAFFIC SIGNALS

This solution has been around for a while but we now see it in more locations than ever. Dedicated traffic lights for bikes are a must in any city, and in Copenhagen, depending on site-specific needs, the bicycle traffic light will turn green before

the lights for motor vehicles. In many cases, it is just a couple of seconds, but in high-volume locations it can last several seconds. The concept is simple. All everyone is doing at the red light is waiting for it to change to green. With this subtle head start, cyclists are already in motion when the motorists take their feet off the brake. This reduces the risk of collision by making the cyclists visible, especially for right-turning vehicles, plus it provides a subliminal benefit—who doesn't like getting a head start?

COUNTDOWN CLOCKS

While the Green Wave is simple, effective, and easy to implement, there is another interesting solution in the City of Frederiksberg. On a similarly long urban stretch of one of the bicycle superhighways leading through the city towards Copenhagen city center, the simplest of boxes hangs humbly on a post about 100 meters (328 feet) from the intersection. It reads, "countdown to next light change." It's a DIY approach that pairs the individual cyclist with the countdown.

You can see the next light up ahead and whether it is red or green. The countdown helps you determine whether you'll make it or not. You might have time to speed up and make it. If you don't, you can slow down and coast gently towards the intersection without having to stop completely.

PULLED-BACK STOP LINES

In the same category are pulled-back stop lines, albeit only pulled back for cars. For many years, Copenhagen's primary solution at an intersection, especially one with right-turning lanes for cars, was to end the cycle track 20-odd meters (66 feet) before the intersection and have cyclists blend with cars. It is a kind of shared-space solu-tion—taking the traffic users out of their comfort zone and forcing them to be more aware. The solution improved safety, but not by the margins the city had hoped. Enter: the pulled-back stop line. The car stop line is moved five meters back from the pedestrian crossing, while cyclists are permitted to stop at their own line at the crossing. Right from the moment everyone stops, cyclists are visible to the waiting motorists farther back. Especially when coupled with pre-greens, safety at intersections has improved exponentially.

TRAFFIC SIGNS SHOWING TRAVEL TIMES

In 2017, Copenhagen installed digital signs in a few places—mostly along busy routes—that

Simple countdown clock in Frederiksberg allowing cyclists to adjust their speed as they approach the intersection—speeding up to make it through or coasting instead of stopping.

show your travel time to destinations ahead, like City Hall Square or Langebro (bridge), for example. Based on congestion during rush hour. These signs double as message boards outside of peak periods, featuring reminders, in Danish and English, to shoulder-check when passing or to signal when stopping. The one I pass each morning on Hans Christian Andersens Boulevard never changes. It's always telling us that Langebro is seven minutes by bike and eight by car. Not a massive win in the time challenge, but it's still good to be reminded of it on the world's first traffic signs of their kind.

DIGITAL BIKE COUNTERS

Digital bike counters, a common sight in a growing number of cities, combine data gathering with awareness about cycling as transport. They were designed in Denmark and first implemented in the city of Odense; in 2009, Copenhagen put in two of them, one on the busiest bicycle street in the world, the aforementioned Nørrebrogade, and another on City Hall Square. The counters were just an addition to the data sensor network, but now they were above ground. While the world looks to Copenhagen as a benchmark city for urban cycling, the citizens here just ride, rather unaware of all the fuss, simply going quickly and efficiently from A to B. The digital "totems," as they are also called, merely brought some civic pride above ground. I remember sitting on a bench next to the counter on Nørrebrogade a few months after the counter was installed, and two young men walked past. They stopped at the new counter and read the number of cyclists who had passed that point so far that year. "That's a lot of cyclists!" exclaimed one of them. The counters reaffirm that cyclists in a city are not alone, and they help convince skeptics with hard, live data.

BIKE BOXES

These dedicated spaces for bikes appear in many cities without bicycle infrastructure in order to give cyclists a head start off the light, but also to help them turn left in the absence of being able to do a safe, box turn—or the "Copenhagen Left," as it is also called. The City of Frederiksberg put in three of them at T-intersections to give cyclists priority turning left, but I think I was only one to bother using them. The City of Copenhagen, however, has put them in place on a number of intersections, and I couldn't figure out why. I asked Marie Kåstrup, head of the bicycle program at the City, what was up, and the answer is simply: *capacity*. The massive volume of cyclists on the cycle track causes mini-bottlenecks at every light. Not every stretch has the Green Wave. Cyclists wait for green in two rows —maybe two and a half when they squeeze more tightly together—on cycle tracks with the average width of 2.3 meters (7.5 feet). Traffic signals are shorter in the city than most other places, so in rush hour you can risk missing a green light. We know this from experience when cycling with delegations of politicians and planners. Bike boxes in these situations allow cyclists to spread out at the light and then "zipper together" on the far side of the intersection, like cars entering a highway from an on-ramp. It has improved capacity through light signals.

The greatest brainstorm in the history of urban cycling was underway.

RIGHT TURNS

As mentioned previously, most countries in the world do not permit a right turn on red, but now it is legal for cyclists to do so in France, Belgium, and a number of places in Denmark, among other locations. It's a simple fix that has clear benefits. One idea that has been around for a while is leading the cycle track to the right with-

Top Left: A car parking spot removed to plant a tree—and add some bike parking.
Top Right: The logo of Copenhagen's Green Wave.
Center: A car parking spot removed to make space for more citizens to park in a shopping district.
Bottom: Pulled-back stop lines for cars provide increased safety.

out forcing the cyclists to interact with motor vehicles. I have seen this in a number of German and Dutch cities, and busy intersections in Copenhagen now have this treatment.

CONVERSATION LANES

On the busiest stretch for cyclists in Copenhagen—and indeed the world—the City has piloted the idea of creating subtle lane dividers. Instead of calling it a fast lane off to the left, reverse psychology was applied. You and a companion can cycle together and have a chat in the "conversation" lane on the right, and anyone who wants to pass can do so on the left. There is no obvious paint, just small chevrons at intervals in a line.

PARKING INNOVATION

While reallocating street space for bicycle parking is nothing new, it has certainly accelerated. Parking zones, inspired by pilot projects in Amsterdam, have been tried out, as have so-called flexzones, especially around schools, where car parking is only permitted outside of school hours to provide a safer environment when parents and kids are arriving or departing and to free up space. One car parked outside a school takes up space that can instead accommodate many bikes and cargo bikes. The best solution is found in Japan, where it is simply illegal in many places to drop off your kid at daycare or school in a car . . . but hey.

On streets that have been traffic-calmed—or given a "road diet," as they say in the United States—space has been created for bike parking, which creates an increased visual narrowing. In my neighborhood, bike racks appeared when parking was removed for tree planting. Every bit of leftover space is considered. As ever, a pragmatic approach is used. Ten or so bikes can fit in the same space as one car. Numerous studies have shown that cyclists spend more money in shops than motorists do, so bike parking in business districts is a given.

One of the more interesting pilot projects was a big pink car that appeared on the street. Copenhagen is a cargo bike city. There are 40,000 cargo bikes in daily use, and 26 percent of all families with two or more children have one. The cargo bike is, simply, our SUV, whether it is a two-wheeler or a three-wheeler. Secure parking is an issue for these bikes. Many people will park them in their courtyard, but that limits the ease of use when you are embarking on the school run or doing errands. By reallocating one and half car-parking spots, four cargo bikes can be securely parked on the street. Here's how it worked. The shell is made of fiberglass and comprises four separate cabins, each with room for one cargo bike. Four solar-powered "headlights" turn on in the dark hours, and a light turns on inside when one of the doors is opened. Hooks and a net are mounted on the walls of each cabin for hanging up rain clothes and other gear.

The countdown helps you determine whether you'll make it or not.

There is an increased focus on cargo bike parking across the board. Outside of Fields shopping center, dedicated cargo bike parking spots are outside the main entrance. Supermarket chain Lidl has also made similar parking spots outside some of their stores, and the City of Copenhagen has a version in place in some neighborhoods.

The primary issue in the neighborhoods is on-street parking where people can leave their cargo bikes overnight. I took a serious look at this and designed the Copenhagenize Bar. Cyclehoop in London helped out with the prototyping. More than 90 percent of the cargo bikes in Copenhagen have a step-through frame, so the design allows for the solid bar to secure the bike with-

A cycle track providing a car-free right turn for cyclists. © Lorenz Siegel

out even touching it. The weak link is always the lock, so I limited the possibility for thieves to use bolt cutters by integrating the metal locking loop in the post. With a heavy-duty padlock, the bike is secure and bolt cutters can't fit in the space.

GARBAGE CANS, RAILINGS, AND FOOTRESTS

It was in 2008 that I suggested to the City that they design tilted garbage cans for use by passing cyclists. I had seen versions in the Netherlands on routes through parks, but I thought it would be a good idea along busy urban routes as well. The City liked the idea and took their standard garbage can and modified it. The tilted cans are now seen throughout the city.

Assuming that cyclists have garbage to throw out is one thing. I was curious, however, about whether or not there was an actual need, and I harbored a strange desire to know what kind of things cyclists threw away. Together with my team, we developed a mobile prototype version of the urban cyclist garbage can and set it up at a strategic location along the Lakes in Copenhagen. No bells or whistles, it just appeared one day on a stretch of cycle track with no pedestrian sidewalk. It didn't take long for Copenhageners to figure out its purpose. We tested it for 10 days and regularly checked the contents. Yes, all this was a bit strange.

To our surprise (although not really), we discovered that cyclists discarded the same things as everyone else. Coffee cups, apple cores, newspapers, cigarette packs, and the like. It was also interesting to see that, in most cases, their aim was true.

TOOL RACKS AND AIR PUMPS

One idea that was tried in a number of Danish cities was public repair stations featuring a rack

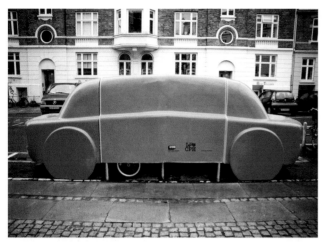

Top Left: *Dedicated cargo bike parking outside Fields shopping center. Concept and photo: Lasse Schelde*

Top Right: *Prototyped cargo bike parking with space for four family bikes.*

Mid Left: *Public repair station in Fredericia, Denmark.*

Mid Right: *Cyclist handle prototype by the author in place in Amsterdam.*

Bottom Left: *A manhole doubles as a ramp for bikes.*

Bottom Left: *Statoil gas station with a DIY bicycle service area.*

on to which you could place your bike and also the necessary tools to do basic repairs. This is an idea that has spread to many cities. It serves a practical function and also sends the message that the City is thinking about cycling. I have heard from many international colleagues that such repair stations suffer from a high level of vandalism. The bicycle offices in a couple of cities that I know of have cheap replacement tools at the ready and regularly check the stations to see if anything is missing. Many repair stations also feature air pumps, either with compressed air or with good old-fashioned foot pumps as an added service.

Sometimes great ideas are of a spontaneous, freestyle nature.

CORPORATE TAG-ALONGS

As the international focus on urban cycling was rising, I noticed that a number of unrelated companies decided to get on board. One of them was the Norwegian gas station chain Statoil. Bicycle service suddenly appeared outside of their gas stations in Copenhagen. Well designed and with bold signage, this initiative was clever. The company knew that providing a simple service for cyclists would increase the odds of them popping into the store to buy a drink or a snack. In a city with one bike shop for every thousand people and incredibly inexpensive prices for basic repairs, many Copenhageners choose that option, but I still see people using Statoil's service areas.

SPONTANEITY

Sometimes great ideas are of a spontaneous, freestyle nature. I can assure you that I am no expert on manholes, but I do know that they are traditionally flat and embedded in the street or sidewalk. On a new street by the new University of

Copenhagen campus, I spotted a manhole bucking the trend. It acts as a ramp up to the sidewalk to make it easier to roll up to the bike racks outside of the building. I did some digging into the plans for the street and found no reference to this design. I wanted to know if it was planned from the beginning or was an idea that appeared in the moment of construction. I really want to think that it was a large, burly construction foreman named Jens, or something just as quintessentially Danish, who said to his team, "Guys, let's make a ramp so they can get to the bike racks."

WEATHER SENSORS

In a climate as moody as an Ingmar Bergman film, every little bit of encouragement helps. Originally an idea prototyped and tested in the Netherlands, adverse weather sensors are appearing in Danish cities. Positioned at traffic lights, they are activated by rain, snow, or temperatures that fall below a certain threshold point. What happens then is that cyclists are prioritized with an increased number of light signals, helping them get home more quickly in the nasty weather. The Netherlands, like Denmark, is at the mercy of the whims of the North Sea.

INTERNATIONAL FOCUS

The Dutch have also been keen to get on board the Innovation Express and contribute to the growing catalog of ideas. For example, they are testing heated cycle tracks to keep the snow melted, inspired by the thermally heated bike lanes and sidewalks in Reykjavik. The goal of black asphalt in the winter is universal for all of us in countries with four-season cycling. Add to that, they are testing cycle tracks built with solar panels that generate electricity for a variety of purposes, and underpasses that allow cyclists, with an app, to choose what color lighting they prefer as they pass through.

The City of Amsterdam expressed an interest in innovative designs focused on urban cycling.

Top left: *Pre-green bike traffic light gives cyclists a headstart and keeps them safe. © Lorenz Siegel*

Top right: *Bike boxes in Copenhagen are for maximizing the number of cyclists through a light cycle, not for turning left.*

Bottom left: *Copenhagenize Design Company concept for used-activated light signal. Visualization: Chris Moir*

Bottom right: *Concept for photo frame for tourists in Amsterdam. Design: Kan Chen*

Top: A bicycle counter gathering valuable
data and boosting civic pride.
Bottom: The Copenhagenize Current design
for cycle tracks combined with stormwater runoff.
Design and concept: The author & Steve Montebello

Copenhagenize Design Company designed a series of ideas for them to consider. In the Netherlands, it is common practice at the stop line for bikes to have posts with a button to press in order to activate the light signal. We suggested that they make it a bit more fun, since every cyclist who stops there inadvertently uses the post for support. Why not add a joystick button that doubles as a handle to hold onto? We also thought that it might be more interesting to have these buttons located on the stretch leading to the intersection. Add a little bit of gamification and understanding of transport psychology, and have the cyclists activate the button with a smack so that they can avoid having to stop up ahead.

It's really important not to lose focus of the beauty of simplicity.

Amsterdam struggles with incredibly high levels of tourism, and dodging confused tourists while you're heading home is a game that isn't always fun. As in Copenhagen, the tourists in Amsterdam love taking photos of the cycling masses. In order to keep them in one place, we developed a photo frame to stand on the sidewalk. On the side facing cyclists, it reads in Dutch: "Pose for the tourists. Thank God they're standing still." On the flip side is some friendly English-language branding of the city as a bicycle-friendly capital.

Maintaining a constant flow for cyclists is a goal, but it is unlikely that this will be possible on every street. There will be red lights to stop at. If a location allows for it, why not design a wind and/or rain shelter, combined with a footrest and railing, for those immobile moments?

BIKE-SHARE

There was bike-share activism in the Netherlands in the 1960s, but really, it all started as an initiative by Mayor Michel Crépeau in La Rochelle, France, in the mid-seventies. The City bought some bikes, painted them yellow, and made them available for people to borrow. I used them in La Rochelle while on holiday there back in the nineties. In 1995, Copenhagen was the first large city to put free bikes on the streets with the Bycyklen program, which was largely a touristy gimmick in connection with Copenhagen as Cultural Capital of Europe in 1996. The bikes were made of parts that were not interchangeable with normal bikes. You put in a coin, as with a shopping cart, and got your coin back when you docked the bike. What happened after that was quite extraordinary. There are now well over 1,000 cities around the world with bike-share systems in place. It has been a veritable game-changer in cities—a strong visual message that bikes are back and are being taken seriously but are also providing vital first- and last-mile transport. Bike-share programs should be normal inventory in a city, along with infrastructure on which to ride the bikes safely.

SPONGE CITIES

There are challenges far greater than reestablishing the bicycle as transport in our cities. Climate change is impacting every corner of the planet. Copenhagen and Denmark are experiencing rainfall levels like we have never seen before, levels that our sewer system is not designed for. Cloudbursts, once rare, are now a regular feature, as is the flooding of our neighborhoods that comes with them. The hot new phrase is "sponge cities," which focuses on the many innovative ways that our urban centers are tackling flood water. Not least in Copenhagen, there is a massive focus on redesigning streets, boulevards, and parks to act as temporary reservoirs in the event of torrential rain. If we put our minds to it, we can think about ways to integrate bicycle urbanism solutions into climate-change-mitigation projects. After seeing the street-level

shops in my building completely flooded and destroyed during one epic cloudburst, I started thinking about how to prevent the water from flowing from the streets to the buildings. My team and I developed what we call the Copenhagenize Current. Virtually every main street in the city has parallel cycle tracks on either side, so with a simple cut-and-cover solution we thought we could create floodwater channels underneath the infrastructure. Prefab slabs of concrete can be placed on top and create an incredibly smooth and comfortable surface to cycle on, all while protecting our homes and buildings from flooding.

KEEP IT SIMPLE

It's really important not to lose focus of the beauty of simplicity—especially in this age of overcomplication. Some of our greatest inspiration is right there in front of us. All the innovation that is coming out of Copenhagen, and beyond, is a gentle manipulation of existing ideas. Many creative thinkers are at work. Nevertheless, it is vital that we seek inspiration from the greatest minds of our age, and indeed, any age. People like Lulu-Sophia. My daughter, she of life-sized-city fame, started her career as the world's youngest urbanist at the age of three and a half. She was in our cargo bike and we were heading to the hardware store on a Saturday afternoon. At a red light, she looked over and saw a motorcycle with a rider and a passenger. She was absolutely amazed. She had never, in her young life, considered the possibility of two people on one motorbike. She pointed and exclaimed, "Look, Daddy! Two people on one motorbike!" It sounded like a massive highlight in her life. I agreed with her that it was cool and that riding a motorbike with a friend must be nice. I also pointed out that we were doing the same thing. We were cycling together, talking and having a nice time. She understood the comparison but remained amazed.

Off we went on our journey. At another red light, farther along, I realized that she had been intensely observing her urban theater, looking for examples of two people transporting themselves together, be it other cargo bikes or pedestrians. She suddenly declared to me, "Daddy, cars are silly." I asked her why. "Because I can't see the people in them." She nailed it right then and there. The social exclusion of automobile society and the anonymity of cars as transport. This little human was seeking out human forms in cars, but she could not see them.

Since then, she has provided me with countless nuggets of wisdom that I've dutifully recorded. For example, one time, while cycling through the woods north of Copenhagen, we got lost. We agreed on a direction, and Lulu-Sophia said that as soon as we hear cars we'll know that we're on the right track to the bike path along the motorway.

Inspired by the observations of this kid, I decided to see what else could be harvested from the minds of children. When my son, Felix, was in third grade, his teacher let me come into the classroom with a project for the class. I briefly explained the concept of urban planning but did not go into any detail, not wanting to influence them. Right outside their school, there is a roundabout that they all use at least twice a day. It has decent bicycle infrastructure and crosswalks for pedestrians, but I don't think it's the best we can do. I asked the kids to study it and propose solutions for making it better for cyclists and pedestrians, and I also asked them to think about how to get motorists to choose other transport forms.

The teacher and I were amazed at their enthusiasm as they divided up into teams and headed out for on-site visits where they took notes, mostly in the form of drawings, and then headed back into the classroom to discuss what they'd observed. They spent a week on the project in between their regular classes. They even designed and built a model of the roundabout out of milk cartons. I then returned to the class to hear about their results. One kid started the

ball rolling by saying that we should just make all cars really ugly so that nobody wanted to buy them. Nobody wants ugly things. That makes sense. Then came their list of potential treatments for the roundabout:

» Set a speed limit of 15 km/h (9 mph) for cars.
» Separate the cycle tracks from the roadway with fences.
» Create a one-way street network for cars.
» Install speed bumps for cars.
» Put in traffic lights instead of a roundabout.
» Cover all the streets, cycle tracks, and sidewalks in the entire city with glass roofs so that they never, ever would get wet in the rain or snow again.

Do you know what? The streets would be beautiful. They would work.

I was amazed at their suggested speed limit and how they decided upon 15 kilometers per hour. They had not been allowed to use Google, so it was an idea from their brains. None of them had a clear answer other than "it just feels slow." They had no way of knowing that the average speed of cycling in Copenhagen is 16 km/h (10 mph), but somehow they figured out that cycling next to cars going at that speed would be pleasant. They're right. All the other ideas make it clear that children are our most rational and logical citizens. They all walk and cycle in their neighborhood, and, unlike my kids, most of their parents own cars. Still, they were in complete agreement that in order to improve conditions at this location, automobiles needed to be addressed. There were no ideas about sending cyclists on an inconvenient detour away from the main street or in any other way limiting cycling. Their last idea is one that I'm sure we can all get behind: staying dry, regardless of how impractical it would be. We have, nevertheless, already been designing "glass roofs" in the form of the Green Wave, rain sensors, and the like.

Working with these children was a massive inspiration, but it also bummed me out in a way to realize that this inherent logic is repressed as we grow into adults. If we could somehow retain this logic and rationality—even just 30 percent of it—we would be able to maintain an important level of creativity and freethinking.

Another source of inspiration is this guy, William of Ockham. He might well have been one of history's greatest bicycle and pedestrian planners, but he will never know that, as he died in 1347. The mathematical principle of "Occam's razor" is attributed to him. In essence, William would have us believe that all things being equal, the simplest solution tends to be the best one. We should, at every opportunity, in all aspects of life, and certainly in urban planning, look at the ideas on the table and choose the simplest one.

All of this begs the question: what would it look like if our main consultants were five-year-olds, third-graders, teams of young design students, and a thirteenth-century religious dude? Seriously. Imagine if this group were hired to redesign a street, a park, or an intersection in your city. While we're at it, imagine how much money we would save. One of them is dead, and all the kids could be bought off with ice cream, so we would only have to pay the design students. But do you know what? The streets would be beautiful. They would work. Most importantly, they would be safer than at any point in the last 100 years. Simple, really.

Top: Lulu-Sophia in a cargo bike.
Center: Kids from Felix's class on a site visit to the roundabout.
Bottom: The class's model of their proposed changes to the intersection.

CHAPTER 18

CARGO BIKE LOGISTICS

Any intelligent fool can make things bigger, more complex, and more violent. It takes a touch of genius—and a lot of courage— to move in the opposite direction.

Albert Einstein

Bicycles, like so many finely tuned string and wind instruments, are rewriting the score in our cities. What we see happening now is that bicycles are finally getting some serious accompaniment from a solid and dependable bass section. Cargo bikes.

At this point, you probably know what I'm going to say. By now, you should be seeing a clear pattern in this book. Cargo bikes are nothing new. They've been around since the very beginning of the bicycle in our cities. Like the bicycle itself,

the cargo bike's remarkable history has been ignored. I'm not pulling any punches when I say that the cargo bike was a primary transport form in cities everywhere. I have scoured archives and seen photos of cargo bikes in so many different cities—in Russia, Australia, France, Mexico, Brazil, the United States, and so on. It was a tireless workhorse for urban transport. In a few cities, the cargo bike survived the onslaught of automobile culture. Interestingly, in Central and South America it continues to serve its purpose for deliveries

A DHL trike competing in a svajerløb
cargo bike race in Barcelona in 2017.

from markets and shops. To this day, over 11,000 deliveries are made each day in the Copacabana neighborhood of Rio de Janeiro on an armada of two- and three-wheeled cargo bikes.

In the first half of the twentieth century, a city like Copenhagen was an extraordinary theater, with cargo bikes pulling the bulk of the weight in goods deliveries. My own father, as a young teenager, was a delivery boy in Copenhagen during the Second World War, riding both delivery bikes—called "Short Johns" in Denmark—as well as the classic "Long Johns." He worked for a greengrocer and rose early each morning to cycle to the market, collect the shop's produce for the day, and deliver it to customers around the center of the city.

Thanks to Copenhageners' collective ingenuity, an incredible number of rolling solutions saw the light of day. You can virtually eat and drink your way through the center of the city.

In another book, *Cargo Bike Nation,* I have presented over 700 photographs that highlight the amazing versatility of cargo bikes in cities. Here in Copenhagen, every time I think I've seen it all, one of my fellow citizens impresses me anew with what they can transport on two or three wheels. As much as I would love to spend an enormous amount of time on the history of urban cargo bikes, I think it best to focus on where we are right now. Between 2011 and 2014, Copenhagenize Design Company was a partner

in the European Union project Cyclelogistics. The declared goal of the project was to raise awareness about the usefulness of cargo bikes in European cities on different levels: private citizens and their families; small goods delivery; and even heavy logistics. It is especially the first two categories that are enjoying exponential growth not only in Europe but around the world.

In Greater Copenhagen, I have calculated that there are over 40,000 cargo bikes in daily use. The primary function is family transport, whether for groceries or moving kids around. As a general rule, when one partner becomes pregnant the other partner starts collecting cargo bike brochures. The cargo bike is a replacement for a car or at least for the family's second car. While the design of most two-wheeled and three-wheeled cargo bikes is over 100 years old, the revival in Copenhagen started in the mid 1980s when a bike designer in the free town of Christiania, Lars Engstrøm, made the first model in the modern era to replace the trailer he and his wife had been using. One of their neighbors was thrilled with the design and functionality, and asked him to make her one as well. The rest is history.

What followed was a veritable cargo bike boom, with many other designers, producing their own models. In 2017, 6 percent of all bicycles in Copenhagen are cargo bikes. In Amsterdam the number is 2 percent, which is still a lot of cargo bikes fulfilling the same role as they do in Copenhagen—transporting kids, moving stuff around, shopping, and even going on dates.

Children are introduced to cargo bikes from a very young age at daycare, and at school there is an amazing selection of cargo bikes and trailers that are pulled out at recess for the kids to use. Many of them are designed to be social and all of them are designed to help the children be active. Small cargo bikes for moving stuff but also for taking your friends for a ride. I don't know for sure, but I have seen at least 30 different models at my kids' schools.

In 2007, the city of Copenhagen loosened and streamlined the rules for selling goods on the streets. This measure was not directly bike-related, but the citizens of Copenhagen, looking at opportunities for selling things, realized that the most efficient way to sell anything on the streets was a cargo bike. Thanks to Copenhageners' collective ingenuity, an incredible number of rolling solutions saw the light of day. You can virtually eat and drink your way through the center of the city by purchasing things from cargo bikes, whether it's coffee, crepes, soup, corn on the cob, or cold water, to name a few. You can also grab a newspaper or buy souvenirs. Many services roll around the city on cargo bikes, as do many plumbers and electricians. The City of Copenhagen even offers mobile municipal services where you can stop and renew your passport or social security card from a cargo bike.

For more than 20 years, municipal organizations have offered citizens free cargo bikes to borrow in the event that they are moving apartments or need to transport things from a hardware store, for example. Many small companies have realized that using cargo bikes instead of motor vehicles is much easier and far less expensive. Nevertheless, there is an enormous growth potential for small-goods delivery in Copenhagen and every city on the planet. We are still far from the levels of cargo bike transport that we enjoyed in the 1920s and 1930s. In the Cyclelogistics project, we conducted research into this potential. It turns out that a whopping 51 percent of all goods transported in a European city be be moved by bicycle or cargo bike. That means we can free up a great deal of space by eliminating many of the trucks on our streets.

The fleet of cargo bikes outside one of the many delivery companies in Copenhagen in the 1930s. © Museum of Copenhagen's Photo Archive

Top: A Copenhagen family heading to the beach on two cargo bikes.
Second: One of the many vendors using cargo bikes to sell their wares. In this case, coffee.
Third: Copenhagenize Design Company's conceptualization of depots on the harbor to connect barges with cargo bikes for last-mile delivery. Design and concept: the author and Adina Visan
Bottom: The percentage of goods in a city that can be moved by bike or cargo bike. Data: Cyclelogistics.eu

The global logistics company DHL was a corporate first mover in realizing the potential of cargo bikes for last-mile delivery. They simply did the math. In their first phase, they saved €530,000 (US$622,000) by replacing vans with two-wheeled cargo bikes—big savings in a competitive market. They also improved their delivery times, which isn't bad either when you are competing for customers. What happened next was as amazing as it was obvious. DHL's competitors looked over the shoulder to see what they were doing and why, and it didn't take long before companies like UPS and FedEx started exploring the possibility of replacing trucks and vans with bikes. This market is developing so fast that it's hard to keep track of how many cities now feature global logistics companies using cargo bikes as vehicles for transporting packages. In 2017, there were at least 50 such cities in Europe. Add to that the many smaller companies that have been doing it for years in cities like Paris and Barcelona. For example, a company called Vanapedal has been operating a micro–distribution center in the heart of Barcelona where trucks drop off packages in the morning and cargo bikes deliver them in the neighborhoods. In 2017, I spoke at the European Cyclelogistics conference in Vienna and was amazed to see so many new faces and companies present. Cargo bike logistics is an exciting area to watch develop.

In so many ways, it's a no-brainer, what with urbanization and the growing number of small

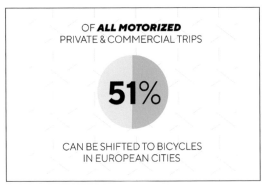

OF **ALL MOTORIZED**
PRIVATE & COMMERCIAL TRIPS

51%

CAN BE SHIFTED TO BICYCLES
IN EUROPEAN CITIES

packages that need to be delivered because of the rise of online sales. In the Netherlands, half of all shoes are bought online. That's a lot of shoe boxes that need to get to a home or office. Our urban short-term memory loss applies here as well. In so many cities, we have long neglected the original transport corridors—the rivers, lakes, and harbors of our cities. While the Dutch are clever at using their small canals for transporting all manner of things, as well as solutions like electric barges for garbage collection, many of our waterways are now deserted. Napoleon built splendid canals leading into Paris from 100 kilometers (62 miles) away to provide the city with fresh water, yes, but also for the transport of food into the city. Now there is little traffic on the canals that flow past congested highways and streets.

As ever, in so many aspects of urban life we simply need to go back to the future, not least cargo bikes for transport.

There is a great deal of focus, especially in Europe, on projects that investigate using alternative forms of transport for goods delivery. Such projects often combine smaller vehicles, including cargo bikes, with distribution centers, ships, and barges. The resourcefulness of the logistics industry is helping to accelerate our efforts. The harbor in Copenhagen was decommercialized 20 years ago and the remaining shipping traffic was moved outside the city center after bustling with life for many centuries. While Copenhageners are gradually figuring out ways to enjoy this vast expanse of water, there is still ample opportunity to incorporate the harbor into our transport system.

The city of Copenhagen has toyed with the idea of a distribution center south of the city. The plans I have seen do not place it near the water, which is regrettable. I developed an idea for combining barges, preferably electric, with cargo bikes for last-mile delivery. Let's face it—trucking companies don't find it cost-efficient to drive in cities, which is the last thing the drivers want to do, and those of us who live in cities wish the trucks were gone. Imagine barges sailing quietly up and down the harbor or rivers and dropping off packages at specially designed depots on the waterfront. Designed, of course, for cargo bikes to roll gracefully in, gather packages, and then head out for last-mile delivery.

As ever, in so many aspects of urban life we simply need to go back to the future, not least cargo bikes for transport. It is a joy for me to see how cargo bikes are truly booming in so many cities in North America and Europe. This is the muscle we need to keep the momentum going.

Street scene in Amsterdam.

CHAPTER 19

CURATING TRANSFERABLE IDEAS

> **Set realistic goals, keep re-evaluating, and be consistent.**
>
> Venus Williams

Two of the major themes in this book are "everything has been invented" and "copy/paste" in order to redesign our cities for the better. However, it might be relevant to highlight an important disclaimer and to squeeze in some thoughts about what is transferable. There are some unique aspects to a cycling life in Copenhagen and Denmark that may not be applicable to other cities or countries.

THE "WHEELBENDERS"

Virtually every bicycle in Copenhagen is equipped with a kickstand and, I've observed, this is the case in many cities in Europe. The idea of parking zones without any physical bike rack, therefore, may not fly elsewhere. Personally, I can't imagine cycling in the city without a kickstand, and the very idea makes me flinch. Many people who visit Copenhagen wander past the filled bike

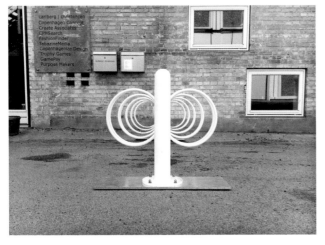

Left: *Standard Danish bike rack.*

Right: *Classic wheel lock on the back wheel.*

racks and are convinced that none of the bikes are locked. But they are—in fact, the vast majority of Danish bicycles are locked with locks that secure the back wheel. While the design of the wheel lock, also called an O lock, is timeless, nevertheless you don't often see them outside of cycling cities in Denmark, the Netherlands, China, and Japan. Due in part to the nature of the democratic perception of bicycles in Denmark, wheel locks are the default. A parking zone is an easy solution when most bikes are mounted with them. Easily 90 percent of the bike racks in Denmark for the past many decades have been the simple design that secures the front wheel and prevents the bicycle from falling over. Your average hard-core bike geek hates such a design and can probably rant for hours about these so-called *wheel benders*. The 99% in Denmark don't seem to mind, though, and I have used them daily for almost 25 years without a hitch. Pretty much everywhere else, apart from Japan, cyclists are used to locking their bike to a physical object with a heavy theft-deterrent chain or a U lock, and fair enough. While I wish that the Danish conditions could be transferred everywhere else, this isn't realistic in the short term. Therefore, there needs to be a concerted effort in cities to provide convenient bike racks with intuitive ease of use.

One of my great urban pleasures is cycling in Dutch cities. The absolute saturation of bicycles is one of the great transportation ballets in the world and it is always a wild, enjoyable ride.

INSURANCE

As an extension of the Danish bike lock culture, the Danish bike insurance system is unique in the world. It has been streamlined over the years to be advantageous to both the user and the insurance companies. As a rule, your bike is automatically part of your home insurance up to a certain amount that includes the bikes you use in your daily life. If you have a fancy sports bike or a cargo bike, you will usually have to buy a supplement. If you buy a new bike in Denmark, it must be equipped with a wheel lock. This is due to lobbying done by the insurance industry, which wanted to sleep a bit easier at night knowing that every bike has a lock. Bicycles in Denmark have had frame numbers etched into the metal since the 1920s, and when you buy a new bike it is registered to you in the system. If my bike gets stolen, the process is simple. I fill out a report on the police website, typing in my social security number and the frame number of the bike as well as details about my insurance company. I copy/paste the case number in the insurance company website when I am making my claim. A couple of days later I receive whatever money I have coming to me and I hurry out to get a new bike—because my daily life requires it.

When the police and the City regularly clean up the bike racks and remove the abandoned bikes, the frame numbers indicate which insurance company technically owns them. This is an extraordinary system that streamlines the process between having a bike stolen and getting a new one. It is brilliant for the individual citizen, but it does pose some difficult challenges and ethical questions. Nearly 400,000 bikes are scrapped every year in Denmark, and Danes buy 500,000 new ones, which means that every decade there are one million extra bikes in the country. It is ironic that the insurance industry has insisted on equipping all new bikes with wheel locks, and yet they are completely indif-

ferent to dealing with the issue of scrapping bikes that could otherwise be put back into circulation either in Denmark or in countries that could use them. Nor do they make any further substantive effort to tackle the issue of bike theft. Indeed, stolen bikes mean more people buying home insurance, especially young people. The police aren't very helpful either, and even if you're standing there having apprehended a bike thief, they are unlikely to send out officers if you call them. It's a big confusing mix of positive and negative and something quite unique in the Danish context.

INFRASTRUCTURE DESIGN

When we talk about the design of bicycle infrastructure, there is sometimes the issue of what is permitted in municipal, regional, or national standards. I'm not going to address those because, with effective lobby work, standards can be changed. As you have probably sensed from my focus on best-practice design, I am convinced that copy/pasting the best solutions into any city in the world is the preferable solution. The experiences of cities like Ljubljana, Slovenia, and Almetyevsk, Russia, are key to understanding that choosing the right designs gets the best results. Copenhagenize Design Company in particular and other organizations in general host hundreds of international delegation participants from around the world every year—whether politicians, planners, engineers, or advocates. The ones who cross an ocean seem to follow a pattern that involves getting the most out of their trip. They will often visit the Netherlands first and then come to Copenhagen afterwards.

I have been asking the same couple of questions for years. First, we discuss their experiences in Amsterdam or one of the other cities they visited, and they invariably talk with great enthusiasm about the wild experience they had and all the things they saw. Then I ask, "If you squinted your eyes in Amsterdam or Utrecht, could you envision your own city?" The answer is always a resounding "No way!" After they have been on one of our bicycle urbanism bike tours or have spent some time in Copenhagen, I ask, "If you squint your eyes here, can you envision your own city?" The answer is just as resounding: "Oh, yes, absolutely!" If, on their trip to the Netherlands, they visited Rotterdam, they are also more likely to see direct inspiration for whatever city they are from.

I'm just convinced that cities are best served by adopting designs that are appropriate and feasible for their own city. We're not redesigning our cities for the next couple of months—we're planning transport for the next century.

While the city center of Copenhagen is well over a thousand years old, with all the winding and confusing streets that that entails, the rest of the city, where the great majority of our citizens live, is a twentieth-century invention. The streets radiating out from the ancient city center are wide and used to accommodate a fine network of trams. At street level, between the façades of

the buildings, it is easy to see how things would work in other cities.

One of my great urban pleasures is cycling in Dutch cities. The absolute saturation of bicycles creates one of the great transportation ballets in the world and it is always a wild, enjoyable ride. The bicycle is clearly king in a city like Amsterdam, while in Copenhagen, I dare say, it remains the crown princess waiting in the wings for her shot at the throne. The daily parasite invasion continues to delay the coronation. While cycling levels are virtually identical in Amsterdam and Copenhagen, it feels as though bicycles are absolutely everywhere in the former. Coming at you from every direction at all hours of the day. It is important to remember that the primary reason for this difference between the two cities is not a question of culture but rather of layout. There is only one Amsterdam and it is quite unlikely that there will ever be another—unless, of course, some crazy Gulf state decides to build one from scratch in the desert outside of Dubai. The same applies to other Dutch cities. But although I enjoy every minute of cycling in Amsterdam, I am always a little bit relieved when I get home to Copenhagen. Due to the layout of the cities, I have often compared the cyclists of Amsterdam to swarming bees, whereas in Copenhagen the biomimicry metaphor of marching ants is more appropriate. You are welcome to your own personal opinion. I'm just convinced that cities are best served by adopting designs that are appropriate and feasible for their own city. We're not redesigning our cities for the next couple of months—we're planning transport for the next century.

Even if we work incrementally due to budget restrictions or whatnot, maintaining a strict uniformity is vital from the very beginning. I usually stay at the same hotel every time I am in Amsterdam, located about 20 minutes from the central station. It's a route that I know very well. I can't help but notice, every time I cycle this route, that I get to experience a wild mix of infrastructure design as well as surfacing. Sometimes it's asphalt, and then it becomes bricks or paving stones. I ride on a cycle track on one side of the street, turn right onto a bidirectional, turn left onto a street with no infrastructure at all . . . and so it continues for the entire route. While it's an interesting freestyle potpourri that keeps me guessing, it is not very uniform or intuitive. We can discuss whether this is due to planners doing their best to squeeze the bicycle into every street or simply to lazy planners and politicians without a clear vision. I have a similar experience in other Dutch cities as well as cities like Strasbourg and Antwerp. If you live in these cities and develop familiar routes on your A-to-B-to-C journeys, wayfinding becomes second nature. The hallmark of good design is how intuitive it is for people who are using it for the first time, be it a smartphone, a coffee machine, or a bicycle infrastructure network.

My own experience after cycling in scores of cities and participating in hundreds of conversations with visitors and colleagues in Copenhagen leads me to conclude that uniformity in bicycle infrastructure design is paramount. You can arrive in Copenhagen for the first time in your life, grab a bike, and head out to explore with a gentle and short learning curve. In addition, you can hop on a train to most other Danish cities and, when you get off the train, the infrastructure is much the same. Enabling you to cycle safely, intuitively, and effectively to whatever destination you choose. Now that the bicycle is returning to emerging bicycle cities, I would hope that the planners and politicians realize the importance of gentle and short learning curves.

I often bring my children with me when I travel for work and, as ever, their observations are worth their weight in gold. When we spent a few days in Groningen, it was absolutely a more positive bike experience than Vancouver. Copenhagen kids can effortlessly weave themselves into the bicycle fabric of a Dutch city, and it was fun to watch them do so. It's worth mentioning that I merely ask questions of the kids, never leading them on and forcing them to think too much about a subject. I only want pure observations. If they don't have any, then they don't have any and I leave it at that. After we had cycled to the hotel from the train station, Felix said, "I was a bit nervous riding on the cycle track from the station and then through the city. There were all these pedestrians trying to cross, so I had to watch out for them. Oh, and there are loads of ladies bikes."

In the evening on the second day, after we had been riding a lot more around the city, I asked the kids if they had any more observations. Felix had put some thought into it.

Felix: "It's like I feel more secure cycling in Copenhagen."
Mikael: "You weren't scared?"
Felix: "No, no, not at all. I just feel more secure." (Here he used a Danish word tryg, which doesn't quite mean safe, but rather indicates a sense of security or feeling comfortable.) "At home I don't need to worry about pedestrians suddenly crossing the cycle track. And here, the cyclists don't signal when they're turning or stopping like they do in Copenhagen. And the cars don't, either."
Mikael: "The cars don't signal?"
Felix: "Many didn't."
Mikael: "Jeroen [our friend and guide] signaled turns all the time, didn't he?"

Felix: "Daddy, that's just because he was at the front and he was showing us that we're turning because we didn't know the way."

Mikael: "But generally you like it?"

Felix: "Yeah! It's cool!"

Mikael: "What do you think, Lulu?"

Lulu: "I don't like those bumpy stones."

Mikael: "Cobblestones?"

Lulu: "Yeah."

Felix: "It's like, in Copenhagen I know where I'm supposed to be and where everyone else is supposed to be. Here, I don't know who is coming in front of me, all of a sudden. At intersections, some people turn on the right side of you and some turn on the left, cutting in front of you. There isn't a lot of . . . um . . . structure."

Lulu: "What's structure?"

Mikael: "It's like in your room when it's clean and everything is in its place. The socks are in the socks drawer, your dresses are in your dress drawer, and stuff like that."

Lulu: "That's not often."
          Uh . . . no.

Felix: "But Copenhagen is a big city. Groningen isn't. Maybe you need more structure in a big city."

Mikael: "What about when we were riding on streets with cars and buses? You kept checking back at me and Lulu to make sure we saw the car coming, didn't you? You called out 'car!' a couple of times to let us know."

Felix: "Yeah, but they weren't going very fast. I was just making sure Lulu was on the right side."

Good big brother. We headed to Amsterdam next, to visit friends. Felix had his own bike and Lulu and I rode an Onderwater tandem designed for an adult and a kid.

Felix: "It's kind of like a mix of Copenhagen and Groningen. Copenhagen feels more like a big city. Amsterdam is like a village, but still a bit like a city. I guess Amsterdam is like 60 percent Copenhagen and 40 percent Groningen, or something."

Mikael: "What else did you notice?"

Felix: "Why did we have to push buttons to cross streets on bikes? We don't have that in Copenhagen."

Mikael: "Good question."

Felix: "We had to watch out for lots of pedestrians, like in Groningen. Oh, and nobody signals here, either. And nobody rings bells."

All in all, interesting observations from the kids. As a balance, I have conducted comparative interviews with kids coming from the opposite direction. For a few years, I rented a large room in my apartment through Airbnb and had a lot of families staying with us, including many Dutch, Germans, and Belgians. If the kids—and parents—cycled daily at home, I would grill the kids whenever I could, asking them for some comparative observations. They were comfortable with cycling at home—we are all creatures of habits—but the majority commented on the ease of use of the infrastructure and the intuitiveness of it when getting around a city they didn't know.

There is an enormous amount of inspiration in Denmark, the Netherlands, Japan, and a growing number of cities around the world. We have to curate it with care and select the right design solutions for the right situations, and we must always choose the best and simplest. We have to be realistic. I would like nothing more than to see every city in the world free of cars and motorized transport and instead embrace a workable, feasible combination of human-powered movement and public transport. But I won't live to see that. Neither will you. We need to work with the ideas that are in place and that apply, using the tools that we already possess and proceeding with a clear and well-defined vision of what is possible. Time is of the essence.

Top: *Felix and Lulu-Sophia in Groningen.*
Bottom: *Cyclists—and friends—waiting for the light to change in Amsterdam.*

CHAPTER 20

COMMUNICATION & ADVOCACY

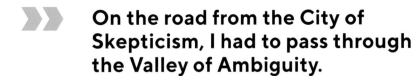

On the road from the City of Skepticism, I had to pass through the Valley of Ambiguity.

Adam Smith

Let's cut to the chase. We have, in our possession, one of the greatest products in history. An innovative, game-changing, life-saving, illness-preventing, city-improving product. I've been describing it as a tool, but for many people it is a hobby and a passion, for others a lifestyle. In this chapter, let's focus on the bicycle as a product. Like all products, it needs customers. In order to get customers we need to talk about it, spread the message, market it. This chapter considers two important aspects of that task: increasing the

number of bicycles in our cities and how to speak to the potential cyclists. With such an amazing product you would think it would be a piece of cake to get people on board, but there are still flaws in the techniques that are being employed.

Luckily, like almost everything about urban cycling, we can harvest inspiration and experience from the past. When the bicycle as we know it today was developed and started to be mass-produced, it quite simply rocked our world. In the halcyon days of the late nineteenth century,

Cyclist in Copenhagen.

when technological advances and new inventions appeared at a constant and spectacular rate, the bicycle rose above them all as a powerful symbol of everything beautiful and useful in the boundless sphere of human ingenuity. No other product in human history has positively transformed society as quickly and effectively as the bicycle did. Let's look at some historical marketing lessons.

It was the so-called *safety bicycle*, featuring the diamond frame, that pushed the bicycle from being a subcultural toy for bored rich boys to becoming a mainstream form of transport. Before that, "bicycles" were an eclectic collection of bizarre contraptions, the most famous of which was the cumbersome penny-farthing, with its large front wheel and comparatively tiny rear wheel. Several inventors and designers were working on an improvement to the penny-farthing, but the first mass-produced safety bicycle was the Rover, invented by John Kemp Starley in the United Kingdom in 1885. Calling it a "safety bicycle" was the first step in marketing the product to society at large, since the penny-farthing had a reputation as a dangerous machine—and rightly so. We can thank the penny-farthing for giving us English expressions like *taking a header* and *breakneck speed*. It didn't take long for the design to catch on and be replicated by companies all over the world. (It became so popular in Poland, for example, that the Polish word for bicycle, *rower*, is a direct derivative of the name Rover.)

By a fortunate coincidence, the invention of the safety bicycle coincided with the perfection of the technique required for the art of lithography, which afforded exciting possibilities in both art and marketing. Artists everywhere desperately tried to figure out how to get on board. They looked around for cool new products that they could produce artwork for, and there was the bicycle, waiting for exposure. Bicycle brands had no problem lining up the top artists of the age to produce marketing material, primarily in the form

of posters. Today we have inherited one of the most spectacular collections of art in the history of consumer society. There were no limits to the use of colors or metaphors in the production of these posters, and artists in many, many countries went all in with their efforts. I have spent years studying this genre and I remain fascinated by it.

I have identified various specific themes that artists, in their collective subconscious across many countries, used when broadcasting the amazing bicycle to an eager and willing populace. In essence, they are: *liberating, modern, elegant, effortless, social,* and *convenient*. Even if you didn't know what I was trying to sell you, you would be interested in hearing more if such keywords were in play.

Let's cut to the chase. We have, in our possession, one of the greatest products in history. An innovative, game-changing, life-saving, illness-preventing, city-improving product.

By way of a comparison, let's look at the sewing machine. Like the bicycle, the sewing machine was the product of technological advances that made fine mechanics possible. Before that, sewing machines were large industrial contraptions operated by men with strong, callused hands in factories around the world. This obviously isn't the place to get into the complex and confusing history of all the people involved in the invention and patenting of the commercially produced sewing machine. It's interesting, however, that the rise of the sewing machine came about in the same age as the rise of the bicycle—and in both cases,

Left: Social, elegant, and effortless. One theme seen in scores of bicycle posters is the woman cycling slightly ahead of the man, showing how effortless it is. This is one of my favorite posters and it dates from around 1900. So simple and calm and yet broadcasting so many fantastic things about the bicycle. Artist: Unknown.

Right: Freedom and modernity. This poster from 1898 is a riot of metaphors. The young woman heading left to right—to the future—and tossing flowers as she goes. The old woman in a bed of thorns, eyes fixed on the past, resigned to the fact that the future is passing her by. Artist: Henri Thiriet.

there was a wealth of beautiful posters to be had. The key point here is that the goal was to sell a lot of sewing machines—indeed, to try and get one into every home. The Singer company, which was synonymous with sewing machines for decades, was the first mover in the mainstream marketing of this invention. Singer identified early on what the target group was: housewives. And just as the sewing machine industry used the same new-fangled lithography techniques as did the nascent bicycle industry, they also understood that the

same keywords were instrumental in getting the message out.

The sewing machine would liberate you from tailors; it was modern, effortless, and convenient. Once the target market was identified, sewing machines were produced with beautiful floral patterns that would appeal to the women who were to buy them, and the machines themselves would become a welcome and aesthetic addition to the home. Elegance on sale. Now let's leapfrog ahead to the 1950s, when the vacuum cleaner became a must-have product in homes everywhere. This brings us to a different age, but take one look at historical vacuum cleaner advertising and you'll see that exactly the same keywords are being used.

Unlike the sewing machine and the vacuum cleaner, whose marketing was clearly aimed at housewives, bicycle brands figured out early on that their target group was basically everyone. Sure, men were the first movers in acquiring bikes, and women, being more risk-averse, needed a little bit of extra coaxing. More often than not, posters were designed to appeal to both genders all at once. In the vast body of work that is historical bicycle posters, at least one of those keywords is present in every example—*liberating, modern, elegant, effortless, social, convenient.*

It's no exaggeration to call this the longest and most successful advertising campaign in history. It was nothing short of extraordinary.

It's no exaggeration to call this the longest and most successful advertising campaign in history. It was unique in that there were so many companies, large and small, international and local, that contributed to this success. It was nothing short of extraordinary.

While the spectacular artwork of bicycle advertising eventually faded away, positive messaging continued unabated well through the 1960s in many parts of the world. In effect, the world was witness to seventy or so years of uninterrupted positive marketing of the bicycle, directly inspiring many other industries, not least the automobile industry, in the marketing of their own products. Think of every car commercial you've ever seen, and it's clear that they are trying desperately to sell us liberty, modernity, elegance, effortlessness, and convenience—not to mention sexy and cool. The same applies to the marketing of whatever smartphone you might have acquired, and indeed such keywords have become the absolute baseline for the successful marketing of *any* product nowadays.

Things have changed. With the advent of automobile culture and the expropriation of urban space to serve cars at the expense of everything else, the popularity of the bicycle waned—especially for transport—and our perception of the bicycle morphed into something else. Two developments were instrumental in causing this. One is such a massive subject that there are several books written about it. The British sociologist Frank Furedi coined the phrase with the title of his book: *The Culture of Fear.* I always recommend this book to anyone working in bicycle advocacy because it helps us identify important developments in our societies. Furedi doesn't write about bicycles specifically but about how we have gone from seven millennia of tight-knit communities to a culture of Every Man for Himself. Despite living in the safest age in the history of homo sapiens, we still apparently possess an inherent capacity and even a need for fear. In a market economy, if you can make someone scared of something by conjuring fear of it, you can sell them a whole host of products to soothe that fear. For most of human history we strove for safety, but now that we are safer than ever we ironically seek fear—and products that will protect us from it.

Against all odds, the bicycle experienced a revival due to the oil crises in the 1970s, re-emerging out of the dusty recesses of transportation. While the 1970s brought the bicycle back, the revival took a different turn. Three decades of car-centric planning had left few places where cycling was safe or feasible. But it was the 1970s, man, with a fledgling focus on the environment and hopes for a better world. In Denmark and in the Netherlands, the bicycle returned to our cities as transport, starting the journey towards the bicycle cities that we see today. Elsewhere, the bicycle also muscled its way back into our consciousness and was warmly embraced by people who used it for sport and/or recreation. It was a big enough boom to signal the rebirth of the bicycle industry in many countries, and they quickly figured out what people were using the bicycle for and started to focus on marketing to this demographic. Their singular focus on the bicycle as a sporty activity was cemented rather quickly, and to this day it remains difficult to change.

With even a cursory glance at the bicycle industry today, you can see clearly how the bicycle is perceived in many countries where the bikes are built for speed and endurance. And it's not enough to sell just a bike; the market for accessories is astounding, mind-boggling. Personally, I don't know what half the stuff is actually for. I seem to recall hearing that the bicycle industry makes more money on accessories than they do on the bicycles themselves. Maybe avid cyclists won't acquire new bikes every year, but they can certainly be seduced to purchase the latest shoes, gloves, helmets, jerseys, etc. If the array of products is confusing to an avid cyclist, imagine what it's like for someone like me, regarding it from afar, who will never own any of these things. My brain hurts just thinking about it.

It's not fair to blame the bicycle industry for charting this course, because all they did was respond to the market. Today, however, things have changed once again, and the bicycle industry—Big Bike—has been slow to respond to the emerging and broadening market.

We have gone from seven millennia of tight-knit communities to a culture of Every Man for Himself.

In cities everywhere, we have millions of citizens who are willing to consider the bicycle as transport. But as they're waiting for infrastructure to keep them safe and make them *feel* safe, I fear that we risk turning them off of the bike-as-transport idea by overcomplicating something very simple. It is fanciful to assume that an entire population will don the complicated uniform of cycling subcultures. I remember browsing an American cycling website that featured a guide to winter cycling, and scrolling past row upon row of photos of men looking like a combination of RoboCop and an arctic explorer. I was unwittingly fascinated by all the strange gear they were trying to sell. I was also bored that day, so I spent the morning Googling all the products on offer and calculating what it would cost me to acquire them. I ended up at about €800 (US$947)—and I still didn't even have a bike. Then I started thinking: If I wanted to take you bowling, we would head down the local alley, rent some stinky shoes, order some beer, and roll some balls. What if, I thought, I possessed a secret desire to become an avid bowler. So I spent the afternoon Googling bowling gear, which was a strange experience. I discovered that if I was serious about gearing up for what would almost certainly be a failed career as a bowler, I would be €450 (US$533) out of pocket. The fact is that most people are not going to do that, nor am I. In its simplest form, urban cycling merely requires a bicycle that can be bought for a hundred bucks at a flea market. That's it and that's that.

Environmentalism is the greatest marketing flop in the history of homo sapiens.

Environmentalism is the greatest marketing flop in the history of homo sapiens. Let that sink in for a moment. I deeply regret this, but it is sadly the case. Think about it. We have had 40–50 years of messaging about the importance of the environment and caring for it. There are very few places in the world where all the things we know we should be doing are actually being done. Scandinavian countries are ahead of the curve, and in a global context there are many initiatives worth copy/pasting into other countries. Nevertheless, we are far from any of our declared goals. From a marketing perspective, environmentalism has consisted of decades of negative messaging, condescension, and guilt trips from groups of people who are often perceived as sanctimonious. None of the keywords that I mentioned above apply here. Sure, this is a different topic and a different "product," but in a modern society overwhelmed by consumerism and populated by citizens who are used to glossy commercials, environmental-

ism has failed to deliver its important message. One of the many reasons you should read the book *The Geography of Hope* is to understand how people will respond to the right kind of communication about environmental issues. The author, Chris Turner, writes from personal experience and offers his important perception that, in short, the protest culture and the type of messaging we used in the 1970s is out of touch with the current reality. A great many bicycle-advocacy organizations were founded—or revived—in the 1970s during the global mini–bicycle boom. They latched on to the same narrative as did environmental activism and never let go.

I follow the tone, technique, and approach of bicycle advocates all over the world and have done so for years. I can see that there is a gradual move towards a more positive approach (I'll get to some of my favorite examples), but so much advocacy today is still rooted in a hopelessly out-of-date narrative. The general message is: "We know better and if you're not doing it like we do then you're doing it wrong," along with incessant messaging about how it's green and healthy and how you have the opportunity to single-handedly save a polar bear on your daily commute. Hallelujah. Unfortunately, society at large has developed a filter . . . which is really just a polite way of saying that people are ignoring the issue because we have irritated them.

The type of messaging we used in the 1970s is out of touch with the current reality.

Broadly speaking, many bicycle-advocacy organizations, like their environmentalist counterparts, are perceived as being *aparté*, speaking passionately but, perhaps, arrogantly about their ideology, all while wearing a uniform that makes them stand out even more. Much of the advocacy is being done by avid cyclists, as opposed to ordinary city dwellers who happen to ride bikes. In addition, there is a lot of talk about safety equipment and potential danger. "Ride a bike! It's amazing for you and the planet! But you'll probably get hurt or even die!"

Imagine, for example, if we sold wine like many people are trying to sell urban cycling. Wine, in moderation, is enjoyable and has some health benefits. It has a mainstream appeal, but it also has a strong subcultural following equipped with an arsenal of confusing and impenetrable terminology. I always try to avoid longer conversations with wine geeks. Even though wine, especially red

wine, is my alcoholic beverage of choice, I will never be an aficionado. Imagine if the wine industry suffered from the same confusing messaging as does a lot of bicycle advocacy.

Drink wine! It's good for you! It's enjoyable! But wait, if you overdo it slightly, it will make you feel funny. Drink a little bit more and it will affect your speech and your judgement. Keep on drinking, and you might experience nausea and perhaps even throw up on your shoes. If you drink too much, too regularly, it can affect your liver function, and turn you into an alcoholic and alienate yourself from family and friends! You might even die! Drink wine! I think it's safe to say that the wine industry has determined that this would not be effective marketing for their product.

White crosses were painted on the asphalt in Copenhagen in the 1960s and 1970s to show where cyclists had been killed by motorists. Photo: Niels Jensen.

In a conversation with one of my favorite bicycle advocates in the United States, Robin Stallings, executive director of Bike Texas, he lamented the fact that the politicians he speaks to in the Lone Star State often opt out of the discussion at the first mention of the word *bike*. We started brainstorming jokingly, perhaps encouraged by our consumption of the aforementioned product, about how to talk about bikes and bicycle infrastructure without mentioning the obvious. For example, we wondered if politicians would be more receptive if we advocated FFTCs, pronounced "faftracs"—Family-Friendly Transport Corridors. Switching up the lingo to dazzle, impress, and confuse.

Design our cities for bicycles as transport and allow the majority to dress for their destination, not their journey.

Indeed, one of the questions I hear most often from bicycle advocates when I'm working abroad is: "How do we get this message across more effectively?" My standard reply is that they should talk less about bikes and focus more on how the bicycle as transport can contribute to the greater challenge of improving city life, and they should also collaborate more with other organizations that have the same overall goal, which is not to attempt vainly to develop an entire population of avid cyclists, but to design our cities for bicycles as transport and allow the majority to dress for their destination, not their journey. In

short, be an avid cyclist if that's your thing. Just don't speak like one to the public at large.

ADVOCATE WITH CARE

For all the talk of the benefits of cycling, there is also the question of activism. The 1970s were a different age and one in which massive protests and campaigns could shift political and public opinion. A hundred thousand people in Copenhagen's City Hall Square demanding a return to bicycle infrastructure and a safe environment for cycling had an amazing effect. White crosses were painted on the asphalt at intersections in Copenhagen where cyclists had lost their lives. In the Netherlands, the famous "Stop Child Murder" campaigns against cars in the city pushed the cycling agenda as well. The sad fact is that society has changed and such protests now have a diminished effect. Some people haven't realized this, though, and thus what I wrote before about the nature of subcultures applies. They are insular and protective.

It was back in 2008 that I first came across the concept—new to me—of memorials to cyclists who had died in traffic. I read about a so-called *ride of silence* somewhere in the United States. I get it, man. Boy, do I get it. You are a member of a passionate, tightly knit group or club and someone you know well dies. It feels like family, and memorial services are a given. We need to broaden our gaze and think about how everyone else is looking at it. On that ride of silence website, I read this: "Someone's going to ride around the lake with us tonight . . . and they won't be here next year." Whoa. If I were curious about cycling and considering taking it up, a line like that would put me off completely. No rational argument about how safe cycling is, statistically, or about the ease of use of using a bike for transport. Nope. Someone you know *will* die.

Roadside memorials to lives lost in traffic is nothing new, but the concept of the *ghost bike* is new, dating from around 2003. A bike is painted white and locked close to a spot where a cyclist died. While this can create traffic-safety awareness and might encourage some motorists to take care, it does little or nothing to promote cycling among people who aren't currently doing it. A ghost bike broadcasts imminent danger.

Society has changed and such protests now have a diminished effect.

While working in São Paulo, Brazil, I participated in the World Naked Bike Ride—a recurring event in some emerging bicycle cities with strong cycling subcultures. I rode with activist friends and kept my clothes on. It was fun reclaiming the streets that night with a whole bunch of people on bikes. But then we stopped at an intersection with busy bars on all four corners. The activists lay down on the asphalt and played dead—it's called a *die-in*. Then they stood up, raised their bikes over their heads and started chanting "Hey motorist, respect the cyclists!" in Portuguese. I studied the crowds outside the bars. Everyone was laughing and filming with their phones. As a protest, it was lively, it was visible, and it had a clear message. However hard it is to admit this, in cities where cyclists are a small fringe group the non-cycling majority stare at cyclists like they're synchronized

swimmers. They're a bit weird and engaged in a sport/activity that seems bizarre. I doubt that any of the spectators who saw the São Paolo die-in are riding a bike in the city today because of it. It was a strange subcultural group shouting at everyone else and demanding respect—but in no way, shape, or form were they inviting people to join their ranks.

As an aside, I should mention that someone tried to organize a naked bike ride in Copenhagen a few years ago. A handful of young activists were outnumbered by a flock of aging, male nudists. We have liberal attitude toward public nudity in Denmark, but the police took one look and shut it down for what might have been their own aesthetic reasons. I doubt we'll ever see such a ride here again.

I get to experience a great many things on my travels with my work. I have ridden in a few critical-mass bike rides around the world. As a protest, it's a brilliant concept and democratic to the core. A celebratory social movement, even. With roots in the 1970s, the modern version dates from 1992 in San Francisco and it spread quickly around the world. The movement evidently split into two styles. In European cities, critical-mass rides are generally true to the original celebratory spirit and very inclusive of the population at large. I rode with over 20,000 people in Budapest—their record is 80,000—and it was a spectacular event. In Prague, though, the organizers ended up changing the name from "Critical Mass" to something akin to "Bike Ride" in Czech. The reason was the bad brand that critical mass was becoming—and as I heard it, that meant the aggressive, confrontational approach that had taken over in American cities.

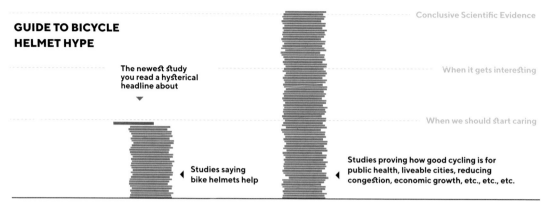

GUIDE TO BICYCLE HELMET HYPE

Conclusive Scientific Evidence

The newest study you read a hysterical headline about

When it gets interesting

When we should start caring

◄ Studies saying bike helmets help

Studies proving how good cycling is for public health, liveable cities, reducing congestion, economic growth, etc., etc., etc. ◄

Let's be rational about helmets and focus on encouraging cycling.

I was in a Halloween critical mass in San Francisco with a number of friends—and several thousand others—and it was festive. As we rolled through an intersection, a female motorist was screaming at one of the cyclists who was blocking the cars to allow the others to cycle through. In her expletive-ridden rant, she shouted about how *you people* (the cyclists) were stopping her from getting home to her kids. From that moment on, as in my awkward experience in São Paulo, I had a bad taste in my mouth—one that I didn't have in Budapest. I realized that I wasn't selling cycling to anyone except people who had already bought into it, and I hated that feeling.

THE H WORD

The bicycle helmet issue slips in perfectly here. Harping on incessantly about how dangerous cycling is, and insisting through promotion or legislation that people should wear plastic hats, does nothing to promote cycling. If you tell people often enough that cycling is so dangerous that you need to dress up like a warrior in order to do

it, you can't expect very many people to ride.

It was in Australia that the first mandatory helmet laws were passed in the early 1990s after a period of intense promotion. Followed by New Zealand. Now, every time helmet legislation rears its ugly head elsewhere in the world, fingers point to Australia and the massive decline in cycling there that started with the promotion of helmets and was completed with legislation. As a result, helmet laws are growing more rare. Virtually every national cycling organization in Europe fights against such laws whenever some hapless politician tries to score brownie points with a band-aid solution.

Uninformed politicians are allied, unknowingly, with a powerful follow-the-money culture. The American bicycle helmet industry is worth, last time I checked, over US$6 billion dollars a year. A colleague of mine in Australia was present at all the hearings leading up to the mandatory helmet law in the state of Victoria. He told me that at each hearing, a vice president from Bell Helmets had flown in from the United States and sat alongside the proponents of the law.

You can't get helmet manufacturers to talk about the capabilities of their products. I once set up a fake email and wrote to all the major manufacturers, under the guise of passionately wanting to promote helmets in Denmark. I asked them to help me with talking points and proof about the effectiveness of their products. None of them would help. Most suggested I google it—hoping, perhaps, I'd stumble across the website of an organization they donate to, which would happily bang on about nonscientific "proof." Clever.

The whole thorny issue is wildly dominated by anecdotes and emotional propaganda as described in the book The Culture of Fear by Frank Furedi. Whenever we hear an anecdote about how someone "saved their life" with a helmet, we should find out who said it was so. Often it was some doctor or nurse, and that, in the eyes and ears of many people, is as close to absolute truth as you can get. Doctors are highly trained, of course, but also highly specialized. Very few of them have any knowledge of the capabilities or the industrial design restrictions of helmets. They stumble across the same websites with select facts that support the profit margins of the industry and the car-centric ideology of the activists who promote helmets. The doctors who treat serious injuries in trauma wards are the drama queens of the medical profession. Unfortunately, they never wander down to the wards where great numbers of people are suffering from lifestyle illnesses that could have been prevented had they been cycling.

As the European Council of Ministers of Transport have stated in their "National Policies to Promote Cycling" that: " . . . from the point of view of restrictiveness, even the official promotion of helmets may have negative consequences for

bicycle use, and that to prevent helmets having a negative effect on the use of bicycles, the best approach is to leave the promotion of helmet wear to manufacturers and shopkeepers."

From an industrial design perspective, a bicycle helmet is designed to protect the head from non-life-threatening, lateral impact in solo accidents under 20 km/h (12 mph). The tests they undergo simulate a pedestrian stumbling and hitting their head. Most serious head injuries are caused by rotational impacts, which helmets are not designed to protect against. The helmet industry knows it. The standards for helmets are weak and the industry fights against every attempt to make them tougher. If the bicycle helmet were a medicine, it would never be approved for public consumption by any health authority. There simply isn't enough conclusive scientific evidence from anywhere in the world.

I wasn't selling cycling to anyone except people who had already bought into it, and I hated that feeling.

Regarding helmets, one of the things I am most proud of is having my expert statement read aloud in the Knesset, the Israeli parliament, and afterwards seeing them vote to repeal their mandatory all-ages helmet law.

At the end of the day, my opinion on the subject is this: If wearing a helmet keeps someone on a bike, great. If not wearing a helmet keeps someone on a bike, great. Unfortunately, the latter group have suffered at the hands of of one-sided, unscientific propaganda for a very long time. This is changing. People are becoming more informed about the subject, and we are moving towards a balance in the discussion.

CYCLING'S SECRET SECT

In the catalogue of bicycle advocacy and activism, there is a chapter occupied by a small and noisy group of cyclists who call themselves *vehicular cyclists,* mostly in the United States and to a lesser extent in Germany and the United Kingdom. Back in the day, I spent four months researching the nature of sects and cults for a screenplay idea I had, and the comparison with these vehicular cyclists is spooky. They are cycling's secret sect.

It is a male-dominated, testosterone-driven club that expect that everyone should be just like them—the classic subcultural point of view—and that everyone should embrace cycling in traffic and pretend they are cars. They are apparently uninterested in seeing grandmothers, parents with children, or anyone else who doesn't resemble them contribute to redesigning our cities for the future.

Like all sects worth their salt, they have a guru or two whom they seem to worship. There's John Forester in the United States and, to a lesser extent, John Franklin in the United Kingdom. Their numbers are few but they are noisy. They are aggressive. And their influence is destructive.

Cyclists participate in a so-called die-in in São Paulo, Brazil, during a Naked Bike Ride event.

The theory about vehicular cycling has been around for more than three decades. And the reason that vehicular cycling cannot be considered any more than a theory is quite simple: there is nowhere in the world where this theory has become practice and caused great numbers of citizens to take to the streets on a daily basis. It remains a theoretical manifesto for a fringe group of cyclists. They often refer to themselves as "bicycle drivers." Vroom vroom.

I asked a leading American bicycle advocate about vehicular cycling and he said, "They have had around 35 years to prove that it works. They haven't be able to. It's time to shelve the idea."

This is largely because the theory appeals mainly just to those very few cycling enthusiasts who like to go fast. Going "fast" is apparently important. This theory is also referred to as "effective cycling," and you can read that "Effective Cycling is Safer, Faster, and More Fun!" on the website of the theory's founder, John Forrester.

If we once again refer to the ignoring-the-bull analogy, the vehicular-cyclist crowd are the Pamplonans of cycling. They enjoy running with the bulls, and bully for them. Completely and utterly useless for the rest of society. The group rejects bicycle infrastructure—it's not for them. Unfortunately, they often stand in the way of getting regular citizens onto bicycles. They come up with all manner of excuses when someone mentions Denmark or the Netherlands or the fact that infrastructure actually gets large numbers of people onto bicycles. "Won't work here," they say. They manipulate studies about the safety of infrastructure and actually spin it to the extreme, calling bicycle infrastructure "dangerous." There are cities that lag behind in designing and building infrastructure due primarily to the lobbying efforts of this group.

The English sociologist Roy Wallis argues that a sect is characterized by "epistemological authoritarianism." According to Wallis, "Sects lay a claim to possess unique and privileged access

to the truth or salvation" and "their committed adherents typically regard all those outside the confines of the collectivity as 'in error.'" The American sociologists Rodney Stark and William Sims Bainbridge assert that "sects claim to be an authentic, purged, refurbished version of the faith from which they split." They further assert that sects have, in contrast to churches, a high degree of tension with the surrounding society. Can we call this group bicycle advocates? I'm not sure. They're more like subculture proponents. Stamp collectors may be "communication advocates," but they don't rant against emails and text messages and other forms of mainstream communication that benefit the common good and ordinary human interaction.

It's as though a group of race walkers are advocating pedestrianism. Telling everyone that it's all about Effective Walking and that it's Safer, Faster, and More Fun! Insisting that the general population should walk just like them.

A male-dominated, testosterone-driven club that expect everyone to be just like them.

Over 35 years of theorizing without any proof that "vehicular cycling" works. How many citizens could have had their lives extended by being provided with safe infrastructure, or lived a life with fewer illnesses? How many overweight people could have had the chance to cycle happily to work on bike lanes and keep fit? Even though their guru has thrown in the towel, the number of potential daily cyclists who have been restricted access to the bicycle must number in the tens of millions. Its influence is now fading, but vehicular cycling remains a dangerous theory and ideology pushed by a self-serving group of people who have no interest in the redemocratization of cycling. Ignore them. Let's move on.

DRAW THE LINE

Long before environmentalism and rogue sects posed challenges to how we talk about cycling, the bike as transport came under threat from sports cycling. In the first half of the twentieth century there were a great many advocacy organizations. As cycle sport grew in popularity, the focus started to shift away from advocacy. Many national advocacy organizations folded or were swallowed up by sport organizations, and cycling for transport was left without proponents. Historically, this was the case in both Sweden and Germany, for example.

Someone who knows how much their bicycle weighs is not someone who should be advocating cycling.

It seems counterintuitive that cycling is compartmentalized, but the fact remains that it is, as I have also tried to outline, above. I have scoured the archives in several countries for years, looking for examples of sport or recreation cycling directly influencing regular citizens to choose the bike for transport—and I've come up almost empty-handed. It's apples and oranges. Two completely different things, only vaguely related. The City of Copenhagen produced a poster featuring a Danish pro cyclist, Jesper Skibby, who won a

stage in the Vuelta d'España in 1995. He was very popular due to his personality. The message rolls off the tongue in Danish, but in English it reads: "It's hard to cycle all around Spain / It's healthy to cycle all year round."

A sporty pro cyclist wearing the requisite uniform is a direct parallel to a Copenhagener muscling into a headwind in her rain jacket. In Denmark or the Netherlands we can see the similarity, but also the difference. Elsewhere, we need to draw a line. If for decades we haven't been using sporty cycling as inspiration for daily urban cycling, perhaps we shouldn't start now.

In 2012, I was invited to go to Paris and meet the head of the company that organizes the Tour de France and that was interested in discussing how they could branch out into advocacy. They were focused on encouraging young cyclists to take up racing, but I explained to them that growing cycling as transport in French cities would have a greater effect on expanding the country's talent base for racing. Denmark and the Netherlands, despite their diminutive size, have both had an illustrious history of winning cycling medals, occupying the top podiums more often that countries several times larger in population.

They listened intently. The CEO, however, said that most of the riders he knew grew up in the countryside cycling 10–20 kilometers (6–12 miles) to school or Grandma's house. I told him that most of the Danes who have cycled in the Tour de France come from towns or cities and grew up cycling to school in their neighborhoods on cycle tracks. By bringing back cycling for transport to the cities, there was a far greater chance of inspiring kids to move into competitive racing. You're simply working with a broader cycling base. But keeping the two separate is important.

Jesper Skibby
Vinder af 9. etape, Spanien Rundt

Det er hårdt at cykle Spanien rundt.

Og sundt at cykle året rundt.

City of Copenhagen poster promoting cycling as healthy.
One of the few examples of sport cycling used successfully as
promotion for urban cycling.

We need to stay focused on our target group: the regular citizens of our cities who won't respond to sport-cycling messaging. We need people who can communicate cycling in cities. Someone who knows how much their bicycle weighs is not someone who should be advocating cycling. Like I said, someone who knows how many groceries you can carry on bike, is.

CLEAR GOALS AND UNITY

The fragmentation continues, even within the ranks of organizations that appear to be working towards the same goal. In most European countries, there are national cycling organizations for both transport and competitive cycling, as well as upstart organizations in some of the larger cities responding to the old-fashioned approach of the larger ones.

In the United States there is a national organization, the League of American Bicyclists, but there are also a great many other bicycle-related organizations and it gets confusing. There seems to be tough competition to dominate the conversation. Off the top of my head, there is 8 80 Cities out of Toronto but operating across North America; the Green Lane Project, which was a branch of People for Bikes; Complete Streets Coalition; the National Association of City Transportation Officials, NACTO; Strong Towns, all the placemaking people, and Better Block Foundation. I'm probably missing some, but the point is that it's incredibly difficult for the outside observer to navigate the messaging from so many organizations intent on *their* angle becoming the standard.

It's not my business to get them all to merge into one super organization, and that is unlikely to happen. The point is that for people outside our bike-happy academic echo chamber, it is

Left: *Felix racing the peloton during the Tour of Denmark.*
Right: *Conceptualization of a bicycle street on Nordre Frihavnsgade. Design and concept: the author, Ole Kassow and Thomas Lygum Sidelmann*

confusing and tiring to try and figure out what is what and who is who. I think that organizations that speak to a wider audience with a clear and intuitive approach are the ones that will experience more success in getting their message across. The ones that embrace the bicycle, but that include it in the grander, more-inclusive vision of city development and improvement. Even just blogs like the *Streetsblog* network, from a communication perspective, have developed a strong voice in their inclusive coverage of urbanist issues. It's not only about the bike. It's about the bicycle's role in our cities and in our lives.

SHOW, DON'T TELL

Talk is cheap. Cheaper than ever now that the Internet is a part of our lives. We talk to drown out other voices, or we talk for ages in the interest of reaching a compromise that keeps everyone happy. While we may not see the scale of demonstrations in the 1970s again anytime soon, we are now seeing smaller-scale activism with far-reaching effect through social media.

While the phrase *tactical urbanism* is new, the idea is not. It is, however, on the rise all over the world as an effective tool for showing, as opposed to telling. The phrase itself, attributed to urban planner Mike Lydon, is both an excellent description of the work being done and a banner slogan to inspire others.

This is one of my key points when giving advice around the world—show people the ideas or plans. Produce professional renderings, and you effectively accelerate the conversation with policymakers and citizens.

There is, believe it or not, a busy street in Copenhagen without protected bicycle infrastructure—Nordre Frihavnsgade in the Østerbro neighborhood. It is a bustling street with many shops, in a densely populated area. The City of Copenhagen gave up on trying to figure out how to put in bike infrastructure, guessing that since the neighborhood is more affluent than others, there would be protests if they proposed cycle tracks at the expense of car parking. My friend Ole Kassow lives in the neighborhood and cycles on the street regularly. In 2014, one of his daughters joined the ranks of people who have been doored, and, together with architect Thomas Lygum Sidelmann, we decided to do something about this street. We were encouraged by speaking to a local politician, Jonas Bjørn Jensen, who was campaigning door to door and asking people about various issues, including whether or not they wanted cycle tracks on their street. The majority replied that they did.

The concept of the *bicycle street* has been around for decades in the Netherlands and is now spreading. We have them in Denmark, and I've seen them in Hanover and Oslo, among other cities. The basic idea is that cars are allowed on the streets, but they are guests. The cyclists determine the tempo, and the motorist must follow it. I decided that we should inspire and provoke by proposing this solution for Nordre Frihavnsgade. Ole and I both blogged about it, and it was picked up first by the local newspaper and then a national one. It led to the City finding 1.5 million DKK (around $240,000 USD) to revisit the street and set up a community-engagement project to investigate solutions. In late 2017, the city council voted to transform the street into our proposed bicycle street. We are proud, believe me, but it all really started with creating a visualization of our ideas that changed the conversation.

The City was also nudged to investigate parking at Central Station after I published my company's conceptualization of those 7,500 parking spots for bikes. The conversation in Paris changed when I published a rendering of what the intersection in front of the Eiffel Tower could look like. With one simple graphic that went viral, Maria Elisa Ojeda Acosta, from Copenhagenize Design Company's office in Barcelona, tackled the ongoing issue of two tram lines not connecting up. Whether they are poignant or humorous, it's amazing to see how simple graphics or actions get legs on the Internet. Images speaking thousands of words.

I have curated my sources of inspiration over the years. Toronto's Urban Repair Squad captured

my imagination early on with their slogan: "City is broke, we fix, no charge!" They have been active for a long time, veritable first movers in the modern age of citizen activism. Painting renegade bike lanes in the wee hours and causing municipal headaches the next day or, as they did when I visited them in 2016, dressing like city workers and changing the speed limits in Kensington Market. "It's better to ask for forgiveness after than for permission before," as they told me. They have inspired many people to paint bike lanes around the world, in countries as diverse as Mexico, Brazil, Latvia, and Japan, to name just a few.

Jason Roberts and his Better Block Foundation are an amazing example of taking tactical urbanism to spectacular new levels. From the simple idea of temporarily transforming a run-down city block near Dallas, Better Block has now expanded

We are now seeing smaller-scale activism with far-reaching effect through social media

from activism to serious urbanism, working tirelessly with cities and citizens alike.

The mayor of the Plateau borough in Montreal, Luc Ferrandez, started transforming the streets soon after coming to power. He made quick work of some of the projects, knowing that showing was much more powerful than telling. Indeed, "do it quick and leave something green behind," as he told me. A painted lane makes a statement, but leaving new trees, grass, or other flora in place as well makes it harder to hate a new idea, especially in asphalt-covered cities.

A group in Berlin decided to hack their system. Berlin has a unique municipal clause that obliges the politicians to discuss a matter if a certain number of signatures are collected. The *Volksentscheid Fahrrad* (Bicycle Referendum) movement mobilized and got the signatures they needed, and they also outlined, in no certain terms, what the City's goals should be for improving cycling. It was a tour de force unlike anything I've seen anywhere in the last decade. You can, of course, just borrow a tank. In 2011, the then mayor of Vilnius, Lithuania, Arturas Zuokas, did just that, taking to the streets in a viral stunt that involved him driving over a car parked in a bike lane. Google it. Never gets old.

Showing was much more powerful than telling. Indeed, "do it quick and leave something green behind."

In Dublin, activists tackled the pressing issue of cars invading the bike lanes by standing on the painted lines and acting as a human shield for the cyclists in the morning rush hour. Original and bold. Transportation Alternatives in New York organized a massive human shield on one of that city's bike lanes, declaring it to be, as is their way in New York, "the world's largest human bike lane shield." Spectacular.

My friend, TV producer Doug Gordon, who runs the *Brooklyn Spoke* blog, took his visionary passion for bicycle activism to the streets of his neighborhood in 2012. Using duct tape, he fixed red plastic picnic cups to the painted lane and observed how motorists respected the physical barrier, however miniscule. Doug was inspired by James Schwarz and Dave Meslin in Toronto, who reacted to the untimely death of a local cyclist in 2011 by using trash to create a physical barrier and to prove that there is enough space for a proper bike lane. They, too, watched as motor vehicles gave the garbage barrier a wide berth.

Simple, creative, effective. Although if you were paying attention to the chapter about best-practice design of infrastructure, you'll remember that physical separation is the gold

Visualization by Copenhagenize Design Company's María Elisa Ojeda Acosta about the issue that two Barcelona tram lines still don't connect.

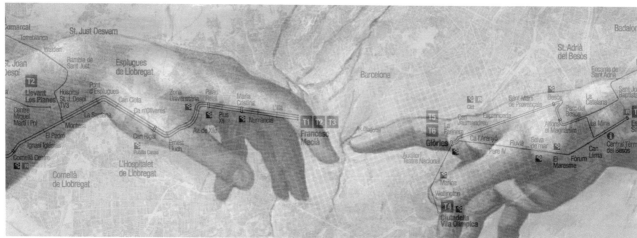

Top: Toronto's Urban Repair Squad in action. Replacing speed limit signs with a safer speed in Kensington Market.
Bottom: A bike lane with garbage used to separate cyclists from motorized traffic after the death of a cyclist at this location. ©James Schwartz

standard. Nevertheless, creative minds are at work and inspiring others around the world through showing—be it the possibilities or the flaws—in ways that our modern communication brains understand.

POSITIVE REINFORCEMENT

The fight for infrastructure and safer conditions for cycling in cities places a focus on safety—it's important and it's important that it's done well. While there is no specific policy in place, the City of Copenhagen has an unwritten strategy that the best communication is non-communication. There are some campaigns, yes, but largely the City prefers to make cycling safer and let people figure that out for themselves. The City never harps on about the perceived dangers of cycling, and they battle the anti-cycling, car-centric propaganda of organizations like the Danish Road Safety Council by continuing to make cycling safer through infrastructure. As Chris Boardman, former pro cyclist and now policy advisor for British Cycling, has said: "That is why I won't promote high vis [high visibility reflective clothing] and helmets; I won't let the debate be drawn onto a topic that isn't even in the top 10 things that will really keep people who want to cycle safe."

Back in 2008, I developed a behavioral campaign for the City of Copenhagen. They had begun using the phrase Hej cyklist! ("Hi, cyclist!"), and I thought that perhaps it was high time to start switching things up and focusing on posi-

tive reinforcement. In a city where few identify as "cyclists," the Hej cyklist! phrase sounds kitschy in Danish, kind of like the voice of a newsreel presenter in the 1950s. The template I designed around it is simple: Hi, cyclist! [insert message from the city here] Thanks for cycling in the city!

It quickly became the default communication template for the city's bicycle office. Every time

No penalty, no punishment, just a message telling you that your bike is okay and parked nearby.

there was something to communicate, the message was bookended by Hi! and Thanks! I knew that banging on about the benefits of cycling for the individual or the planet was ineffective and that it wasn't the City's style, either. We are well aware of the massive benefits, so why not just say thanks to the cycling citizens for all the amazing things they do, and get on with it? There will be a need for other campaigns, but why not have a positive baseline in the majority of the City's communication? Those pesky Norwegians borrowed freely from my idea, translating it to "Thanks for cycling" in Norwegian and featuring it on bike infrastructure and in campaigns in a number of cities. Whatever helps to communicate with positive reinforcement wherever people are cycling.

The City of Copenhagen further developed its positive approach in its communication with cyclists. There was an issue with bike parking during some roadworks in the city center awhile

back. There were signs in place asking cyclists not to park there, but many still did. Instead of removing the bikes, the City merely moved them.

"Hi, cyclist. Can't find your bike? It's now parked in Rosenborg Street. In order to make space for everyone, we made a temporary bike parking zone by Købmager Street where you can park your bike. Bikes parked outside the zone will be moved to Rosenborg Street."

No penalty, no punishment, just a message telling you that your bike is okay and parked nearby. Similarly, many bikes were being parked by the emergency exit to the metro by Nørreport Station—which, unfortunately, suffers from a drastic lack of bike parking despite a recent renovation. It's also the busiest station in the nation. The City launched a charm offensive aimed at nudging people to park elsewhere so as not to block the exit. If you do so anyway, City workers will move your bike to the bike racks, whereafter they will oil your chain and pump your tires for you. They leave a note on your bike telling you they did so and asking you to avoid parking by the exit in the future. They are called the "bicycle butlers." The number of people parking illegally dropped drastically in just a few months, and by all accounts, nobody has been angry at having their bike moved.

POSITIVITY

There's never enough positivity in the world, but with regards to bicycle communication, things are improving. The City of Malmö, Sweden, has run a great campaign for several years called Inga löjliga bilresor ("No ridiculous car trips"), which was focused on the urban folly of driving a car on trips under five kilometers (three miles). Motorists were encouraged to send in their most ridicu-

Top: A Norwegian version of the
Thank You for Cycling campaign
developed by the author.
Bottom: A recent poster for
Copenhagen Capital Region's
bicycle superhighway that reads:
"Thank you for still cycling."

lous car trip, and the craziest one would win a bike and accessories. One winner described how she would back out of her driveway onto her one-way street and back up for 200 meters (about 650 feet) to the school to drop off her kid before heading to work. The campaign was a massive success. Its reverse psychology was refreshing.

In the heady days after Klaus Bondam became mayor in Copenhagen, the city starting to recognize the value of communication. The international success of the *Copenhagenize* and *Copenhagen Cycle Chic* blogs had placed the focus firmly on the city. The City decided to develop a logo to represent their growing efforts to improve cycling in the city. At the time, all bike-related activities were gathered in one place—the Bicycle Secretariat. The logo was meant for communication with the citizens, but it ended up inspiring many people around the world. It is no secret that the "I bike CPH" logo—"CPH" being the airport code for Copenhagen—was freely influenced by the "I ♥ NYC" logo designed by Milton Glaser in 1977. But the simple message resonated internationally. I have lost track of how many city variations I have seen on every continent. Here in Copenhagen, the logo features on all communication from the City regarding bikes. In a city where

so many cycle daily, it has been difficult, in my opinion, to completely nail the branding in the eyes of the citizens. I have asked dozens of people what they think the logo represents, and the majority assume that it's a product of the tourism office, as opposed to the municipality trying to engage the citizens in communication. Nevertheless, the logo is still going strong.

The number of people parking illegally dropped drastically in just a few months.

Others have tried to develop their own logos in order to draw attention to themselves. In Luxembourg, the Ministry of Sustainability established an office dealing specifically with bike and pedestrian transport—or "soft mobility," as they call it. They wanted a bold statement without the usual clichés of bike-related logos, and Copenhagenize Design Company created one for them.

We were also hired by the city of Groningen, in the northern part of the Netherlands, to boost their international profile. They wanted a share of the many international delegations on study trips who regularly arrive in Amsterdam and Copenhagen, as well as cities nearby to those. Indeed, Groningen deserves its space in the limelight, even if it's a small city that is relatively unknown outside the immediate region. They have many stories to tell and much experience to share. I went to work designing a logo and a visual identity for them, aimed at attracting professional tourists on study trips to the city. Groningen uses the letter *g* freely in their other

Left: *The City of Copenhagen's logo for their bicycle office, designed by Troels Heien, on a poster in Copenhagen.*
Top right: *Logo for the bicycle and pedestrian office in Luxembourg's Ministry of Sustainability.*
Bottom right: *Proposed logo for the City of Groningen's bicycle office.*
Opposite: *Friendly signage by City of Copenhagen informing citizens that their bikes have been moved using the "Hi, Cyclist" campaign.*

logos and communication, so employing that was a given. After much discussion or infighting (depending on whom you listen to) in the city, they decided to make their own logo. What is not obvious to anyone outside of the Netherlands—which, from the beginning of the process, was the primary target group—is that 050 is their telephone prefix. However you do it, a logo can be an important tool for cementing the fact that bicycles are here to stay and that a city is working towards creating a framework for bicycles as a part of the transport equation. The City of Trondheim, Norway, has been producing campaigns that follow all the necessary guidelines for positive communication, and they are inspiring to see. They pull out all the stops when communicating the vision of their Miljøpakken project (Greener Trondheim) focused on all aspects of urban life, including bikes.

As municipalities go, it has to be the City of Vienna that tops the leaderboard for the most concerted effort to promote cycling positively. They have a complete grasp on the concept of selling cycling, using techniques that society at large will be receptive to. They have used regular citizens and well-known personalities alike. For example, a photo of the head doctor of the national hospital cycling with his statement about his bike as the tagline blazed across the poster: "My cure-all remedy." Or a high-ranking priest declaring the bicycle to be his passion, and a young couple in love with the bike called their "wheel of fortune." The City of Oslo's bicycle office produced a campaign directly inspired by Vienna, recognizing the value of the Austrian approach. The Hungarian Cyclists' Club, Magyar Kerékpárosklub, has been a leader among advocacy groups for using professional graphic design and,

Top Left and Center: *City of Vienna campaign to promote cycling.*
Bottom Left and Right: *Great campaign from BikePGH that humanizes cyclists.*
Right: *Poster by Miljøpakken (Greener Trondheim) promoting cycling positively. It reads: "Faith, Hope and Bicycle" and features an imam and a priest.*

not least, commercials produced by top advertising companies with a production value equal to anything we see on television. They produced an annual commercial for their Bike-to-Work Month campaign, and they are consistently brilliant.

One of the campaigns out of the United States that has impressed me is from Bike Pittsburgh. Simply highlighting the fact that cyclists are regular citizens just like everyone else. One poster for Bike Month in New York amused me. It highlighted that it is only 12 minutes by bike from Bed-Stuy to Fort Greene. Except it featured three people walking their bikes on the sidewalk. Talk about trying to keep everyone happy all at once. It's a positive ride a bike message, but they made sure that all these groups were covered:

» helmet advocates (there was a helmet dangling on the man's handlebars)
» anti-helmet advocates (the two women didn't have one)
» age-diversity advocates (old dude, middle-aged woman, young woman)
» racial-diversity advocates (an African American woman)
» gender-equality advocates (two women)
» pedestrian advocates (they were walking their bikes on the sidewalk)
» urban-transportation advocates (the general message)
» hipsters (it's outer Brooklyn they were talking about)

While it isn't difficult to find many campaigns worth mentioning in a positive light, there is still a disturbance in the force. Far too many campaigns still push a negative cycling agenda to the extreme. We have all seen them. You can find one of the worst in recent years by googling images using the search words *Phoenix bicycle*

safety. Then you'll understand what we're up against. Prepare to facepalm yourself.

Because we live in a society dominated by marketing, we are subject to spin. I look forward to the day when headlines in mainstream media have a different focus. Like one campaign from the City of Copenhagen's health department that stated:

"You're safer on a bike than on a sofa! / This just in! 2,000 Danes extended their lives this year because they cycle daily! / You have to cycle 4,000 years in Copenhagen before getting into a crash! / Shop revenue up after cycle tracks were put in! / Children who cycle to school are more alert and healthy!"

I look forward to the day when headlines in mainstream media have a different focus.

And so on. We're getting there. While some struggle to bust their way out of the tired circle of environmentalism's influence on messaging and a narrow focus on cycling as sport or recreation, others have done it and done it well. Nevertheless, the ultimate goal is that we no longer need to communicate cycling as transport.

Conclusion

 The fact is that cars no longer have a place in the big cities of our time.

Bertrand Delanoë, Mayor of Paris 2002–2014

We are in the midst of a new, fascinating, and challenging urban age. The quote at the top of this page says it all. It's not a brash quote by me or a dreamy quote from a transportation advocate speaking at a conference somewhere. It's a sober and pragmatic quote from the former mayor of Paris. *That* Paris. He was in office from 2002 until 2014, and in that time he steadily worked towards his vision of what his city could be. Bicycles led the charge in his urban revolution, flanked by traffic calming measures and bold political decision making.

He is not alone. Municipal politicians around the world are saying similar things. When people like that say things like this, it is safe to say that we are shifting determinedly towards a new paradigm. One that will take us back to the future. Back to a place where we were rational about urban development. To my mind, there is a constant boxing match between realistic and impatient. Between optimism and frustration. When I started this journey over a decade ago, I didn't understand why every city wasn't just doing it. Why they weren't just happily copy/pasting Copenhagen's solutions into their own city. I have since learned volumes about the intricacies and challenges faced by cities around the world. I know that the municipal structure in some cities is complex and restrictive, while other cities enjoy a wider margin of flexibility. The idealist my mother raised can still be heard sighing in frustration, but the inspiration I gain from having such a passionate, diverse, and international network frequently gives me cause to fist-pump enthusiastically. Working closely with my company's client cities, seeing in their eyes their determination to make their city better and to use the bicycle as the fantastic tool it is, is a gift for which I am so incredibly grateful.

The fast track that I secretly suspected was possible when I began has proven itself to exist. For every Seville, Buenos Aires, Minneapolis, Almetyevsk, or Bordeaux, there are 50 cities still sitting on their hands. But man, there is Seville, Buenos Aires, Minneapolis, Almetyevsk, Bordeaux, and many other cities in the same vein. These bicycle-urbanism zeroes-to-heroes are leading the way just as much as Copenhagen or Amsterdam. Without them, our journey would be far more arduous.

The conversation has changed around the world. In 2006, few cities on the planet were thinking bike. Now there are few cities where they have *not* had the discussion about how to reestablish the bicycle as transport. The process is improving. It's never quick enough for my liking, but we are spreading the narrative farther and wider than ever before. The number of people, whether citizens, advocates, activists, or policymakers, who are now on the same page grows daily.

I noticed back in 2010 that the conversation specifically in North America changed radically. That year Copenhagen was the host city for the Velo-City conference, and never before had so many participants made their way from North America. After they returned home, having experienced the cycling life in the Danish capital, I registered a buzz on my radar. It is perfectly summed up in a film by Clarence Eckerson from Streetfilms entitled *Copenhagen through North American Eyes*. *That* was the catalyst. *That* was the tipping point.

It is pure poetry that a nineteenth-century invention is capable of solving complicated twenty-first-century issues. Just as countless scholars continue to dissect, study, and analyze the complete works of Shakespeare, we are doing the same with the bicycle. We understand its importance and relevance, we have figured out the rhythm and structure of its poetry, and we recognize its timeless contribution to our society. Nevertheless, the challenges we face are daunting. We have to overturn at least 70 years of destructive traffic engineering, we have to convince an entire generation to reacquaint themselves with the bicycle as transport, our cities are facing the greatest wave of urbanization in history, and we have to battle a plethora of lifestyle illnesses that have already reached epidemic proportions. We believed so fervently in the bicycle when it was launched upon us and our cities in the late nineteenth century. Now, more than ever before, it's time to believe in it once again. Let me say it again: If you don't see cycling as part of the solution, you are part of the problem. There is no gray area here.

My hope with this book is to simplify a subject that has been needlessly overcomplicated. To boil it down to something concrete, useful, human, and quite beautiful. We possess a tool of such amazing versatility—a Swiss army knife to help get us through the next century. I want to highlight in no uncertain terms that the task ahead need not be difficult. The cycle track before us has been paved with the finest asphalt by generations of citizens, planners, engineers, and politicians. Let us embrace their knowledge and dedication and not disrespect them by thinking we can reinvent their wheel. It's all right there before us, ready to use. It is also my hope that the word *copenhagenize* fades into obscurity because it is no longer needed. Because the bicycle has been returned to the urban pedestal that it deserves, and citizens around the world rely on it like a fifth limb to get things done in their daily lives. Perhaps one day we will speak about Barcelonification, Montrealifying, Mumbaism, or whatever you like. That will be fine if their work is worthy of the moniker.

Cities are erected on spiritual columns. Like giant mirrors, they reflect the hearts of their residents. If those hearts darken and lose faith, cities will lose their glamour. That is one of my favorite quotes about cities, by the Turkish author Elif Shafak. For far too long, we have allowed our urban hearts to darken and our faith in our cities to be lost. It is time to polish our mirrors and to renovate those supporting columns. The monument most often associated with Copenhagen is a little, naked, green lady lounging on a rock, who has been staring longingly out to sea since 1913. "The Little Mermaid" is a brilliant fairy tale, but the statue, in my opinion, is a lame monument for a city like Copenhagen. I firmly believe that the greatest monument we have ever erected is our bicycle infrastructure network. It is an intricate and complex work, ever changing and in constant motion and constantly modified and improved by hundreds of thousands of citizens and visitors alike who use it each day. An organic structure of such overwhelming beauty.

There is no ownership of this monument. It is completely open-source and it's not reserved for Copenhagen alone. The Dutch have raised theirs, as have other cities around the world. The foundations are being laid in many others. Let these monuments rise. They are monuments to human ingenuity, monuments that improve city life and human lives instead of destroying them or wiping them out. These are life-sized monuments that will define our age for centuries to come—if we so choose. You and I are the designers, architects, and builders of them, as is every urban citizen.

Let these monuments rise and let us do it together.

About the Author

MIKAEL COLVILLE-ANDERSEN is a Danish-Canadian urban design expert and CEO of Copenhagenize Design Co., which he founded in 2009. He works with cities and governments around the world, designing their bicycle infrastructure and communications and coaching them towards becoming more bicycle friendly. He is a sought-after keynote speaker at design and architecture conferences and events around the world and is the host of the global television series about urbanism, *The Life-Sized City*. His writings include the popular blog *Copenhagenize* and the books *Cycle Chic* and *Cargo Bike Nation*.

Island Press | Board of Directors